THE HELPING INTERVIEW
WITH CASE ILLUSTRATIONS

ALFRED BENJAMIN

HOUGHTON MIFFLIN COMPANY   BOSTON

Dallas   Geneva, Illinois   Lawrenceville, New Jersey   Palo Alto

To Aliza Joyce
Wife, Mother, Grandmother,
Helpmeet, and Beloved Life Companion

Printed in the U.S.A.

Library of Congress Catalog Card Number: 86-82663

ISBN: 0-395-43725-3

BCDEFGHIJ-A-8987

CONTENTS

PREFACE

The summer is just about to end. It has been peaceful here in Nahariya — on the seafront and only ten minutes by car from war-torn Lebanon. I love listening to the waves at night when quiet reigns. It is then that I think of the dead and the living and reflect upon what existence is all about. I am at peace with myself this summer and feel the urge to write and create.

I have been thinking of *The Helping Interview*. A new edition is overdue but I do not want to write one. I like the book as it stands in the third edition and prefer not to touch it. Yet, I cannot leave it. And so the idea has gradually crystallized: I shall write a new volume to reaffirm my beliefs and apply learnings from my personal experience as therapist-interviewer over the past twenty-five years and more.

By now the outline is ready and I can feel the book taking shape while the waves roll in. As I cannot be a resource person to many, let me, at least, write a resource book — one the reader will be able to turn to whenever so inclined. I shall hold to the outline of *The Helping Interview* for easy cross-reference.

The Helping Interview first appeared in 1969. Additions and revisions were made in the second edition (1974) and the third (1981). I have decided not to tamper further with the book lest I spoil with good intention what would better be left alone. I trust that this new volume will prove a suitable companion to the earlier one and that together they will be of genuine help to the interviewer and therapist.

I have chosen to remain within the framework of *The Helping Interview* (1981) because I continue to find its approach very congenial. Therefore, nearly all of the original text is included in the present volume, interspersed with the new material. The new material consists of further elaboration of the topics discussed in *The Helping Interview* along with case illustrations that add a sense of immediacy and reality to the discussions. What I most definitely wish is to reaffirm the basic beliefs and values expressed in the earlier book because I consider them indispensable in the relationship between client and therapist. In this book, the participants in the new dialogues are no longer referred to as interviewer and interviewee because I have moved increasingly in the direction of personal counseling and psychotherapy.

Over the years I have developed a style that I hope reflects the credo expounded in the first edition of *The Helping Interview* back in 1969. It is my intent to show how I apply my recent learnings to the interviews I conduct and to share these, as much as possible, with the reader. If I perceive my own development correctly, interviews flow now; they have become much more spontaneous. Frequently "technique" is put aside when I sense that doing so will assist the client's quest for growth, health, and self-realization. More specifically, I shall share my experience as it applies to marital therapy and to the area of loss and separation — be it through death or divorce — as these have become a major focus of my clinical work. Reaffirmed and applied, *The Helping Interview* remains at the core. In these pages I have tried to be frank and specific, genuine and intimate. Essentially, *The Helping Interview* has been brought up to date and become more therapy-oriented.

Once again I wish to thank my editors at Houghton Mifflin for their constant support and encouragement. They have provided much constructive thinking for this new project and their skillful editing contributed immensely toward integrating and unifying a text that seemed at first disparate and cumbersome.

My deepest thanks go, today as in the past, to my clients who have taught me so much and teach me still. I shall quote extensively from our joint endeavors, but in such a way as to preserve their anonymity.

A. B.
Nahariya, Israel

1 • HELPING

Helen said: "I shouldn't have come. I can't let you share what goes on inside; I don't even let myself in. The worst of the matter is that I know I need help and I don't know where to look for it or even if it exists."

Sandy said: "I don't want to continue as I am. For over twenty years I haven't been satisfied with myself. I need to talk things through and discover new ways for myself. I really hope you can help me do that."

Who Can Be Helped?

It had been very hard on both of us. We had talked for a while — disputed, rather — and then fallen silent. After a few moments she had slowly risen and, without another word, begun to leave. Helen had insisted that she could not be helped, but I kept hearing that it was I who could not help her, who was disappointing her so deeply. After all, she had come to me and was obviously suffering.

1

Helen's husband had died suddenly a few years before, and she was still unable to pick up from there. They had been close but uncommunicative even with each other and had shut out most of the external world. She wanted to talk, to cry, to get things out of her system, but she could not. She did not know how and never had. She knew that she had turned herself into a fortress, but when it came down to brass tacks, she preferred its ostensibly protective walls to any alternative for which, presumably, she had come.

Helen did not accuse me and I did not feel guilty. I felt bitter, however, and dejected and emotionally drained as I saw her out and closed the door behind her. I knew that my desire to help was not enough, could never be enough, and yet . . . I had suggested various ways of working and she had rejected them all. Perhaps I had not tried hard enough. She had hinted that she was looking for a friend, not a professional. I thought I had been tactful and kind, but . . . I could feel my sadness changing to anger. Was I on the verge of playing God? I knew that I cannot help everyone, that no one in the helping professions can help at all times. And I considered Helen herself. She had confessed that the slightest personal revelation had cost her nights of sleepless anxiety. Perhaps she did best to remain behind that fortress so painstakingly built over the years. I remembered my last words to her to the effect that my door would always remain open for her . . . and my thoughts and feelings determinedly passed on to the next client.

I thought of Sandy, although she was not due for several hours. From the first session she had grasped eagerly at the help I proffered. She was really — slowly but surely — moving from an external to her own internal frame of reference. She was discovering new things about herself and others and was just beginning to change in a direction meaningful to her. I allowed myself to relax.

In the last resort, do we really know who can be helped by us or, better still, can help himself through us? I doubt it, and from that doubt arises my need to write this book. Much will depend on the client and much on me; even more on the two of us as quantity changes into quality. I want to be able to feel my way in this new situation and to enable him to feel his. At the outset all I need are name and phone number and we are on our way. Should we decide upon psychological or vocational tests — and this is rare in my experience — the decision will be a joint one and test results will form part of the process of our enterprise.

Is the capacity to be helped really a matter of diagnosis? My personal experience shouts an overwhelming *no.* Therefore, I do not seek diagnoses and find little comfort in them when available. I want to meet the new client and decide with her. Yes, the client who had attempted suicide tried it again, but then, at last, she had had enough and our real work could begin. The young man diagnosed as psychopathic or manic depressive was definitely neither, though his problems were real and deep. And the one diagnosed as "merely" neurotic tried several times to hang himself and has been hospitalized ever since. Frankly, the less I hear about the client and the more I hear with her, the better for me and, I believe, for her as well. That is my belief, and the years have only strengthened it.

Some time ago I had almost reached my home after the day's work when a stranger accosted me. He asked me if I knew the whereabouts of a certain street he was looking for. I pointed it out to him: "Straight down and to your left." Assured that I had been understood, I walked on. As I did, I noticed that the stranger was walking in the opposite direction of that I had indicated. "Sir," I said, "you are going in the wrong direction." "I know," he replied. "I am not quite ready yet."

I stood flabbergasted. Here I was. Over and over again I had tried to point out to my students that everyone possesses a life space of his own, that everyone is unique, and that we can best help others by enabling them to do what they themselves deeply wish to do. This man had asked me for direction. I had given it to the best of my ability. He had understood — I had at least made sure of that. But this had not been enough for me. Well, no harm had been done. He had told me he wasn't quite ready yet, and that was that. But I was uneasy. How thin the sands on which we build! How continuously on the watch we must be in order not to help too much, not to help to the point of interfering where we are neither wanted nor needed! This wasn't technically a helping interview, of course, but did that matter? We shall always be beginners, I thought to myself as I opened my front door — meaning, I suppose, that I was.

Many elements help to shape the helping interview. One must begin somewhere, and a convenient starting point is the optimal conditions we should like to create for the interview — conditions that will facilitate rather than hinder this serious, purposeful conversation we shall be embarking on once the client arrives. He is not here yet, and that is rather comforting because, truthfully, we are a bit afraid of him — not of him really, for we know nothing or very little about him, but of our interacting with him and his with us. We are just a bit anxious. As we become more and more aware of this uneasiness, we may begin to relax somewhat. Now, at least, we know how we feel. We do not know just how he feels, but we venture the guess that he feels pretty much like ourselves, if not worse.

Soon he will be here. What can we do to make this interview as helpful to him as possible? I am not suggesting that when we have more practice and interviewing has become a part of the daily routine, we shall always go through the same feeling of tenseness. I am certain, though, that both the external and internal conditions we create for the client before his arrival and while he is with us are of tremendous significance. The atmosphere that will result if we succeed in our purpose will be intangible and yet will be felt by the client during the interview itself, or if not then, will possibly be sensed in retrospect.

External Factors

The Room

External conditions are difficult to specify, since the way in which you arrange and decorate your room is a matter of taste and sometimes of necessity — of making do with what you can get. I am assuming you have a room. I once helped to set up a rehabilitation center in Israel. The buildings were far from completion, but the people in charge wanted immediate action and wired us, "Interviewing can be done in tent." We wired back, "Send tent!"

Of course, a helping interview can be carried on almost anywhere, but we usually presume that it occurs in a room. I have never been able to tell people what this room should look like. The only thing I can say is that it should not be overwhelming, noisy, or distracting. What belongs to the room belongs, and the client will adjust to this. Under ordinary circumstances nothing that is part of the interviewer's professional equipment need be hidden away. What we do not wish the client to see — files of other clients, papers of other students, electrocardiograms of other patients, the remains of a late lunch — should be put away before the client enters the room. The professional atmosphere of a room need not hinder. After all, the client knows he is coming to a professional person, and this sort of room may even help him to focus on what he wishes to talk about.

Our goal is to provide the atmosphere that will prove most conducive to communication. Each interviewer will decide what this should be. The room has to be right for her, too, since she is in it most of the time. If she feels best with a cluttered desk, this will not bother most people, I suppose, unless she begins rummaging through her papers while the client is talking. As to the clothes the interviewer should wear, all I can suggest is that they be appropriate. Here, too, everyone must decide what this means for him. After all, one can neither guess nor meet the expectations of all clients, so he may just as well fall back on his own personality and minimal professional standards.

The question of how to arrange chairs often arises. Most of the time no more than two people are involved, and usually the interviewer decides where both will sit. There is no definitive answer here either, as far as I know. Some interviewers like to sit behind a desk facing the client and think that this arrangement is desirable for both parties. Others feel best when facing the client without a desk between them. Still others prefer two equally comfortable chairs placed close to each other at a ninety-degree angle with a small table nearby. This arrangement works best for me. The client can face me when she wishes to do so, and at other times she can look straight ahead without my getting in her way. I am equally unhampered. The table close by fulfills its normal functions and, if not needed, disturbs no one.

By gesture and word I offer new clients the choice of where to sit. Most choose one of the armchairs, and as long as they come — whether it be weeks, months, or years — they will always return to the same armchair. Some, very few, choose the couch that stands at the opposite side of the room. I can think of three female clients who did so consistently. They were all rather rigid and tense and ambivalent about the encounter. One woman sat on the couch but each week moved a bit closer to the door, till one day she left and never returned. In couple therapy I have known several men who sat on the couch. It was manifestly clear that they did not wish to be present at all but came only to seem cooperative. They gave me the feeling that they were sitting on the "hot seat" and the sooner off, the better they would like it. All of these couples eventually separated.

The couch has served well in an entirely different function. I do not recall exactly how the practice began, but once I suggested to a very tense client that he might wish to lie down on the couch, take his time, collect his thoughts and feelings, and try to relax. It worked. This approach is by no means to be confused with psychoanalysis. I am not an analyst and do not practice analysis. For some clients a few sessions on the couch are sufficient, after which they return of their own initiative to the armchair. Others remain on the couch to the end of therapy, while still others lie on the couch for the first part of the session, moving to the chair when so inclined.

Some clients reject the suggestion out of hand because to them it smacks too much of what they've seen in the movies. Others try it for a while but then decide against it. Those who have found the method congenial maintain that they have benefited from it. My suggestions are very simple: remove shoes if desired, relax as much as possible and say whatever comes to mind, and do not fear silence (should it ensue) but try to concentrate on what occurs inside and verbalize it.

This method enabled Natalie to begin grappling with her feelings about her father and helped Linda to discover her anger toward her dead husband. Harry gained control over his headaches, and the spots he had seen in front of his eyes disappeared. Joe, very reluctantly, could express negative feelings concerning me and begin to relate to his father, mother, wife, and the many mistresses he had needed to keep from perceiving himself as a failure.

No one has ever suggested lying on the couch on his own initiative, and I myself propose it most infrequently, preferring by far the face-to-face encounter.

I have had two doors installed in the work apartment. One is for everyday use and the other is reserved for those rare occasions when clients might meet. Thus, while one client sits in the waiting room, the other can exit without possible unpleasantness to either party.

A shaded lamp stands on the table between the armchairs. Only one client, Tom, has asked me not to light it — preferring to sit in the dark. He came for several years, two and three times weekly. The dark helped him to unleash much repressed anger. It exploded from him in bursts of invective and torrents of tears. He hated his father and me and yearned for mother and the womb. As we were approaching the end of our sessions, he requested that all the lights in the room be turned on. Shortly after this he left to finish therapy with a female therapist. But more of that anon.

Interruptions

External conditions that can and should be avoided include interruptions and interferences. About these I feel rather strongly. The helping interview is demanding of both partners. Of the therapist it demands, among other things, that she concentrate as completely as possible on the present situation, thus establishing rapport and building trust. Outside interruptions can only hinder. Phone calls, knocks on the door, people who want "just a word" with us, secretaries who must have us sign this document "at once," may well destroy in seconds what we and the client have tried hard to build over a considerable time span. The helping interview is not sacred, but it is personal and deserves and needs the respect we wish to show the client herself. Once we appreciate this fact, we shall find a way to achieve the necessary cooperation from our associates.

I experience few interruptions at work. This was not always the case. When I first began seeing clients at home, the living room was my workroom. This arrangement worked well enough for clients but not at all for our young daughters, who wanted their daddy and had no compunctions about letting everyone, including the neighbors, in on the secret. Eventually, we built a work apartment downstairs. In the meantime our daughters have grown up and gone their separate ways, and Sivan, our granddaughter, who is a frequent visitor, does not tend to interrupt. As a matter of fact, when she is downstairs with me playing and a client approaches, she scurries away.

Possible sources of interruption are the telephone, the doorbell, and clients who arrive early. Work sessions generally start on time. I am punctual and so, too, are most clients. Nevertheless, should they appear early, I show them into the waiting room and finish the session with the client I have been seeing, who then uses the exit door previously described. If the doorbell rings, I excuse myself to check who it is. Ignoring the first ring simply provokes further ringing. The intruder has usually made a mistake or else has come to collect funds for a charity. The former leaves, the latter is referred upstairs, and work resumes.

Concerning the phone, I recall one client who vehemently demanded that I ignore it: "This is my time and I want you all to myself. It may be an illusion but that's the way it is. Whoever it is can call again." Another client claimed he liked listening to me answer the phone. It taught him, he maintained, to be brief, concise, and polite as well.

Unless doing so might sabotage the sessions, I excuse myself, repeat the last words of what has just been said so we can easily pick up the thread again, and answer the phone. Such interruptions occur very seldom, as every new client is told the hours I can be easily reached. Still the phone does ring occasionally. If the message is brief, I take it. If more is involved, I defer it to a later time. Sometimes the client herself is wanted; she is relieved I picked up the phone.

Many interviewers who do not work privately make a practice of putting on the door a sign reading "Do Not Disturb" or something similar. Although this might be helpful, it could possibly frighten off the client waiting outside or, at least, make him feel more anxious than he already is. Staff will generally cooperate if they know what is involved and are informed that you are interviewing. We need communication more than signs.

Internal Factors and Atmosphere

It is no easier, I find, to be specific about the most desirable internal conditions of the helping interview than about the external ones. I firmly believe, however, that these are more important to the client than all the external conditions put together, for the internal conditions exist in us, the interviewer.

Bringing Ourselves; Desiring to Help

The question is, What do we bring with us, inside of us, about us, that may help or hinder or not affect the client one way or another? Here again I do not have the answers but want to cite two internal conditions, or factors, that I have found to be basic:

1. Bringing to the interview just as much of our own selves as we possibly can, stopping, of course, at the point at which this may hamper the client or deny her the help she needs.
2. Feeling within ourselves that we wish to help him as much as possible and that at the moment there is nothing more important to us. This attitude, communicated nonverbally, will be sensed by the client.

These are ideals we seldom realize entirely, but when the client perceives that we are doing our best in this direction, it will be meaningful to him and prove helpful. Although he may not always be able to state it, he will probably take away from the interview, if nothing more concrete, the feeling that we may be trusted as a person and the conviction that we respect the client as a person.

Trust in the interviewer by the client and the conviction that the interviewer respects him are, of course, only part of the goal of the helping interview, whether it be between teacher and pupil, supervisor and worker, doctor and patient, rehabilitation worker and client, or therapist and client; but without these, little that is really positive will be accomplished. Our saying assuringly, "I can be trusted" and "I fully respect you" will certainly not help if the client does not sense this to be true. On the other hand, if mutual trust and respect are clearly present in the interview, felt by both parties, they will not require expression in words. I think it is to the establishing of trust and respect that those who teach and write in the field of interpersonal relations primarily refer when they speak of "contact," good "rapport," and a good "relationship"; and the atmosphere that may bring these about is what we must further consider now.

This intangible atmosphere is probably determined most by the interest we take in what the client is saying and by the understanding we show of her, her feelings, and her attitudes. We communicate these, or the lack thereof, by diverse and frequently subtle nonverbal cues (Comp. Group Studies, 1972) that the client may be more aware of than we ourselves are. Our facial expressions (Ekman, 1971) reveal a great deal. Our bodily gestures contribute to the picture — supporting, denying, confirming, rejecting, or confusing. The tone of our voice is heard by the client, and he decides whether it matches our words or whether they are a mask that the tone of our voice exposes, whispering, "Sham, camouflage, beware." For better or for worse, we are exposed to clients; and nearly everything we do or leave undone is noted and weighed.

And so we come back to ourselves. What of ourselves do we bring to the interview? We are the only known in the equation. In a way this is what the following chapters are about. But this is begging off. Beyond our assumed professional competence certain internal conditions or attitudes may aid us. Knowing, liking, and being comfortable with ourselves is one.

Knowing Ourselves; Trusting Our Ideas

Platitude or not, the more we know about ourselves, the better we can understand, evaluate, and control our behavior and the better we can understand and appreciate the behavior of others. As we become more familiar with ourselves, we may feel less threatened by what we find. We may even get to the point that we genuinely like some of the things about us and, therefore, become more tolerant of the things we like less or do not like at all. And, then, as long as we continue to examine, discover, and explore, it is possible for us to grow and change. Oriented to ourselves, we become comfortable with ourselves and thus are able to help others become comfortable with themselves and with us. In addition, because we are at ease with our own self, there will be less of a tendency for it to get in the way of our understanding another self during the interview.

I have been aware for years that I come across very strong to people at times. I have known myself to be assertive, determined, and stubborn. I am not always tolerant of what I perceive as stupidity or vulgarity, but I have tried to combat these tendencies in myself in diverse ways, including an attempt to adopt the Rogerian philosophy. It is only rather recently that I have been able to accept these characteristics in myself without feeling guilt or anxiety. I possess other qualities with which I am far happier, but I am one person and I can now live comfortably with both sides and enjoy the whole.

Quite early on in the game, I impart to clients what they must be aware of in me: my quickness and assertiveness and that lack of patience and tolerance that I occasionally display. I am sincere in my belief that unless client and I can work together as distinct personalities, we had best part soon.

Such an attitude will help the client to trust us. He will know who we are, for we, having accepted what we are, shall feel no need to hide behind a mask. He will sense that we are not hiding, and as a consequence he will hide less. He will feel liked and may reciprocate our feeling, not knowing, perhaps, that we can really like him only because we feel positively toward ourselves. I am suggesting that our necessary presence in the interview need not be an encumbrance, that we need not be preoccupied with ourselves but can concentrate wholeheartedly on the client. We can be free to listen, to attempt to understand just as much as possible, to try to find out what it is like to feel the way he does — in brief, to be genuinely interested because nothing in us gets in the way of what comes from him. We can never completely achieve this goal, but only by trying can we approach it.

Trusting our own ideas and feelings constitutes another important internal condition. Relatively comfortable with ourselves and concentrating on the client, we shall find that ideas and feelings will well up in us. We ought to listen carefully to these ideas and feelings of ours as well as to those coming from the client. It will always be up to us to decide if, when, and how to express these to her. I believe it to be true that once trust and respect have been established, voicing our feelings and ideas as ours and hence not binding on the client may frequently help rather than hinder. I assume that such communication on our part, of course, will occur only when the client cannot feel threatened by it, when she is ready to hear it and feels assured of our continued respect no matter what she does with our expressed feelings and ideas. To me this in no way entails telling her what to do. We would not do that even if she should ask us to. Rather, such communication helps us fulfill our role of an active, cooperating, present agent during the interview.

Experience has taught me increasingly to rely on my intuition — to trust my thoughts and feelings and to act on them. Paul was referred to me after what was described as a serious anxiety attack. He was tense and fearful and had lost confidence in himself as a baker, a husband, and a future father of a family. He needed — only for the time being I was sure — someone strong to rely on, and I was prepared to provide, temporarily, the authority figure required.

After a few sessions Jane and I agreed that something would have to change if we were to push ahead. We felt comfortable with each other, so that was not the obstacle. What was it then? It took Jane a very long time to warm up each session, and when she finally did it was time to stop. She was familiar with this tendency in herself, and she was slow in everything at the start. There was nothing she expected of me except, perhaps, to propose a change of format. I suggested we meet once weekly for a long session of ninety minutes rather than twice a week as we had been meeting. This proved to be the solution for Jane and thus for both of us.

Serge worked with me such a long time ago that he may well have forgotten most of our sessions. I have not, simply because he taught me to trust my feelings. He came for merely eight sessions. He always complained about my silence and insisted he wished to hear more from me, to obtain more direction, and especially to have me sum up his learnings. He complained but went right on examining, exploring, and getting closer to himself, his feelings, and his internal frame of reference. I knew intuitively that I should not interfere but felt a bit anxious about his reproaches. I held myself in check while he continued to rebuke and to work. During the eighth session, he informed me that this was our last meeting; he was much better, indeed fine now, and could confront life alone. Even as he left he still reproved me, but his handshake was warm and firm.

Rita fidgeted in her chair. She found it hard to begin, to continue, to concentrate. She tried smoking, chewing gum. She played with the clasp of her handbag, the links of her bracelet. She went to get a drink of water and returned only to begin sobbing. She was pathetic and miserable and far too agitated to work meaningfully. I suggested she might want to stretch out on the couch to relax a bit and collect herself. Rita lay on that couch every weekly meeting for an entire year, and rose, thanked me, and left. Some time later she brought me a record I still cherish.

My good friend Ely died of cancer suddenly at the age of forty. Some years later his wife, Shosh, came to consult with me. She had firmly decided to remain at the kibbutz where they had lived together and to continue to bring up her children there. However, she could not make up her mind whether to go on working on the kibbutz or to resume her studies as she had planned just before Ely's death. We tried to examine all angles of the picture, after which Shosh began to make inquiries. I was certain of the direction she should take. I now meet her occasionally at the teacher training college where we both work. She is a qualified, mature professional person and finds great fulfillment in her work.

Being Honest; Listening and Absorbing

Another internal condition logically follows the condition of knowing ourselves: being honest with ourselves so that we may be honest with the client. If we did not hear or understand something, if, absorbed in ourselves, we could not listen to her, if we have become aware that we were not completely with her, it is far better to say so than to act as if we had been there, to pretend that she did not make herself clear or that what we missed was probably unimportant anyway. I think most clients feel best with therapists whom they perceive as human beings with failings. This makes it easier for them to reveal their own fallibility.

Reciprocal honesty of this kind may at times involve telling the client that we do not have the solution to his difficulty. Instead of inhibiting him, such frankness may encourage him to confront his situation more energetically. Again I am assuming that we have accepted ourselves sufficiently so that we do not feel we need appear to others as all-wise, all-knowing, near-perfect. Here I am primarily concerned with integrity toward ourselves. Everyone will have to decide, of course, the point at which honesty borders on imprudence. For example, we may genuinely feel that the client is arrogant or dependent, but it may not be appropriate or helpful to her to state it in that way or even to state it at all.

Risk Taking

Risk taking is part of living. Never get out of bed if you do not wish to take risks, I have told my students for years, but even remaining in bed entails risks. I take risks when I express myself frankly and openly, I take risk when I initiate, I take risks when I state my position firmly, and strangely enough, I take risks when I refrain from risk taking.

Many years ago Nathan came to see me. Unhappy, depressed, unable to concentrate on his studies, he came for help. To my lasting regret it took me far too long to put my finger on the source of his difficulty. True, he did not provide many clues — he couldn't. It took him months till he dared even to admit to a conflict and much longer till he was able to face it. He was enrolled in a teacher training program. His kibbutz had chosen this profession for him, and being a faithful kibbutz member, he had consented. The trouble was that he hated not only teaching but also the very idea of it. However, he dared not admit this even to himself, much less to the community in which he functioned. Ultimately, I had to fight his battle for him and understandably so. It took me, a professional outsider, months of persuading until Nathan was permitted to drop his studies and return to work in the fields as he wished. The framework of kibbutz life has changed much since then. Nathan's tale could not be told today. Back in the sixties, however, he was the victim of rigid norms that he dared not flout unaided.

Susan's story had a sad ending. I had liked her very much as a student. When, some time later, she came for therapy I readily agreed, and we got off to a fine start. Gradually, disturbing signs appeared in her behavior. I feared a potential psychotic episode and tried with all my might to help her ward it off. She believed in me and I in her sanity. We were both mistaken. Her eventual hospitalization was probably unavoidable, but today I know that I should have been less obstinate. I hate to see patients hospitalized, especially youngsters.

When Sol, who had made the appointment for himself, brought his wife, Erna, to our first meeting and insisted she stay with us, I had my doubts. I met with Sol — a weak and dependent person full of repressed aggression — until one day Erna called. She wanted a report on my diagnosis of Sol's condition, a description of what methods I was using, as well as a detailed prognosis. Restraining my annoyance, I told her I could not discuss Sol behind his back but would be pleased to tackle her questions in Sol's presence. This infuriated her; after all, Sol was her husband and she had every right to know and who did I think I was . . . Sol left therapy soon afterward.

Henry falls between two stools; he sees too much to be considered blind but too little to function as fully sighted. When he came to me he was working at a menial job that required almost nothing but a bit of muscle and good sight. It was obvious that he would have to find another job. He looked around but found nothing at which he lasted more than a few days. One day I went out on a limb: since the world of the sighted was proving too difficult, perhaps he should try the world of the blind. To make a long story short, he is now a most efficient telephone operator, using his sight when possible and his fingers when necessary. But his resentment towards me lingers. He still fantasizes about the Garden of Eden from which, he insists, I evicted him. There he carried suitcases in and out of the hotel. True, he could not always read the labels, but this was infinitely preferable to . . .

I met with Bea, a social worker, for supervision of her rehabilitation cases every week. We both looked forward to these sessions until Bea became morose, reluctant to talk, nervous, and tense. I said nothing at first, but when things got worse, I risked telling her what I perceived happening and asked if I could be of help. Bea did need help — and fast. We had to decide whether to continue supervision, move over to therapy, or to continue the supervision and look for another therapist. Bea preferred the last course of action.

When for financial or other reasons, potential clients inquire about the length of therapy, I will sometimes risk an estimate. Alexandra came with painful somatic symptoms believed to have originated from emotional turmoil. As I listened to her, I thought that twelve sessions or so would suffice. I told her that we would probably finish within three months. And so we did. Alexandra later revealed to me that she had begun to feel better the very moment I estimated three months; she had feared that it might take three years!

When Bertha, between sobs, begged to know how long it might take to improve relations with her son, I could rather confidently promise amelioration within three weeks. Actually, three sessions sufficed.

Atmosphere

Far from having evolved into a science, therapy still remains an art. Science explains; words can only hint at what art is about. There is much of the intangible in art, and so it is in our profession as well. The atmosphere we create for clients is one of these intangibles. We wish that atmosphere to be supportive and non-threatening, promoting search and discovery. We want it to be neutral yet warm, all-encompassing yet limited in time. We try to create the unique and the universal simultaneously. And to what purpose? Basically, so that the client may dare face, confront, and ultimately change the reality that makes up his world. He needs a milieu where he can let down his defenses and where real coping can begin. If we succeed, both of us will sense the challenge in the air, the tension, the dread, and the hope.

I first met Albert at the university, where he participated in a T-group I was offering. He impressed me as intelligent and talented, yet immature and without direction. As our group drew to a close, some members suggested that Albert might profit from therapy. He rejected the idea vehemently at the time, but a few years later he got in touch with me. He was tense and guarded and did not wish to be seen arriving or leaving. He maintained that he trusted me yet was suspicious that I might record our sessions without his knowledge or consent. He radiated anxiety and fear. For months the subject of sex was avoided, yet eventually Albert allowed himself to face reality: he had been denying strong homosexual tendencies.

Morris loved writing music but hated teaching it. He could not make a living at the former and resented the hours he considered wasted at the latter. He angrily accused others of plagiarizing his lyrics and melodies and denounced their perfidy. When, eventually, he calmed down he began to confront the actual state of affairs. Morris did possess talent but had already reached middle age and was still unknown. Perhaps teaching had more to offer than he had been prepared to admit. Less time devoted to execrating his fate might improve both his composing and his teaching.

Oliver is a giant of a man. His coming to therapy was a secret between us — no one else must know. Although he squirmed restlessly in his seat, he commented upon the "soothing effect of the room." He felt at ease; the threatening world seemed light-years away. He wanted nothing more than to sit and soak up the calm and the silence. The reality big Oliver had to face was that he saw himself everywhere as a small boy; the adults about him were viewed as infallible and threatening parental figures whose commands and norms had to be anticipated and conformed to. At first he had perceived me thus, as well, but now he wasn't so sure anymore . . .

Learning to face reality can be very upsetting. When Selma faced her inadequacy as a mother she consented that her parents should bring up little Rebecca. She shook with sobs while deciding, but soon after comforted herself by taking off for Europe.

Gordon and I met over a period of two years. It took him months to feel more or less at ease. A gentle person, he radiated kindness, and our smaller daughter, a toddler then, would run to him when he appeared. Gordon was terribly shy and slow and afraid of all members of the opposite sex. His educators nagged at him for having so little ambition. It was clear that he preferred working to studying and listening to the radio to reading. In his own way, he was ready to accept his reality. His teachers and especially his parents found it much harder. Gordon is married now and has children of his own. He still works hard, reads little, and in the evening watches TV.

Intangible or not, atmosphere matters. For reasons of convenience, I began to meet Abe for his weekly session at the teacher's college where he studied and I taught. We met late in the afternoon when there was no one about and had a classroom to ourselves. Nevertheless, we both felt something was lacking; the room seemed anonymous and cold. In spite of the hours of travel involved for him, Abe decided to come to my clinic. Even there he found it hard to open up, but at least we began to establish a closer rapport. Unfortunately, soon after this Abe became fatally ill and a few months later passed away. Esther, his wife, told me that he had described the room to her in great detail. Although he was sparing of words, she could sense the support the surroundings afforded him.

One last point. Beginning therapists are often so concerned with what they will say next that they find it difficult to listen to and absorb what is going on. This is understandable but not beneficial. It takes time, perhaps, to find out that what we say is generally much less important than we think it is. When we start out, we may be so enthusiastic that our own eagerness gets in the way. We may be so unsure that we feel the need to prove how confident we are. I know of no remedy for this except patience and awareness of ourselves. The client will usually set us straight — if we only let her.

Lewin (1935) and others speak of the life space each one of us occupies. What I have been trying to say comes down to this: It seems to me that when we are interviewing, it is best to act in such a way that we do not impose our life space on that of the client, that we do not confuse ours with his, and that we behave in a manner that will enable him to explore his own life space because of our presence and not in spite of it. Sensing trust and respect, he may be able to launch upon this exploration in a way never attempted before — a new experience for him, then, and one he may well treasure way beyond what we say or leave unsaid.

Coping Versus Defense Mechanisms

Sigmund Freud (1955, 1936) and his daughter Anna (1970) have given us rich, new insights into defense mechanisms — steps we take unconsciously to protect our ego. More recently, students of human behavior have been stressing coping mechanisms, steps we take consciously to meet the demands of reality (Allport, 1961; Maslow, 1970; White, 1966; Wright, 1960). Without denying the existence and vital importance of defenses, they point out that it is possible at times, for example, to cope with disappointment instead of repressing or rationalizing it away. In the type of atmosphere I have tried to describe above, it may be possible for the client to cope with reality rather than defend himself against it, deny it, or distort it out of recognition.

Everyone is familiar with the old tale about a fox who wished to get at some luscious-looking grapes. When he discovered that they were too high for him to reach, he decided they were sour. Not admitting that he did not have the necessary skills or tools and instead disparaging the desirability of the grapes, the fox provides for us an example of typical defense behavior. To cope, on the other hand, is to face facts and then decide what to do about them. If we are able to create the atmosphere in which coping can be achieved, our helping interview may help more than we anticipate.

A Personal Note

I am blind and have been so from birth. Blindness is a relative concept. As a child I saw a great deal compared with the very little I see today, and the remaining sight decreases steadily. I mention this disability here because I feel bound to reveal it to my clients at the outset. Few are surprised; most of them know already since Israel is such a small country. To the best of my knowledge, no client ever left therapy with me because of my blindness, though I am certain that some who were put off by it never came.

I try to handle the situation matter-of-factly: I cannot be aware of facial expressions. I shall never know what the client looks like. I shall, naturally, miss some nonverbal cues. Compensations — I know of none. On the other hand, if I felt that blindness created an unsurpassable obstacle, I would have chosen a different profession. At this point in the interview where the issue arises, I invite questions and reply as succinctly as possible. If the client remains I return to her and keep her central from then on.

I can recall two clients who remarked that they were pleased that I am blind. What they meant, of course, was that they felt more comfortable knowing that I could not see them. Milly was glad I could not look at her in the manner she felt all men did. Seeing without being seen gave her a sense of having the upper hand. Carl felt relieved that his blushes went undetected, as did the trembling of his hands. Obviously, these admissions proved very useful in their therapy.

Two of my present clients are amateur photographers. I find their hobby fascinating and enjoy hearing them talk about it. They, in turn, like talking to me as the explanations required frequently sharpen their own perceptions.

Albert is a sculptor. One of his pieces resides in our living room. Some time ago he held a one-man exhibition and invited me for a privately guided tour, enabling me to examine every sculpture by touch.

Summing up the reactions of clients to my blindness, I conclude that it becomes quite irrelevant to most, although some express astonishment at forgetting that I am blind, while others find it difficult to hide their irritation at my not being able to see — especially as they claim that I appear as if I do indeed see them. Some show an interest in how I read and write; others are too shy or preoccupied with their own concerns to bother. Some even brag about the fact that they are in therapy with a blind therapist who can see.

2 • STAGES

Well, the great day has finally arrived. It may not seem so great to you at the moment, but it will soon be over and your first interview will have become a part of your past. The client is waiting just on the other side of your door. In spite of inclement weather he has come. You were hoping that perhaps . . . but still you are glad he is here. This is, after all, the moment for which you have been waiting. You have studied and read and practiced — all or some of these — and the time to act is at hand. As you cautiously approach the door to admit him, you feel that everything is ebbing away — all you have learned about human development, the psychology of personality, the cultural milieu; all you have practiced in role-playing or in practicums; all the things you repeatedly told yourself you would or would not do when interviewing. All this and more besides are gone now, and you feel entirely alone and unprotected with just a door between him and yourself. But, after all, it is you he has come to see; and so you let him in, learning one of the most important lessons you will ever learn about interviewing: in it there is no one but the client and you. As time goes on, you become accustomed to this fact; and with a little more time you begin to accept it for what it is: the basis of the helping relationship.

You undoubtedly have interviewed before now, but you were not so conscious of it as you are at this moment — or perhaps you were not conscious of it at all. Now you are a bit frightened and uncertain. You have only yourself to rely upon — yourself and him, waiting on the other side of the door. If you could only rely on him. . . . But you can, I believe, and you will increasingly as time passes. Since he has come for a specific purpose, he may know best how you can help him. So if you can learn to rely on him, this will help you to give him the aid he requires. This important lesson may take time to learn, for right now you are very much concerned with yourself and your feeling of being completely exposed and alone.

One more word before you turn the knob. I have said and shall continue to say in this book many things that I sincerely hold to be true. They are true for me, and I find they usually work. But these very same things may not prove to be true for you, nor may they prove workable. The answers suggested here — to the extent that they are answers — may not be answers for you. Surely they need not be. But if they stimulate you to question them and come up with answers meaningful and workable for you, I shall feel more than rewarded for having put them on paper. The helping interview is more an art and a skill than a science, and every artist must discover her own style and the tools with which she works best. Style matures with experience, stimulation, and reflection. I am not interested in your adopting my style, but I am very much interested in stimulating you to develop and reflect upon your own.

Miriam phoned as arranged. She said: "I've finally decided not to get involved. It's too hard for me, at my age, and too dangerous. I'll just have to live with the mess I've made of my life. Thanks anyway. . . ."

Carl said during our first session: "I've been waiting for something like this for ages. I've been carrying this load of junk around much too long and I'm hoping to drop it right here. I'll be wanting to know your reactions, but now I just want you to listen."

How We Get Started

Sometimes we never do get started. Much information about the client has been provided via telephone, mail, or a third party, but the client himself never materializes. At times he does call to make an appointment but cancels at the last moment or has someone else do it for him. At still other times I just wait, keyed up as always when anticipating the arrival of a new client and he simply doesn't show up. I become angrier and more frustrated as the minutes pass, I seem never to learn not to count my clients before they arrive.

Often the first interview turns out to be the last as well. Florence came looking for a fast and safe cure to lose weight and had no intention of getting involved more deeply. Blanche just wanted me to hold her hand and sympathize. Ben needed reassurance and encouragement in order to dare go back to a job where he had been disparaged. He called later to say that things were now fine. Another client, certain he needed help, said he would think over the possibility of therapy. He called to inform me that he was getting married instead. The brother of a well-known public figure came to bemoan his brother's success and his own failure. He considered himself weak, inadequate, cowardly. He never returned.

Some, like Miriam, seriously consider therapy and, for one reason or another, decide against taking the plunge. Therapy is too expensive, too difficult, too dangerous. It threatens whatever stability has been achieved, be it ever so far from satisfactory. It demands hard work and promises relatively little in return. Therapy is not a science and can work only for those who believe in it — and even then is not a sure thing. Many potential clients leave disappointed but never attempt to discover why this is so.

And, finally, there are those who come to the wrong address. They are looking for pills that I am not authorized to prescribe. They wish tests that I do not administer. They are seeking a cure through a faith I do not possess.

Of all interviews I most look forward to the first one. It is exciting and challenging — full of hope and expectation. We can never be sure that the last interview will, in fact, remain the last, but there is only one first interview, and neither client nor therapist can ever forget it. Most clients come prepared. They are more or less familiar with the therapist's role, their own task, and our joint enterprise. They are eager to get started immediately, and I try not to get in their way. Later on in the interview I shall ask for full name and phone number. We shall discuss fees and look for a suitable time for our future sessions. I shall want to know if the client has been in therapy before or whether she is in therapy now. But all that can wait for a while, since she is tense and nervous and ready to begin.

Opening the First Interview

I like to distinguish between two types of first interview: the one initiated by the client and the one initiated by the interviewer. Let us start with the former.

When Initiated by the Client

Someone has asked to see you. The most sensible thing to do then, it would seem, is to let him state what led him to come. Simple, but not always easy to do. Sometimes we feel we should know and should let him know that we know. So we may say, "You must want to find out how Johnny is getting along with his new teacher." This may or may not be correct. If it is, it gains us nothing except perhaps a sense of perspicacity. If it is not, the client may be put in an awkward situation. He may feel that this is what he should be concerned about; and so, not wishing to contradict, he may agree even though he wanted something else entirely. The more confident client will simply say, "No, I came about . . ." But he will undoubtedly be thinking: "Why must you tell me what I'm here for? I'll tell you soon enough if you'll let me."

At times we may be positive that we know what has led the client to see us and may indicate this to her at the outset. It may turn out, of course, that we were right, and telling certain clients why they have come may help them to get started. However, my conviction is that if someone has asked to see us and has come, it is better to let her state in her own words just what brought her, what in particular is on her mind. Once the formalities of greeting and being seated are over, the most useful thing we can do is to help her get started if such help is necessary (it usually is not) and to listen just as hard as possible to what she has to say. If we feel we must say something, it ought to be brief and neutral, for we do not wish to get in her way: "Please tell me what you wished to see me about" or "Mm-hm . . . go ahead" or "I understand you wanted to see me" or "Please feel free to tell me what's on your mind."

I strongly object to all formulas in interviewing. Thus I am wary of such openings as "I'm glad you came in this morning," because I may not be or may not remain so for long. Nor do I like "Please tell me in what way I can be helpful to you." I do not mean in the least to challenge the interviewer's genuine desire to assist. The point is that the client does not always know at the outset what help you can give him. He may know but not be able immediately to verbalize it. He may know but hesitate to state it bluntly so soon. Then, too, we cannot be sure how much he likes the idea of having to come for help or what connotation the word *help* holds for him. Finally, our culture is so permeated with "May I help you's" whose intent is so clearly something else that it is probably best to try to help as much as possible without using the word.

Nor do I feel at ease with the word *problem*. "What is the problem you would like to discuss?" This kind of opening troubles me for several reasons. First, the client may not have a problem. Second, she may not have thought of it as such till we put the word in her mouth. Third, the word *problem* is heavy, loaded, almost something to shy away from rather than to confront. I am not suggesting that people do not have problems. They may have them and not know it or not wish to face the fact that they exist. But I feel that to use the word *problem* at the very beginning, out of context and without knowing how the client reacts to the word, will hinder rather than help.

And now a paradox. When someone comes to see us because he genuinely wants to and because he initiated the contact for this purpose, almost whatever we say will go unnoticed because he is anxious to get started. As long as we do not get in the way too much, he will begin to talk.

Sometimes at the outset there is room or need for small talk on the therapist's part, something to help the client get started. But we should attempt this only when we truly feel that it will be helpful. Brief statements such as the following may break the ice: "With traffic the way it is around here, you must have found it hard to get a parking place" or "It's nice to have a sunny day after all that rain, isn't it?" or "It's hard to begin, I see."

Occasionally a client will begin by asking: "Is it up to me to talk?" or "Are you waiting for me to begin?" or "Am I supposed to be saying something?" Here, I feel, the only possible thing to say is "Yes" or "mm-hm" with or without a nod of the head and to add, if necessary, something to the effect that it is probably not easy but that only she, the client, knows for what purpose she has come and what she wishes to discuss.

Marie has brought a list of topics with her that she begins to run through hastily. Jane, who has been in therapy before, still has trouble expressing herself. Martha bombards me with questions. No, she does not wish to talk about herself; I am to question her as little as possible and guide her as quickly as possible and as much as I can since she can no longer go on "this way." Laura is very articulate at first. She speaks of husband and children. She hints at marital difficulties and suddenly comes to a halt. She sits bolt upright and says — practically shouts — that the truth of the matter is that she has come for herself, and herself alone.

We have, indeed, begun. Clients come in order to talk, and most of them do so. A few may require a bit of encouragement, but that generally suffices.

Not so with Dick, who sat immobile and silent. All my attempts to guide, encourage, probe; my own silence; nothing helped. Dick just sat as immobile as a statue and refused to break his silence. He arrived faithfully for his weekly appointment and continued to sit, immobile and silent as the tomb. Months passed in this manner, till one day he began to open up. He had needed all that time to test himself and me. Now he was ready. We had both passed the test.

Carl immediately expressed the need for long weekly sessions, knowing himself to be extremely verbal. To this day he has much to impart.

David had come some years before with his wife. This time he wished to come alone and "set my house in order," as he put it.

A sensitive man, very easily wounded, David has a low estimate of himself. Now he, too, was on his way.

From the first interview on I endeavor to enable each client to express himself in the manner most conducive to his way of being and behaving. In other words, my style is to bring out his and to work along with him; by no means do I wish him to adapt his style to mine. As a result, since every client is different, I work differently with each one. I want, so to speak, to enable him to lead and to follow his steps unobtrusively in order not to cramp his style.

Sandy appeared for her first session with a tape recorder. She needed to go over our sessions at her leisure and to learn further from them. Knowing that the interview was taped, she felt relaxed; there was no necessity to attempt to remember everything because it was all on the tape.

Bob absolutely refused to meet on a regular basis. When he felt like coming, he would call and make an appointment. This might occur three times in one week or once in two months. Bob knows that he has a tendency to run away from confronting himself but so far has always managed to come back.

Laura insisted that I not interrupt her. This request actually made both of us laugh, as so far I had hardly uttered a word. Laura wanted to do everything herself, but in my presence because she needed to hear my reactions! We both laughed again.

Sam never arrived without his list. Before coming, he would jot down the topics he meant us to discuss, as well as the order in which they were to be tackled. List in hand, Sam felt safe. What really needed working on did not appear on the list for a long time. I might have pressed him but decided against it. The list was his shield; he needed it for the time being to ward off reality. Eventually, the shield was turned into a sword and he was then ready to attack his major problem.

Dora insisted that I begin each session. Although she would eventually take over, I had to initiate because she simply could not. All the well-worn explanations were of no avail, and I reluctantly began each of our many sessions. Dora did take over in time, but it was a hard struggle. She still tries now and again to have others do her work for her but is fully aware of her game and is even prepared to lose at times.

When Initiated by the Interviewer or Therapist

The interview starts off on a different note when the interviewer is the one who has initiated it. Here I discern both a rule and a danger. The rule is simple: to state at the outset exactly what led you to ask the client to come to see you. Thus the interviewer at the employment bureau may say: "I've gone over the form you filled in the other day, and I wanted you to come in so that we might talk over the types of jobs you're interested in and see in what way we might be of service. I see you noted down here that . . ." The doctor may remark: "The results of those tests are in, and I asked you to come here so that we can talk about them. Now let's see . . ." A counselor in a rehabilitation center may start by saying: "You've been here a week now, Betty. I've asked you to drop in to see me so that we can talk about your impressions of this place and anything else you may want to discuss." At this point the counselor should begin to do the very thing she said she wished to do — listen to Betty.

The great danger in these interviewer- or therapist-initiated sessions is the possibility that they will turn into monologues or lectures or a combination of the two. A father remarked to a teacher who had invited him to discuss his son's problems, "If you asked me to come in just to listen to you, you might have written me a letter instead." We can avoid this danger if we are careful to stop after we have indicated the purpose of the interview and furnished the information, if any, that we intended to give. The client will usually have a great deal to say if he feels we are ready and willing to listen to him. If we want a conversation and good communication, we shall see to it that the client has the opportunity to express himself fully. This is the only way to discover if and how he has understood us, what he thinks, and how he feels. Otherwise, I suppose, a letter may indeed be preferable.

"I suppose you know why I asked you to come in" or "We both know why you are here" or "Can you guess why I asked you to stop by" are openings that if meant seriously can come across in a threatening light. Such pointless coyness has no place. The client may not know and yet fear our disbelief. She may think she knows and not wish to tell. She may imagine several reasons and become confused. She may consider this a challenge and react in kind. She may then and there decide to fight rather than co-operate. It is very doubtful that this sort of opening will bring two people together. It may well force them apart or keep them apart. I believe that the client is entitled to know immediately our purpose in calling him in. If it is our intention to assist him, the more honest and open we are, the more honest and open he can be. The result will be a real interview, one in which two people converse seriously and purposefully.

Explaining Our Role

Two further reflections about this initial phase. I feel it is best not to involve the client in the intricacies of our role, profession, or professional background. These are of concern primarily to our employer. The client may wish to know just who we are in a given agency or setup, but in that case he usually is simply asking whether he has come to the right person, whether we are the one he should be seeing rather than someone else. We need only identify ourselves and state our role in the agency in order for him to proceed with ease. If our role does come up for discussion, it will frequently be in terms of what we can or cannot do. This should be clearly explained when such a situation arises. Some examples:

> "I'm Miss Frank, the school counselor. You can discuss with me whatever may be on your mind about Jane."

> "Our agency does supply the service you are interested in. Miss Smith is the one who deals with it, and, if you like, I can arrange an appointment for you."

> "I understand that we would both like a medical opinion on this. We don't have a medical department here, but we work with X hospital. Would you like me to arrange for you to be seen there?"

Making Use of Forms

Finally, there is the matter of forms. To be frank, I have little regard for them, even though I appreciate the function they serve in our society. The information called for is too often reluctantly given and prejudgmentally received. As a result, forms may come between interviewer and client. I think it is best, therefore, to have necessary forms filled out during and as an integral part of the interviewing process. At times this can be effected quickly and unobtrusively: "Before we proceed, Mr. Jones, there is a short form we must fill in. Should you have any reservations about any of the questions, please let me know as we come to them, and we'll try to see what's involved."

If the form is lengthy, complicated, or both, the interviewer may want to arrange a special meeting with the client to work on it together, using the occasion to begin establishing rapport. Generally, people simply submit to answering questions as an inevitability of life, unless they have been asked the same questions over and over again by different agencies or by different people in the same agency. If they then balk, one can hardly blame them. But if this is not the case and if the client can perceive from our behavior that she can state her reservations — that she can, so to speak, question the question — there should be little difficulty, provided that we as well can accept forms as important or at least as one of those inevitabilities of living. A good initial relationship can be built if both partners in the interview accept the procedure in this manner. As they work along, they may discover a lot about each other and create the proper atmosphere so that when the form is completed, the interview can flow ahead smoothly.

The Time Factor

Our culture measures much in terms of time and sets a great deal of value on time. We say: "A stitch in time saves nine," "Time waits for no one," and "Time is money." Therefore, in our culture time is an important factor in the interview. We wonder about the significance of the client's coming so early or so late and of the meaning this has for him. In other words, we are conscious of time, and we assume that he is as well — and usually he is. He notices our behavior in this dimension, too. When we schedule an interview for ten in the morning, are we there and available to the client at ten in the morning? This is more than merely a matter of courtesy. The longer he is kept waiting after ten, the more he will wonder whether we have forgotten him, whether he is of no importance to us, whether we are keeping him waiting for some dark purpose unknown to him, whether we are being fair with him. What this means in terms of trust and respect is obvious. Appointments should be kept on time or a good and sufficient reason provided. "I know we have an appointment at nine, Mary, but something has just come up that is entirely beyond my control, and you'll just have to excuse me for fifteen minutes or so. Terribly sorry, but this cannot wait."

On the other hand, when Shirley's mother rushes into school and insists on seeing you at once, there is usually no reason to drop everything and see her. No appointment was made, no emergency exists, and you are legitimately occupied. If she must see you that day, she will have to wait until you are free to see her. She should be told this politely but firmly. Were you to see her when preoccupied with other concerns, you would be too distracted and tense to listen to her in the way you would like. Honesty has a way of smoothing out relationships.

You should usually tell clients explicitly or implicitly how much of your time is theirs. This provides an important framework for the interview. "I'm sorry, Mrs. Brown, but in ten minutes I must leave for a staff conference. Should we not finish by then, we can make another date to meet." This is preferable to continuing without saying anything but feeling increasingly pressed and wishing Mrs. Brown would get up and leave. You are no longer listening to her by this time, and perhaps you are even feeling angry with her because she hasn't finished yet and you have an important meeting (about which she, of course, knows nothing). A social worker may say: "So we have agreed, Carol, to meet for the time being every Monday at four in the afternoon. We'll have about forty-five minutes each session to talk over whatever is on your mind."

When several interviews are involved, the time factor becomes part of the general atmosphere, part of the relationship. In one-time interviews this sort of time structuring is not so important, but even here boundaries must be clearly drawn. People sometimes go on talking without realizing they are repeating themselves. They may not know how to end, get up, and leave. Being products of our society, they may feel that the polite thing to do is to sit and await a signal from us that the interview is over.

I do not mean that we should rush the client, but I do mean that we should make clear to him the time available so that he can orient himself within it. I have no precise answer as to how long an interview should be. My feeling is, however, that forty-five minutes should generally suffice. What is not said during that period would probably remain unsaid even if we extended the interview time, and much would be repeated. This is an upper limit; if after ten minutes both of you feel you have finished, there is no reason to sit there just because the allotted time is not yet over. "Well, Mr. Kay, if there is nothing to add, I suppose we have finished. Thanks for coming in."

However, there is room for some leeway. I also schedule sessions of ninety minutes, an hour, or only thirty minutes. I have already referred to Jane's and Carl's preference for a long session. As ninety minutes is a long time even for them, we take a short break. With couples, in most instances I find a session of sixty minutes very adequate as it enables both partners to have their say without feeling rushed. I try to leave some free time after these sessions in case it proves advisable and profitable to extend them somewhat. For Gordon forty-five minutes was much too long. Half-hour sessions seemed sufficient. I prefer these shorter sessions for clients who have little to say and for whom silence is a burden.

My personal needs enter the time equation as well. Usually I have fifteen minutes to myself between clients. I need them badly. Barring inclement weather, I spend this time strolling up and down in the garden outside my office. Reflecting upon the session just ended, I go over in my mind certain aspects I want to remember, and I listen to my inner feelings. Presently, I leave that client and think of nothing or else of trivia from my personal life. Then I prepare myself for the client about to arrive. I try to pick up the thread of our last meeting and to recapture the atmosphere. The client may not refer to any of this and, in that case, neither will I — except when absolutely necessary. I want her to lead and me to follow.

Once, in Los Angeles for a few hours between planes, I was invited out for dinner by another therapist. We had corresponded but never met previously. Hardly had we ordered drinks when he excused himself and disappeared. Just before coffee he once more disappeared. Returning, he explained: he was seeing a very anxious patient right then and another so depressed that he feared for his life. He spoke to them on the phone every evening in order to reassure them and himself.

Clients rarely phone me and never turn up without an appointment. I regard the telephone as an instrument for delivering messages and not as a medium for the helping interview. I can be of minimal help on the phone and have no need to intrude myself into the lives of clients beyond what is necessary.

Of course, clients do call to cancel, change, or confirm appointments; to give or receive information; to express a request. I call them as well when necessary and for the same reasons. Some clients — a very few and always the same ones — try me and their luck: they must relate an incident, get immediate advice on a matter that brooks no delay, receive sympathy, reassurance, a ready ear. My responses leave little doubt as to my attitude:

> TH.* I am sorry to hear that, Howard. And just when we thought you had overcome the booze. Of course you're upset. When you come in on Friday we can look further into things

Sol, whose wife, Erna, I had felt compelled to rebuff, attempted several times to obtain my sympathy via the phone:

> CL. I couldn't fall asleep last night. I perspired and shivered and at work today, naturally, I couldn't function. People are beginning to suspect there's something wrong with me. I don't feel we're making any progress. I can't go on much longer like this. Isn't there something you can suggest?

> TH. Last time you were in to see me, you began to understand the meaning of your symptoms. All I can suggest now is that we continue to work hard. I hear your reservations about therapy. And yet, you refuse medication. If you want an earlier session . . .

Esther had met my wife at a university seminar. When she gave up on me, she turned to her. Long telephone monologues ensued that my wife was too polite and considerate to cut short.

Emergencies require that we suspend rules. I once received a call from Bolivia in the middle of the night. My recollection of

---

*TH. stands for therapist, CL. stands for client.

the incident is hazy, but my professional opinion was needed and I hastened to provide it.

Charles has lived for years on the borderline of sanity. He called to check whether I was still against his joining a week-long group dynamics laboratory. I was still very much opposed. Feeling his disappointment and anger at me, all I could do over the phone was to reflect these and accept them.

Peggy, who had never before called, tracked me down at our summer home. She was distraught as she had to decide that very day whether to accept her parents' conditions for studying in Tel Aviv. Familiar with the background, I was able to help her reach a decision.

Once Dick had broken his silence, he thought that he could phone at any time, day or night:

> CL. What do you think? Shouldn't I fire the foreman of the metal section — the one we talked about last time?
>
> TH. I don't have the slightest idea, Dick.
>
> CL. But you remember what I told you about him?
>
> TH. Yes, I do remember. He's been working for you for years and you'll have to decide. We can discuss the pros and cons again when I see you on Monday.
>
> CL. I had hoped for more from you.
>
> TH. Sorry to disappoint you.
>
> CL. I'll let him stay. There's always time to fire him.

We shall return to this topic when discussing closing. Here I wished to stress the importance of the time factor to both therapist and client and to demonstrate that it can become a bridge on which to meet. Both should feel comfortable within the time framework; and when the need exists, the therapist can assist by verbalizing what she sees the client is feeling but is unwilling or unable to express himself: "I have the feeling, Jim, that you'd rather we stopped right here." "You keep looking at the clock, and I'm just wondering whether there is something else you must attend to. We can continue with this some other time, if you like." Such sensitivity and openness on the therapist's part will surely not diminish trust and respect but may well add to them.

A practical point: if you must interview several persons in one day, allow a few minutes between interviews to write or fill in your notes, think over what has gone on, or relax and get ready for the next person. Otherwise you may keep on talking to client A in your mind while client B is sitting there and entitled to your full attention. Get client A off your mind before seeing B. To do this you may well need a few minutes to mull things over, note on your calendar what you promised A you would look into, or just sit back or walk about to get ready for B.

On Money

Remuneration for services rendered is also measured in terms of time. Clients pay for sessions we spend together — be they fruitful, fruitless, or downright harmful. And we charge what we think the market will bear. We even charge for sessions that never take place, unless canceled in time or due to force majeure.

I work hard for my living and feel I deserve what I earn. I experience no guilt or embarrassment accepting money for services rendered and can handle check or cash with equal equanimity. Some clients deposit their fee gingerly on my desk so that I have to feel around for it. Much better, I tell them, to hand it to me. In order not to waste time on fees at each session, I suggest a monthly bill followed, upon payment, by a receipt. Most consider this a suitable arrangement. Some clients pay less than others, either because they can afford less or as a result of compromise. I generally "carry" one client who cannot pay right then. Eventually, he either pays or does not. Clients rarely elude payment. I can think of only four or five instances over the many years I have been working when clients simply ignored bills. Their feelings toward therapy and therapists are not too difficult to surmise!

Anal or oral implications aside, I find it true that the manner in which clients pay reflects their personality. Morris, disorderly in general, is erratic about fees, too. He never pays exactly what he owes; either less, making it up later, or more, thus forcing me to keep accounts.

Dependent, shy, and insecure, Dick is a businessman, and when it comes to money, he perks up remarkably. He checks every bill minutely and postpones payment as long as possible.

Howard is affluent and perhaps because of this attaches no great value to money. He may pay for a few sessions at a time if he happens to be carrying cash with him. If not, he'll pay another time.

Henry hates parting with money. I charge a low fee, knowing of his small income, but he still finds it hard to part with it and counts it over and over, lest he overpay. He "saves" by skipping sessions.

Dora always pays promptly. It is clear that she considers this her main contribution to our joint task. Beyond that, she still awaits miracles.

Three Main Stages

Like Caesar's Gaul, the interview is divided into three parts. Unlike Caesar's Gaul, these divisions are not always clearly visible. Sometimes they fuse into each other to such an extent that it is difficult to tell them apart. These divisions, or stages, indicate movement in the interview. If they are absent, this may indicate that there was none, that we never got past stage one, for example. On the other hand, movement may be so swift that it is very difficult to determine just where one stage ends and the next one begins. The three stages are:

1. Initiation, or statement of the matter
2. Development, or exploration
3. Closing

Initiation

In the initial stage the matter about which the therapist and the client are meeting is stated. This phase generally ends when both understand what is to be discussed and agree that it should be. (If they disagree, they may well part right then and there.) In actuality, the interview may not deal exclusively or even primarily with this matter. Other points may arise, and what seemed so central at first may diminish in importance and be replaced by another subject. It may develop that as the client feels more at home in the interview, she will allow herself to discuss what the real matter is, thereby changing partly or entirely the focus of the interview. Thus you, the teacher, ask Dick to see you, telling him when you meet that you have noticed that he hasn't been doing his homework as assiduously as he used to. If Dick feels that you really wish to help him, that you are genuinely interested in him and not merely in his homework, he may tell you of the difficulties at home. As a result, you may find yourselves discussing primarily these difficulties and what can be done about them, returning to the almost forgotten subject of homework only when both of you, having explored the situation, see homework as part of a wider picture and plan accordingly. Here, incidentally, all three stages were covered. The matter was stated, then it was explored, and closing followed.

To illustrate further: A man ostensibly looking for a job comes to see you at the employment bureau. While the two of you are exploring possible employment opportunities, it turns out that he is actually interested in further vocational training but does not know how to go about obtaining or financing it. In closing, both of you are planning around this. The need for a job, supposedly the matter, has been replaced by something more important to the client at this juncture. The real matter is further vocational training.

Mrs. A. visits her physician and complains of severe headaches. As she is encouraged to describe their manifestations — where, when, under what circumstances — Mrs. A. mentions that she thinks she may be pregnant again and . . . The real issue has been reached, and the interview proceeds accordingly.

Development, or Exploration

Once the matter has been stated and accepted, it is then looked into, explored. In this second phase — exploration — the main body of the interview has been reached. Most of our time will be spent in this mutual looking into the matter — trying to examine all its aspects and reach certain conclusions. Here, just where you may feel most in need of help, I shall have to disappoint. I cannot tell you what to say or not to say, what to do or leave undone. You may wish to consult some of the many excellent casebooks available. These present case material gathered from many professions and representing various interviewing approaches. (See the Supplementary Reading List at the end of this book.) However, Chapter 7, "Responses and Leads," should be of help here.

Learning from Past Interviews   Intending no disparagement of other sources, I should say that you can best help yourself by using your own interviews as guideposts — thinking about them, discussing them with colleagues and supervisors, and listening to your own recorded interviews and those of others. Every interview is different. As time goes on, you will perhaps discover a pattern; but this will take shape because of the way you function, the way you are. Discovering, examining, and deciding what to keep and what to change in this pattern will provide the sort of professional and personal growth that, I feel, will be most meaningful for you.

Certain aspects of this main phase of the interview deserve careful consideration. I shall point out some of them, knowing that there are others I can only touch upon. Again, my wish is to stimulate — not to present answers but to help you find your own.

Question: Did you help the client open up his perceptual field as much as possible? Was he able to look at things the way they appear to him rather than the way they seem to you or someone else? Was he free to look squarely at what he sees and to express it, or did he perceive himself through the eyes of someone else? Did he discover his own self, or did he find a self he thought he should be finding? Did your attitude prevent him from exploring his own life space or enable him to move about in it, unhampered by external influences?

When Lucy said, "I'll never get married now that I'm crippled," what did you do? You know you felt terrible; you felt that the whole world had caved in on her. But what did you say? What did you show? Did you help her to bring it out; to say it, all of it; to hear it and examine it? You almost said: "Don't be foolish. You're young and pretty and smart, and who knows, perhaps . . ." But you didn't. You had said similar things to patients in the hospital until you learned that it closed them off. So this time you simply looked at her and weren't afraid to feel what you both felt. Then you said, "You feel right now that your whole life has been ruined by this accident." "That's just it," she retorted, crying bitterly. After a while she continued talking. She was still crippled, but you hadn't gotten in the way of her hating it and confronting it.

When Charles, a black youth from Harlem, told you he hated Jews and would gladly strangle them all if he could, there was much you wanted to say. It was all on the tip of your tongue when you recalled that you were here to help him if you could. How could he realize you wanted to help him if you wouldn't even listen to him? If this was how he felt, you decided, it was better to listen and try to understand what it meant for him. And so you did not scold; you did not criticize; you did not tell him not to talk or feel that way. You did not moralize about Judeo-Christian values. Instead, you opened his perceptual field even wider by saying, "Right now you hate the Jews desperately." He poured out deep feelings of rejection, bitterness, and hopelessness. Gradually you began to see, to understand. You did not agree; you did not condone; but you began to feel what he had gone through and was still going through. You saw how full of hate and resentment he was against the Jews he knew and how totally unaware he was that you were Jewish.

Question: Did you help the client move from an external to an internal frame of reference (Rogers, 1942, 1951)? Did you help him come closer to himself, to explore and express what he found there rather than enmesh himself in platitudes and the evaluative labels others had been all too ready to bestow upon him? Did you enable him to tell you how he genuinely feels, how things truly look to him?

When Michael said that he knew it was wrong to steal, did you reply, "Why do you do it, then?" Or did you perhaps try to get him to sense and express what went on deep within him — his internal frame of reference — by saying something like: "You say this is wrong, but you go on doing it. I wonder what this means to you and how you understand it." You are glad you didn't probe or moralize — your internal frame of reference — by asking, "Do you have any brothers or sisters, and do they also . . . ?" or by stating, "I'm sure that since you know this sort of thing is wrong, it won't happen any more."

Interested in his internal frame of reference, you are concerned with what is central to him, not what is central to you; for the latter may be peripheral for him and in that event will shift him away from himself to you. If he says, "I hope for your sake that you don't have any sisters; they're all damned pests" and you reply, "It so happens that I have a sister, and we get along very well; your sisters may feel that the pest is you," you shift the frame of reference. But if you remark, "You and your sisters aren't exactly hitting it off right now," you do not shift but remain within his internal frame of reference.

Question: Did you let the client explore what she wanted to in her own way, or did you lead her in a direction you chose for her? Did your behavior truly indicate the absence of threat? Was she afraid to express herself, and if so, what did you do to relieve this fear? Did you really want to listen to her, or did you want her to listen to you because you already had the answer to her problem, because you were anxious to "give her a piece of your mind," or because you really didn't want to hear more as you wouldn't have known what to do with it anyway?

You will have to answer such questions when evaluating yourself and your interviews. There will be different answers with different clients; you will not always respond in exactly the same manner.

Question: Did you go along with the client, or did you force him to go along with you? Which do you prefer? What is better for him?

CL. When I was in the war, I had two buddies, and we used to —

TH. Well, you are back now, and I feel we must get on with your educational plans. I have the results of those tests here, and I'm sure you must be interested in them.

This sort of cutting off goes on in interviews more often than we may think. Sometimes we intend it so, and even then the procedure is debatable. At other times we don't; we just get carried away with ourselves, and later in reflecting upon it, we wish it had been otherwise. Occasionally we feel pressed for time or suspect that the client is telling stories. But sometimes we are not sufficiently aware of our own behavior in not being willing to find out what is really happening.

> CL. Last night, for the first time in weeks, I slept perfectly well without taking the medicine.

> IER.* That medicine is very important for you to take. Now, let's see, you are getting . . . three times a day, right?

I wonder how much we may be losing by such insensitiveness. I wonder what the patient feels about the doctor's genuine interest in him and how important this may be for restoring him to health.

Going along with the client means listening and responding to what he is saying and feeling. It means enabling him to express himself fully. It means following him rather than asking him to follow us. It entails clear-cut decisions: Are we prepared to let the client take the initiative and keep it as long as he needs to? Are we prepared to let him assume responsibility for himself, or do we feel we must assume it for him? Are we prepared to let him lead, or do we need to have him follow us? Ultimately, these are philosophical questions, but we answer them in one way or another every time we interview.

Frequently as we look deeply into the matter under discussion, we find that topic fuses into topic, thought elicits thought, and feeling brings forth more feeling in much the same way that stage fuses into stage in the interviewing process. However, this does not always hold true; at times the flow may falter and eventually halt. The client may look at you as if to say, "Where do we go from here?" and you yourself may be wondering, too. Again I have no conclusive answer but can offer several suggestions. For one, you might express what you are feeling, "You are looking at me, I feel, as though to say, 'Where do we go from here?'" Another possibility is to ask yourself and the client what is happening, "I wonder whether we have said all we are going to say today." Or you might say, "Unless there is something you'd like to add, perhaps we have talked enough about your latenesses; I wonder if there is anything else on your mind." Expressing puzzlement or

*IER stands for interviewer.

incomprehension on your part, you might observe, "Frankly I don't understand what is making it difficult for you to continue." By stating this in a slightly different way you will give it a different bearing altogether: "I feel it's kind of hard for you to go on. If it will help just to sit and think things through a bit, I don't mind at all." You have invited silence.

Silences Few areas of the helping interview have concerned me over the years as much as that of silence. I used to grapple with client silences and with my own as if they were natural disasters that just had to be endured. I often felt extremely uncomfortable but believed I was bound to endure client silence and that which I imposed on myself for the sake of the client and the ongoing therapy. Silence had always to be respected, I thought, to be held in awe rather than to be examined like every other aspect of the interviewing process.

Where this attitude originated, I cannot definitively say. It may have had its roots in my Rogerian background. I did not realize for a long time that silence is multifaceted. Silence may express the desire to listen rather than speak. Silence may mean evasion and escape. Silence may indicate resistance, hostility, aggression. Silence may signify lack of interest and even boredom. Silence often expresses confusion, lack of direction, lost bearings. Silence may, of course, communicate ineffable grief that should command our respect. It may ultimately denote deep concentration and thought on the client's part that we ought not interrupt. In short, silence conveys many varied messages that we must learn to decipher and respond to in accordance with the interpretation we have reached. We have, possibly, misread the message; this can always be checked out.

Many Kinds of Silence My experience has been that most beginning interviewers or therapists find silence hard to bear. They seem to think that if it occurs, they are at fault and the lapse should be remedied at once and at any cost. They regard it as a breach of etiquette that must be corrected on the spot. In time therapists learn to differentiate between silences, to appreciate and react to them differently.

There is, for example, the silence the client may require to sort out his thoughts and feelings. Respect for this silence is more beneficial than many words from the therapist. When ready, the client will continue, usually quite soon — in a minute or so. This minute will seem quite long to us at first, but with experience we shall learn to measure time internally. Should the silence endure, we may want to interject a brief remark to help him go on; one can get lost in silence and appreciate the indication of a possible way out. For example, we might say: "There must be lots going on within; I wonder if you are ready to share some of it with me" or "I can see by the expression on your face that there's much going on behind the scenes; I'm ready to participate if you're ready to have me." Silence of this sort can be most helpful if the therapist does not feel threatened by it or uncomfortable with it but can handle it with ease as part of an ongoing process.

Occasionally a silence arises, the cause of which is quite clear to the therapist. In fact, she, needing the respite as well, may share it. The client may have related something heartwarming, tragic, shocking, or frightening, and both partners feel the need to absorb it to the depths in mutual silence. If after such a silence the client still finds it difficult to continue, a comment such as "It must have been a heartwarming experience for you" will often help him pick up the threads again.

Confusion will frequently lead to silence. A given situation may be confusing to the client. She may have come out with something that confused her, or you may have inadvertently done so. Here the shorter the silence the better, lest confusion compound confusion. You will have to act to alleviate the tension in a manner appropriate to the situation and to your appraisal of it. "What I said just now about you and John seems to have confused you." This alone may be sufficient; if not, you might add, "What I meant was . . ." and then rephrase your statement. Most likely this will elicit a response.

In an entirely different situation you may feel that the client — after he or you have stated the matter to be discussed — may be confused as to what to do next. Often in this case you can help by structuring the situation a bit for him: "I see you don't know what to say or just where to begin. Here you can say whatever you like or begin where you choose. I really want to try to understand what you think and how you feel about this matter and to help you if I can."

The silence of resistance is something else again. The client may be silent because she is resisting what she considers to be probing. She may see in you an authority figure to be opposed or avoided. She may not yet be ready to reveal what is really on her mind. The therapist may well find this type of silence the hardest to deal with because he himself tends to feel rejected, opposed, and thwarted. Everyone will do what he considers best under the circumstances, but it is most important (1) to see the situation clearly for what it is and (2) not to respond as if he were being personally attacked. Showing the client that we can accept this form of resistance may be an effective way of breaking her silence: "I don't mind the silence, but I feel you are resenting me in some way. I wish you would tell me about it so we can discuss it together." Or perhaps: "I don't feel that either of us is particularly comfortable with this silence. I can wait; but if there is something you're feeling, expressing it so that we can examine it together may help."

It was fascinating to contrast Dick's behavior when he came with his wife Betty with his demeanor when he came alone. Alone, he could now talk, but in Betty's presence he regressed to his former, silent self. Dick explained that there was no need for him to talk, because Betty did so for both of them. Furthermore, he felt that she was pressuring him. His way out was his old familiar escape into silence.

Martha's silences frustrated me totally: she had told everything and there was nothing to add — it was up to me now. Yes, she hated her father but she had no intention of saying anything more on the subject. She would certainly never divulge what he had done when she was a child. Men were too threatening, false all of them, and not to be trusted. Yes, that included me as well. There was nothing more to be added; she had said what she intended to say and now it was my turn. Silence. My interpretations of resistance produced silence. My expressed desire to help if she would only . . . silence. She was obviously in dire need of help, so I suggested a change of therapist. More silence, which was finally broken with "I knew right along you'd want to get rid of me. Just say so in plain words and I'll go." Eventually, I had to say so; not because I wished to get rid of her but because I could not help her. She left, as always, in silence.

Tom refused to let me intrude into his protracted silences. He would sit in the dark silently, session after session, until the dam burst and the grief and anger poured out.

Elaine lost her young husband in the Six-Day War of 1967. "I don't know how I'll cope now or if I'll ever be able to cope again." She needed many periods of silence to reorient herself after the first sharp pangs of grief had given way to an ever-present ache. She needed to mourn for Gary; to think of the children and the future, of herself carrying on; and, part of the time, simply to sit in healing silence.

Eve was the mother of two teen-age daughters. There had been a son, too, but he had recently died at just two years of age as the result of a debilitating illness no one had understood or been able to diagnose. She did not want to see me or anyone else, but her husband had insisted. And so she came, merely to sit in her chair frozen, remote, and silent. I could persuade her to talk only about her little boy, and this she did, meeting after meeting, in great detail. She spoke of him as if he were still alive, as if she would find him waiting for her when she returned home. About his illness and death she could not speak until months later.

Finally, there are the brief silences, the short pauses, during which the client may simply be searching for more thoughts and feelings to express. He may be thinking of how to express them or he may wish, first, to decide what he thinks and feels before continuing. This is the point at which we most often get in the way. We say something meaningful or meaningless — and destroy his train of thought. Therefore, it is best not to rush, not to interpret a short silence as a command from above to act, but to wait a bit and be prepared for what will come. Usually something will follow these short "thinking silences." Then, instead of hindering, we shall have assisted the client to express an idea with which he may have struggled. We shall not have interrupted him nor made him feel that here he cannot wrestle with ideas and feelings without being pounced upon.

Inevitably both client and therapist will sometimes speak at the same moment and both then retreat with apologies and encouragements to the other to continue. This can be awkward, and a bit of humor may assist us. I am assuming, of course, that we are interested in listening to the client and do not feel that we must have our say just then. We can interject a short remark: "I'm sorry, go ahead." Frequently just a smile with an encouraging nod will be sufficient. Or: "I was just wondering aloud what you would say next when you said it, and now I've missed it. What were you saying?"

I have learned to tackle silences. I do not let them endure just because they have occurred. I make use of my intuition, check my intuition out with the client, and proceed. Profound silences do exist, of course, but shallow ones exist as well. Today I can cope with them better than I once could. I differentiate now; that enables clients to differentiate as well. I can respect silence and tolerate it for sessions at a time, but I must feel that it is purposeful. I am able now to break silences and to assist the client to move ahead. No longer do I believe that silence is always golden. Frequently it is merely gilt.

Personal Experience Having searched my files, tapes, and memory, I still cannot discover a single instance where, engaged in therapy, I initiated relating a personal experience. Upon further reflection, I still consider this the correct course. I do not mean the normal chit-chat that accompanies all human encounters and that occurs in therapy as well. Should the client mention a novel, play, or concert that I too have read or attended, I may discuss it with her briefly. Should she ask to hear about my latest visit to London, I will touch upon the highlights. But I will take care to make the client central again as soon as possible: We managed to see eight plays and heard six concerts in two weeks. London has so much to offer that we had difficulty choosing. The National Theatre was especially good this season. We heard Perlman, who was really superb. I could go on for the entire session . . . but tell me, what's been happening to you while I was away?

When the temptation to use a personal example or experience arises, it is up to you to decide whether to yield to or rise above the temptation. Not everyone agrees with me, I know, but my conviction is that for several reasons it is best not to yield. My personal experience or example holds meaning for me. I am not convinced that it will for the client. Furthermore, he may well hesitate to express how he honestly feels about it lest he offend me by casting aspersions in some way on my example. In addition, in presenting my own experience I may unintentionally be threatening the client. He may think to himself, "Well, perhaps that worked for you; but if I were you, I'd be sitting where you are now and not be in this mess." If he is able to express his resentment, so much the better. However, if he denies himself such freedom of expression, he may appear to accept what I have said and cause me to believe that I have helped him when I have not.

If requests seem to me inappropriate, I block them:

> CL. Did you have trouble raising your children?
>
> TH. Now and then, I suppose. How are things going with John?
>
> CL. When you first came to Israel things must have been very different.
>
> TH. I suppose they were. We felt more like one large family then and lived more simply. How do you find it as a newcomer?

When clients encroach upon private grounds, they are probably fantasizing about me or else seeing in me some other significant person in their lives. Needless to say, I respond to the underlying implications rather than to the remark itself:

> CL. I saw you with your wife last night. She looks so pretty and gentle.
>
> TH. When you think of my wife and myself together, what associations does that evoke?
>
> CL. That's a new picture you have hanging on the wall. Did one of your talented clients paint it for you?
>
> TH. I hear envy and jealousy in your voice. . . .

When clients expressed concern and interest during and after my hospitalization for a heart attack, I felt grateful. Since a coronary is a most common occurrence, questions about treatment, doctors, and nurses naturally arose, as well as comments upon the relative merits of other hospitals. During the visits at hospital and home I responded to these remarks as any other convalescing patient would. Back at work, I returned to my customary practice:

> *CL.* Don't you think that you returned to work a little too soon?
>
> *TH.* I hear you saying I should not repeat the mistake you made last year after your surgery. You are still not back to being your old self.

I do not mean to suggest that the experience of others may not benefit the client. It may indeed. I do maintain that I hinder her when I place myself with my personal experience and example into the spotlight. However, if the client solicits them, the situation is thereby changed, and I may choose to comply with her request. But even then I think it is prudent to qualify my words with a remark such as: "This has worked for me, but I can't say whether it will work for you" or "This helped me, but I wonder how you feel about it as regards yourself." In this way I indicate that it is she who is central in the situation and that she need not copy my example. She will realize that I do not look upon my experience or example as necessarily providing the solution for her.

A less confronting way is to draw upon the experience of others by means of generalization and depersonalization. For example: "I have known many students who when faced with a similar situation have found it helpful to . . . How do you feel about this?" or "People do come up against obstacles like this. They often feel better when they are able to . . . How does this strike you?" There still remains the danger that the client will think he ought to adopt the course mentioned because others have and particularly because I have pointed this out, but it is only a minimal danger.

I have no mixed feelings about the following attempt at encouragement. The therapist should avoid it like the plague. "Well, you know, everyone has to go through this sooner or later. Every cloud has its silver lining, and by tomorrow morning you'll feel much better. A good night's sleep always helps, so why don't you try that?"

The area in which my personal experience is most often solicited is, naturally, blindness. Here, at times, I feel trapped. If a sighted person expresses curiosity about a specific aspect of blindness and I sense no affect behind it aside from purely human interest, I have no problem providing the information and moving on, back to him. But should the request come from a recently blinded client, the matter is more complicated for me. On the one hand, since I do possess experience of a most personal nature, I find it unnatural to ignore the request. On the other hand, I realize that what works for me may not work for the client. I also know that some, consciously or not, may resent me for already having passed the hurdles that still lie ahead of them. Therefore, I must tread warily.

Earle lost his sight as the result of an accident in the army. He can never regain his sight, both eyes have been enucleated. One day he questioned innocently enough:

CL. How do you get around?

TH. Most of the time I use a cane — the long one you are familiar with from mobility training at the Rehabilitation Center. Sometimes I go with my wife or a friend.

CL. I want a dog. That's safer and with a dog I won't be so dependent on people.

TH. Fine, but we are all dependent on each other.

CL. Maybe, but I want to minimize it. Where did you study?

TH. In the States at Cornell, Columb —

CL. I'm going to study in England. I'm going to study computers. They didn't have that in your day.

TH. No, they sure didn't.

CL. Before all this happened I wanted to become an architect. I don't believe in the "helping" professions. No one has ever helped me. I've had to do everything on my own. Everyone tells me I have to accept my new condition but that's a lot of crap. I'll never accept it and I bet you don't either. You just pretend because your job requires you to.

TH. Accepting may be impossible but coping is not.

CL. That's a lot of crap, too. It's really the same thing. Does your wife see?

TH. Yes, she does. We met —

CL. I bet that makes even you feel inferior — her seeing, I mean.

TH. Do you think you'll always feel inferior to the sighted now?

CL. All blind people do, I'm sure. I don't want to marry a blind woman either. That's all I need — two of us groping around. So I'll buy any services I need with good old hard cash.

TH. I know blind people who used to —

CL. No preaching, please.

TH. In my experience —

CL. Your experience means nothing to me. You were born blind, you said. How can you compare that with me?

Zella had to travel a long distance to consult with me but had chosen to come because of my personal experience. She had recently lost her sight due to a severe diabetic condition. However, she was certain she would regain most of her vision after surgery. Zella worked as a school counselor and wanted assistance in organizing her work while in her "present condition."

CL. How can you tell when you reach the end of a session?

TH. I carry a braille watch in my pocket so I can know the time merely by touching it. Here, look.

CL. But I won't need braille. Isn't there another alternative?

TH. You could use one of those alarm wristwatches that are so popular these days.

CL. Do you mind showing me how you dial the phone; you do dial yourself, don't you?

TH. Let's go into the other room and I'll show you.

CL. Not that I think I'll ever need either, but what are the pros and cons of guide dog versus cane?

TH. ... but the choice is a very individual matter. How do you plan to get about?

CL. My husband does all the shopping now and drives me to and from school. At school, friends are always ready to help.

TH. You're getting lots of help.

CL. Yes, but there are things I prefer doing alone, if possible. What do you do about taking notes after sessions?

TH. I type up summaries or tape sessions.

CL. I don't touch-type so I'll just use tapes I guess. I don't know how you've stood it all these years. For me it's a temporary situation. If it isn't, I won't want to live.

TH. You seem to feel that it isn't worth living if one is blind.

CL. Exactly, and I do admire you but . . .

TH. Is there anything else you wish to talk about today?

CL. No, thanks. My first operation is scheduled two months from now. I imagine I won't have to come again.

Now for two more ghosts that loiter in the background of the typical interview and must be put to rest. The first is, "If I were you, I should . . ." The client's reaction: "Well, I just don't believe it. If you were me, you'd feel just as confused and unsure as I do, and so there would be two of us, neither knowing what to do. If you were me, you wouldn't say that. If you were me, you wouldn't know what to do any more than I do. But if I were you, I would never say to anyone, 'If I were you, I should . . .'" Far better to come out with it straightforwardly: "I think your best bet at this point is to . . ." or "I feel that right now the wisest thing you can do is . . ." This, at least, sounds sincere.

The second ghost needs only a coup de grace. His name is "I know just how you feel." The client thinks: "I'm not taken in. How can you 'know' how I 'feel'? And if you know, so what? You don't feel the way I feel or you would never think of saying that you know." This ghost is cold and remote. If he has a mind, he surely has no heart, and so away with him.

If we genuinely feel with the client what she is feeling, if we can let her know by our behavior that we are feeling with her just as hard as we can, and if we are able to show this without getting in her way, we shall not need to tell her, for she will already know. She will understand that we shall never know just exactly how and what she feels but that as another human being we are trying our best and showing her that we are trying. "I know how you feel" really says, "I don't know how you feel, and I'm not willing to go out of my way to find out."

I may have given the impression that in my opinion the therapist should never either lead or question. What I do believe is that therapists lead and question to such an extent that the role of the client is subordinated. Naturally we must lead and question at times; but when we overdo this, we do not enable the client to express himself as fully as he might. Some clients require leads and like to be questioned. But such individuals probably expect us to solve their problems for them rather than help them arrive at their own, more meaningful solutions. When we attempt this, no growing experience is provided the client to help him meet future situations.

Closing

Stage three, closing, is in many ways similar to stage one, initiating contact, but operated in reverse. Now we must fashion an end to the contact and separate. Closing is not always easy. The beginning therapist, especially, may not be adept at letting the client know that the time is about up. She may be fearful that she will make the client feel that he is being pushed out. The therapist herself may not be ready to close. Both may find it difficult to part.

Much needs to be said about this closing phase of the interview, but I have found that two factors are basic:

1. Both partners in the interview should be aware of the fact that closing is taking place and accept this fact, the therapist in particular. It is a bad prognosis for therapy if it is the client who terminates sessions. If it is he who gets up and initiates leaving, we had better check things out fast; the process is endangered.

2. During the closing phase no new material should be introduced, or at any rate discussed, for closing concerns that which
   has already taken place. If there is more new material, another
   interview will have to be scheduled.

It is the therapist's responsibility to deal with these two factors
as effectively as she can. The task becomes easier as she increasingly appreciates its importance and feels comfortable with it.
Unless the client is especially experienced or sensitive, he will
not always know how much time is still at his disposal, and you
can help him by indicating that closing is imminent: "Well, our
time is just about up. Is there anything you'd like to add before
we try to see where we have arrived?" Frequently you and he will
have really finished, and you can avoid a great deal of stumbling
about and awkward silence by remarking, "I have the feeling that
neither of us has anything useful to add at this point." Sensing
relief and agreement, you continue, "Well, then, let's see . . ." I
think most of us feel better with this sort of simple structuring.
Knowing definitely now what we previously feared, anticipated,
or assumed — that the interview is about to end — we can act
accordingly.

There are cogent reasons for avoiding the introduction or discussion of new material at the closing stage. What happens if you
do permit it? Conscious that you must shortly see someone else
or keep an appointment at another place, you will not be attending as closely as you should. Before you realize it, you will be
angry at the client for coming up now of all times with new, important ideas he might have introduced previously. There you will
sit, inwardly writhing, while he goes on talking. This state of affairs is unfair to both of you and can be avoided easily enough.

I carry a braille watch in my pocket so that I can keep track of
time without disturbing the client. This "uncanny" ability to
sense time amazes clients until they raise the issue and I produce
the watch. As the session approaches its close, I give nonverbal
hints to that effect. I may straighten up in my chair or rise to
accompany the client to the door. I may add:

TH. The time passed so quickly that it's hard to believe the
hour is up. We'll have to stop for today. I can see you have much
more to say. We can continue from here next time if you like.

Or

> *TH.* Sorry I have to break in on your silence. Our time is just about up.

To close in spite of the presentation of new material at the end of the interview is easier when both sides know that another meeting is scheduled.

> *TH.* Our time is just about up for today, Mrs. Keen.
>
> *CL.* What about camp for Betty this summer?
>
> *TH.* I didn't realize you were considering it. We won't be able to discuss it now, but we can start from there next week, if you like.

You do not know why Betty's mother waited until the last moment to bring up the subject of camp. She herself may not know. Perhaps she did so because she wasn't ready sooner, because she was afraid to discuss it, because she hoped that you would do it for her, because she wanted you to herself a little longer. You could go on speculating. You might choose to make a mental or written note of these reflections, but you know you cannot pursue them now. Both Betty's mother and you realize that the interview has come to a close.

I will seldom allot more time to the client even when he has arrived late. This is his responsibility, not mine. Here, too, there are bound to be exceptions. I can cut down on my break between sessions if this seems important, but I will do everything to assure the next client of her full time and my undivided attention.

Dick resents it when I bring sessions to a close. He wants to squeeze out a few more moments even though he may have sat silent for half the session. After all, time is money — my time and his money.

David cannot bear abrupt closing. He has told me so:

> *CL.* I don't like the way you bring sessions to a close. Right along I feel you are with me and then, suddenly, you practically throw me out. I know someone is due after me, that I

am not the only one you see, but you rub it in a little too hard for my liking.

TH. I didn't realize I was being so abrupt. I'll try to remember that in the future. How do you feel now that you've told me?

Anne finds it hard to spend money. She pays promptly and fully but admits that she hates doing so. Every minute of our time together is valuable to her, partly because every minute costs.

TH. O.K., Anne, I see that's it for today. See you next week.

CL. You still owe me three minutes.

TH. Do I? Well, let's go on then.

CL. But I have nothing to add. You say something.

TH. I have nothing to add either. How much time do I owe you now?

George goes right on talking as I accompany him to the door. He always has more to say. So I ease him out of the door and into the garden and we part there — at times I feel as if I were fleeing back to my office for shelter.

I am not suggesting that we be inflexible and work mechanically, keeping one eye on the clock. I am convinced, though, that the interview is most helpful when limited in time and when both partners accept and work within this time structure. Acceptance of the time factor is important, especially in a series of interviews. It helps us to recognize that being together is a delimited situation and that beyond it both of us are persons with professional and private obligations that must be respected. In one-time interviews closing is more difficult to handle. But if somewhere along the line we can ascertain approximately how much time still remains available to both of us and if we can begin closure early enough, allowing ample time to pull things together, closing should prove relatively easy.

Styles of Closing There are many styles of closing. The style used will depend on the interview itself, the client, and the interviewer. Sometimes the ordinary courtesies will suffice to bring the interview to an end. Under these circumstances a closing remark such as the following will serve: "I believe that does it; we know how to get in touch with one another should anything else come up" or "Thanks for coming in. I feel that this meeting has been a fruitful one for both of us." I don't mean to suggest formulas but want to stress the fact that closing statements should be short and to the point. When we have nothing else to add, the more we say, the less meaningful it becomes and the more drawn out and painful closing is.

At times in closing you may wish to refer back to the matter discussed in the interview with a concluding statement, in effect a restatement of the way you have both agreed the matter is to be dealt with. The school counselor may conclude: "I know now how you feel about Bill's college plans. When he comes in to see me, he and I will be able to take your reservations into account. You two will carry on from there, as you suggested." The doctor may say to her patient: "Now that we've decided on the operation, I'll make the necessary arrangements. Then you'll get in touch with the hospital, as we agreed." Or the placement officer at the employment bureau may conclude: "O.K., then, I'll look into the possibilities we've discussed. Unless you hear from me before then, I'll see you next Tuesday."

Occasionally a more explicit summation is required to check whether you and the client have understood each other: "Before you leave, I just want to make sure I understood you correctly. You can't go back to work for a while because of the baby. You feel that John should shift over to night school in the fall and get a job during the day. Until then his family will go on helping. If I left anything out or didn't get it quite right, just set me straight."

A somewhat different approach is to ask the client to state how he has understood what has been going on in the interview: "We've had quite a chat, Jack, and I'm wondering what you are taking away from it. It hasn't been easy for you to talk, I know, and I'm not certain I understood everything you tried to express. So if you could sort of summarize things out loud, it might help both of us. If I want to add anything, I'll do so."

Sometimes in closing we may want to point up matters that were mentioned but not discussed because of lack of time: "There's the bell, and we haven't even gotten around to talking about the French or your work on the paper. We can do that next time, if you like. You know my hours; when would you like to come in again?"

Finally, when definite plans have been made during the interview, it may be well to recap them briefly during closing, especially if both client and therapist or counselor have agreed to carry out different tasks. This is a kind of mutual feedback to verify that both understand what they are to do. "Now let's see. You agreed to talk to your mother about the allowance and to try to turn off the TV by ten. I'll speak to Miss Barrett about having your seat changed. Was there anything else?" Similarly, mutual feedback is provided when the counselor first states his part in the task ahead and then encourages the client to state his: "I suppose that's it for today. We've made quite a lot of decisions. As I understand it, I am to look into the possibility of evening electronics courses and to check about the grant. As you see it, what are the things that you're going to look into before our next meeting?"

Closing is especially important because what occurs during this last stage is likely to determine the client's impression of the interview as a whole. We must make certain that we have given her full opportunity to express herself, or, alternatively, we must set a mutually convenient time for this purpose. We should leave enough time for closing so that we are not rushed, since this might create the impression that we are evicting the client. Whatever remains to be done at the end in the way of reviewing steps to be taken or summing up matters should be attended to without haste and preferably as a joint venture. With patience, practice, awareness, and reflection, everyone can develop a style that satisfies him and facilitates the helping interview.

Trial Period

It is a custom of long standing in many colleges and universities to let students try courses and professors for a short period at the outset of each term before settling down to a firm program. We are offered trial periods for subscriptions to newspapers, to magazines, and to much else in the world of merchandising. However, in the helping profession the prevailing attitude seems to be "take it or leave it." If you can tolerate the idiosyncrasies of the therapist you stay; if not, you go. As for the therapist, it is taken for granted that she can work with every client.

When beginning with a new client, I suggest a trial period for both of us: "You've come to work on matters that are very important to you. In the process, you'll have to reveal much of yourself and allow yourself the freedom to examine afresh many things in your life. After a while you'll probably want to make decisions about yourself and others in your life. You've got to make very sure that I'm the sort of person you feel you can do this with. It's a risky and expensive undertaking and you should make this journey only with someone with whom you feel comfortable and whom you feel you can trust. I know Penny recommended me to you, but what was good for her may not be good for you. I, too, have to feel that we can work together; that I can be of use to you. I can't work with everybody either. So my suggestion is that we meet a few times and consider this a trial period. We'll check things out as we go and if we click, fine; if not, let's say so frankly. If necessary, I'll help you find a more suitable therapist."

This seemingly endless speech takes about one minute. I am firmly convinced that it is essential. It opens up options and allows us both to relax. It encourages examination and mutual feedback. It legitimizes personal preferences and removes the "No Exit" sign. Usually things do work out. The checking at the end of sessions takes a very short time. Thus I asked Sandy:

TH. How did things go for you today?

CL. Pretty well. I feel comfortable

In another early session she stated:

CL. I was glad you were more active today. What you said about my mother and me sure shook me up. I'm glad it's on my tape.

Contrast this with Sara:

TH. How did things go today, Sara?

CL. Well, you know, you were here. I don't feel you always understand me and I think you side with Andy. It's easy for him. Away all day at work, he can be friendly and patient with Louise in the evening — by that time I'm totally worn out.

TH. I felt your resentment and it made me quite uncomfortable.

Shosh volunteered:

CL. It's hard; it's as if Ely were here with us. Still, I'm glad that I came to you. The fact that you two were friends makes it easier, not harder for me. A total stranger . . .

The final decision is not formal, but both sides are aware that it has been taken. Obstacles in communication may remain, clients may still leave, but at least we have given ourselves and each other a fair chance. Sandy continued to tape our sessions:

CL. I'm going on. I don't mean it as flattery but you are just what I need.

Sara and I arrived at a dead end:

TH. If during my vacation you made no attempt to reach me and turned, instead, to another therapist . . .

CL. I think you're right. I feel better with him. You and I just didn't hit it off.

TH. Fine. I wish you luck.

Shosh did not refer to our trial period, but we both knew that it was over and it was okay.

Comings and Goings

At times, there is movement: in and out of therapy and from therapist to therapist. The latter concerns me at this point. Clients have left me for a variety of reasons. Howard left to combat his alcoholism in a program employing behavioristic techniques. Earle, as might have been expected, went over to a sighted therapist. Pat and Peter left because Peter thought I was partial to his wife and, in addition, incompetent. Peter complained in a like manner about their next therapist, after which the couple separated. I only learned of Henry's departure from his new therapist, who called, wishing to consult. As already indicated, Martha left in silent despair. I hope that somehow she found her way in life.

As part of the groundwork for this book, I prepared a list of the clients for whom I felt genuine liking. To my amazement I discovered while going over it that Tom was not among them. For I had genuinely liked Tom. We had worked together in darkness and in light. I accompanied his silences, tears, and outbursts of rage and then his calmer reflections. I admired his determination, wit, and courage. But, obviously, I had never really forgiven him for the way he left and, unaware, resented it still.

During his third and last year of therapy we could both see the light at the end of the tunnel. Tom's therapy was, at long last, coming to a close. His battles with the past were over and won; he could now look and plan ahead. He could communicate with and at times even share personal experiences with his father. And then one day Tom disappeared. He missed sessions — he who had always been compulsively punctual. He did not get in touch — he who had sent me innumerable letters during the worst crisis of his therapy. He did pay his fee by mail, without a word of explanation. From others I learned that he had turned to a female therapist and within five sessions had concluded therapy with her!

Some years later, Tom got in touch. He wanted to see me for one long session. He came, never referred to the past and unburdened himself of his current conflict. He brought an attractive plant for my wife. To this day he owes me for that session.

Clients who have been in therapy before tend to reveal this at the outset. When necessary, one of the very few questions I pose concerns previous therapy and therapists. If the client has been in therapy before, there is no need to explain the process. In addition, it is important to examine with him the reasons for his changing and his choice of me as therapist. The reason may be very prosaic: Morris moved to my town from a larger city. He had abandoned therapy some years before and felt a need to renew it. He had no desire to travel back and forth to his former therapist and he had heard favorably of me.

Experienced therapists know better than to associate a client's leaving with personal failure or another's moving over to him as an accomplishment. On the contrary, generally speaking, I find that those who were not helped by other therapists are likely not to be helped by me either. But there are exceptions.

Jane had seen a therapist for one year when she was eighteen years old. Now, at twenty-two, she felt more mature and more ready to involve herself in the therapeutic process. This time she deliberately chose a male therapist.

Regina's catalogue of therapists she had consulted could compare favorably with Leporello's catalogue of Don Giovanni's conquests in love. Having time and money to spare, feeling bored once again and ailing with minor symptoms, she decided that my turn had come. We lasted all of five sessions together.

Eric arrived S.O.S. on the recommendation of his psychiatrist. He had gradually gone blind and, now that his job was in jeopardy, had gone into a deep depression. The psychiatrist and I agreed to cooperate but, as will be seen later, it was in vain.

I wanted to know whom Gerda had seen, not to judge or criticize but, just in case I was acquainted with the therapist involved, to imagine their interaction and fantasize as to what had taken place between them. Gerda's former therapist was highly qualified but known in the field as somewhat dogmatic and rigid. Gerda required an entirely different atmosphere, which, in her case, I could provide.

Dora is an experienced client. As a child she saw two therapists. She worked with two more during late adolescence and now, a young married woman, she has come to me. Neither of us is too optimistic. She lacks energy, fears change, and still requires Mommy nearby. Her symbiosis is a deep-rooted plant. Dora comes faithfully twice a week but still feels that this, in itself, should perform the long-awaited miracle. Unfortunately, miracles are rare.

Is Clienthood Teachable?

Although I hate to admit it, I fear that clienthood is rarely teachable. Those who are highly motivated may learn to some extent; others may take much that is meaningful with them from therapy while remaining "bad" subjects for therapy. Basically, people are either born good clients or not, just as they are born liberals or conservatives, if one is to believe Gilbert and Sullivan. So we proceed by trial and error. We try to instruct; we hope that time may help; but, deep down, we know better — by now I recognize a "good" client when I meet one and a "bad" one as well.

The talking cure we are engaged in seems to work best for talkers. Clients either possess verbal ability or they do not. Some were brought up on conversation, others on captions. Some find it easy to express feelings; others find it difficult or even impossible. Some can clutch at the enabling act and be aided, while others are just not built to respond to our cues or to profit from the atmosphere we create. We all have our own, very personal ways of learning. Therapy does not speak to all. Some learn from books, from religion, from the experience of others. Some are taught by the arts or by esoteric beliefs. Some claim to learn from life, while still others feel no need at all to learn. "Good" clients must be made in heaven. It is our luck when they come our way.

Shirley explained that she needed a "general cleaning — from cellar to roof," as she put it. No, she had never been in therapy before but had often considered the possibility. Lately she had been feeling so dissatisfied with herself that she experienced it as a physical pain in her gut. She was cross with Dan, her husband, and resented her two small boys who were impeding her career. She hated housekeeping and had no intentions of becoming a slave like many other women she knew, including her mother. Shirley, obviously, did not need to be taught clienthood; she was already a master.

Glenn sat looking somber and morose. A humanities professor, he knew about therapy, having read much. Glenn had undergone open heart surgery and thought he needed help. There was not much he could say; he slept too much, ate too little, did not enjoy life the way he used to. He found it difficult to expand, answering questions briefly and succinctly. He possessed an incisive mind and soon "understood" that we were getting nowhere. He "knew" what I meant when I tried awkwardly to "teach" him therapy. He just wasn't cut out for it. He had always managed on his own and would just have to continue that way.

Olga did not bring a tape recorder as Sandy did, but she took copious notes during and, she claimed, after every session. She was so busy with her notes that she seemed to have hardly any time left over for our interacting. Olga taught special education. She could analyze the therapeutic process beautifully — when it related to others. She even knew, cognitively, that her strength lay in analyzing others. She was unhappily married, but for the children's sake . . . She loved her profession and that gave her the strength to continue. Meanwhile, she buried herself in her notes. Sandy profited from her taping; for Olga, her notes provided yet another defensive wall. We went on dabbling at therapy for a while, but we both knew it was pointless.

Some clients are not really teachable but seem to hang on for dear life. They have never completed the therapeutic process but cannot leave therapy entirely. They will show up now and again for a single session or even a period of weekly meetings. They are not therapy addicts but require a booster shot now and then.

I never know just when Evelyn will appear, but that she eventually will is beyond doubt. She holds a responsible position in a large company but has no real friends at work. Except for an aging mother and a few acquaintances, she lives a lonely existence. Evenings, she drinks a bit and talks to herself for lack of better company. At times she has hallucinations. Whenever she has difficulty making a decision on her own, she calls for a single appointment, after which she again disappears into anonymity until the cycle repeats itself. I never mind seeing her. Evelyn possesses wit and charm and I have fantasized helping find her a mate. Unfortunately it has remained at that.

Betty first sought therapy with me twenty years ago. Eventually she married Dick, who came alone for a time, after which they started therapy together. Lately they have been coming individually or as a couple on an irregular basis, as the need strikes. She is volatile and tends to hysteria; he, stubborn and depressive. They both tend to feel inadequate. However, they have succeeded in bringing up two children reasonably well and have kept their own heads above water. It would seem that we have set up a silent partnership: before they jump, we always consult.

Elsa and Charles are also eternal visitors. They were referred to me after Charles's brief hospitalization and have come ever since, off and on, for many years. So far we have succeeded in keeping him this side of sanity and her flexible enough to cope with him

and with her own anxieties. I am very fond of Charles. He is original, creative, and often fun to be with. When he feels jealous,
deprived, or hounded, our encounters are difficult. He and Elsa
have lived together for over thirty years. They have three married
sons and many grandchildren. Charles always knows when he
needs me. He is hostile and counterdependent at times, but basically we have established good rapport.

Is therapisthood teachable? I doubt this as well. Therapists, I
guess, are also made in heaven. However, learning skills, acquir-
ing experience, and gaining perseverance can improve existing
therapeutic attributes. Still, the art of matching the right client
with the right therapist remains a mystery and entails more luck
than brains.

My own therapisthood has taught me two lessons: first, beware
of the pitfalls of diagnosis. Trust your own judgment. Ask yourself: can I reach this particular client and can he reach me? Above
all, do not panic. The second lesson concerns authority. I have
finally grasped and accept the fact that I am or represent an authority figure to the client. If she believes in me and I do not
prevent her from leaning upon me temporarily, I may help assuage her pain, enable her to gain strength and, paradoxically,
grow into a more independent human being.

Easing pain, providing strength, and enabling independence are
metagoals of therapy. Even if clients can only approximate them,
it is worth putting our authority on the line. Therapy remains,
ultimately, a matter of belief. If the client believes in me and I do
not abuse that belief but, rather, employ it to eventually
strengthen him, I shall have played my role to the hilt.

Esther could not lean on Abe at all. He was a very good husband
and father but weak, and now she was in need of someone strong.
She needed someone who believed in her, would fight with her
and, if necessary, for her. She just could not go on working inside
the kibbutz; she was stifled there. She had a profession,
physiotherapy, and she wished to work and advance in it — but
outside the kibbutz. She loved kibbutz life and the education it
was providing her children. But she had ruined her relations with
the medical staff and considered this irrevocable. Of late her rages
had become uncontrollable; hospitalization had been suggested.
Esther leaned upon me heavily for over a year. The compromises

proposed were rejected. Esther considered leaving — kibbutz, family, everything. Today she still lives on the kibbutz though Abe has passed away. She pursues her profession successfully "on the outside" but returns home every day after work and helps out in the communal dining room on weekends. Esther has not needed me as therapist for many years. Her family and mine have become friends. This is a rather unusual development to which I will return later.

Carla's therapist had recently died. She sought me out in the hope that, with time, she could believe in me as she had in her. She needed the assurance that there existed someone to whom she could turn in case of need. In five sessions she "brought me up to date." She came once more after a few months' interval. Since then she has managed on her own.

Paul came to Israel from Morocco as a small boy. Money was short in his family and he went to work at an early age. Today he owns a pastry shop and loves his trade. Suddenly, for no apparent reason he developed severe anxiety symptoms. Anything remotely smacking of violence or death frightened him. He could no longer read newspapers or watch TV without trembling uncontrollably. He could not go near cemeteries. Heart palpitations and stomach pains appeared. All medical tests returned negative. Paul knew nothing of therapy. For him I was the doctor — a different kind of doctor, perhaps, from the ones with whom he had previously come into contact, but a doctor nevertheless. I had to ask the questions. He dutifully provided answers. Whatever I "prescribed" in the way of exercises and activities for reinforcement or extinction he unquestioningly carried out. When I was certain he would completely recover, I told him so. His deepest fear had concerned paternity. Today he is the proud father of a son and heir.

CL. I am no longer an "invalid" as you used to call me. I've come a long way, but I still need to have you tell me what to do sometimes. Telling myself the very same things just isn't the same. I don't know how that happened. I never saw my parents in that light. Ever since I realized that Bert had taken advantage of me for years by pursuing his career at my expense, he, who had been an authority for me, is so no longer.

One day I'll let you "order" me not to regard you as an authority any more but not quite yet.

Anne has put it in a nutshell. At first she had to be driven to and from sessions. Now she takes the bus. This summer she even flew to Europe with Bert and enjoyed herself. She is much less self-centered, although she still has to make a real effort to think of Bert and the children first.

3 • ATTITUDES AND BEHAVIOR

Every therapist or interviewer engaging in the helping interview brings along with him attitudes in terms of which he functions. Whether he is aware of it or not, whether he can put it into words or not, these attitudes influence what he does or leaves undone and in what manner he accomplishes his task. In terms of his attitude he determines his own behavior in the interview to a great extent and, thereby, that of the client as well. His attitudes in the interview, which may be explicit or implicit, expressed or unexpressed, are his philosophy regarding both help and interviewing. Everyone deeply interested in his work will wish to discover the attitudes in terms of which he operates. Furthermore, once aware of how he behaves, he can decide if he wants to act thus or if he would like to behave differently.

My Own Approach

My approach has everything to do with how I wish to behave in the helping interview and surely colors everything I have written so far and am still to write in this book. I am not endeavoring to prove that my approach is right or wrong, good or bad; nor can I determine its relevance for you. Nonetheless, I feel that I must attempt to state it so that you will know what it is and be stimulated to learn what your own approach is. In other words, I shall state mine not only because you are entitled to know it but primarily because I should like to encourage you to think more deeply about your own. Such introspection, in turn, may enable you to state your attitude and even to change it now or in the future should you feel so inclined.

At best, the helping interview will provide the client a meaningful experience leading to change. The experience is the relationship with you; change is what we hope results from this relationship: a change in her ideas, a change in her feelings about herself and others, a change in the information she possesses about a topic important to her — a change in herself as a person. Change is possible for the therapist as well if he can participate in the interviewing process with his entire being, but it is intended primarily for the client. The latter has come so that as a result of her relationship with you in the helping interview, something about her may alter. Here two basic questions arise:

1. What sort of change do we wish to help bring about?
2. How can this best be accomplished?

Type of Change Desired

Aaron bursts out: "No, I'm not going to change. I can just about manage without changing anything. Judy wants me to change for the kids and for her but I can't. You can't help me but you can help her because she believes in change. I believe in just keeping going. If not that, then nothing."

Tom marveled: "I never, never would have believed that this would happen to me. I am really, truly changing. I sometimes hardly recognize myself. I am still Tom but not the Tom I used to drag around. I feel lighter and more optimistic. I've finally been able to throw away lots of the old garbage. Now I need new tools and I'll go on in therapy till I get them."

Bringing About Desired Change

Therapy addresses itself to change more than to any other goal. Therapist and client examine the changes the latter wishes to introduce into his life, while the therapist attempts to enable the client to make this change possible. How it is done, and the extent to which it can be done, is the subject of this chapter and the main theme of the entire book. But first let us look briefly at examples of change clients wish to bring about.

As we have seen, Dora wants change but cannot muster the energy to bring it about. She would like to be able to drive the car on her own. She would like to be able to enjoy being home alone instead of worrying when her husband will return. She would very much like to distance herself from her parents. She would like to be able to travel by plane. She expresses her desires, comes twice weekly, pays promptly, and waits for miracles.

Bertha wants to get along better with her son. She is prepared to change her behavior towards him to make this possible. In a very short time she learns to set limits, to listen to her son with more understanding, and not to insist that he take a sweater to school because she feels cold.

Ruth is a young social worker who already enjoys an excellent reputation in the field. She loves her husband and small daughter and participates in a rich and varied social life. Ruth wishes to change. She feels the need to explore her relations with her mother, sensing that they must inevitably affect hers with her own daughter. She wants to become more aware of her ambivalent feelings toward these two central female figures in her life. She wishes to learn and, as she puts it, "to grow up."

Some clients come because they were sent, specifically, to be changed. Rachel is not stimulating enough sexually for Ted. Altogether, she is too reserved, quiet, and morose. Rachel comes because she would like to be different for Ted's sake — not her own. But she tries hard and Ted notices improvement.

Art is sent to stop devoting his life to mourning his daughter, who died on the operating table. He must learn again to think of the living and not live only with and for the dead. Art comes, tries, and fails. Something has frozen within him.

Ralph is sent because Miriam, his wife, claims to be still in love with him and wants him to love her as he once did. He, however, exploits our sessions to insist that for him the marriage is dead. Miriam's strategy has backfired. Only the fate of the children remains to be discussed. They quarrel, blame me, and do not pay their fee.

Ben was sent by his parents. He is the skeleton in their cupboard. He neither works nor studies. He lives on relief and stands at street corners watching little girls. The police know he is harmless but keep an eye on him anyway. With me he discusses philosophy and Far Eastern religions. He had a friend once but they fell out. He might be able to change, perhaps, but things are so convenient as they are that it isn't worth the effort.

The themes which I am about to discuss and illustrate seem to comprise some, at least, of the major ingredients necessary for change. Somehow — and we still do not fully understand how — they enable the client to explore himself and the world about him; to become more aware of his feelings, needs, desires, defense mechanisms, thoughts, and ambitions; to learn and grow and sharpen his reality testing. During this process, we witness the changes that take place in him. It is beautiful to observe.

At first, the change desired is not toward but rather away from something: physical pain manifested through specific or generalized symptoms, a life without direction, fears and anxieties that — as they are temporarily warded off — drain mental and physical resources, strong feelings of ambivalence that paralyze action, a joyless existence weighed down by repressed burdens from the past. Only by tackling the present and past can we welcome the future.

The change we want to help bring about is basically one upon which the client will be able to build — one that will be meaningful to her and will permit her to function more successfully as a person in the future. The change in which we are interested involves learning. The client should take away from this experience useful information — cognitive or emotional: new facts and ideas or more realistic feelings and attitudes — or all of these.

At the moment, it is clear that the client needs us, and we may need being needed. Engaged as we are in professions focused on the amelioration of the human condition, we obviously need being needed and must always be aware of this need lest it intrude upon our efforts to help the client not need us any longer. We must constantly ask ourselves to what extent we have a need to control her life, to tell her what to do and how to do it; to what extent we can tolerate her disagreeing with us; to what extent we can encourage her to find her own way, not ours, and become self-functioning, independent of us, as soon as possible. Helping can take place, it seems to me, in three main areas: information and resources, self-awareness and awareness of others, and personal growth.

Helping to Effect Change

I feel we can best help the client to help himself through behavior that creates an atmosphere of trust, in which he feels wholly respected. Rogers calls this "unconditional positive regard" (Rogers, 1951). We can best help him through behavior which demonstrates that we consider him responsible for himself and his actions, thoughts, and feelings and that we believe in his capacity to use his own resources increasingly. In such an atmosphere he can confront himself and those thoughts and feelings that govern his behavior but that he hides, distorts, or denies to himself and to us. We provide information when required; but realizing that this has come from us, we wish to find out how he understands it. We offer the resources at our command and discuss their potential benefit for him, but we believe the decision as to their applicability is his to make. We act in a way that will help him become more aware of himself, his life space, his own frame of reference. We want to help him learn that change is possible but that it is up to him to decide if and when and how to change.

We behave in a way that will prove least threatening for him so that he can go on deeply exploring himself, his relation to others, and theirs to him. We genuinely feel that to learn to change in this way is good and will pave the way for more learning and more change. We do not tell him what to think or how to feel; but our behavior reveals that we value thoughts and feelings, our own and his. It indicates that the more he can discover about his own, the more he will be able to act upon them or modify them, should he so choose. We wish to help him come closer to himself and thereby to others. Being looked upon as a responsible person, he may learn to see himself as such and to enjoy applying this new learning. The interview or interviews concluded, he may continue to grow.

Playing a Vital, Active Role

I do not see the therapist as passive in the least. On the contrary, I perceive her as active at all times. I am not implying that she should talk a great deal, but I am saying that she should make her presence and interest continuously felt. The therapist is active in gaining as deep an understanding as possible of the client's world, in encouraging him to discover what it is like and whether he feels at home in it. The therapist is active in her interest and participation in the client's searches for meaningful change. The therapist is active in giving of herself when she feels this to be helpful and appropriate. At all times she is active in revealing herself to be a person deeply involved with another person (Burton, 1975).

The therapist is and acts as a genuine person. She has authority from which she does not shrink, but she employs it so that the client will become the authority in his own life. The therapist uses her authority to put the client in the center of the stage and to keep him there. She contributes of herself and her professional knowledge to help the client, not simply to display her wisdom or her splendid personal qualities. She wields her authority in such a way that the client may come to trust himself in finding his own way and his own direction. The therapist reveals what she herself sees and understands, what she thinks the client is thinking and feeling, in order to help him look deeper and try harder to reach his inner self — not in order to impose her own interpretations on the client, to tell him how he should be thinking, feeling, and behaving. The therapist puts herself entirely at the disposal of the client in the latter's search for solutions, for ways to change and move forward. She creates an atmosphere in which the client has genuine interest in the therapist's awareness because he knows that the other does not wish to impose herself upon him. In his struggle the client finds it important to have the therapist react to his thoughts, feelings, and behavior.

The therapist wants the client not to become dependent on her, but to rely more and more on himself. She does not deny her authority but uses it to understand and be understood and to provide the information and resources at her disposal. On the other hand, she does not hide behind this authority to make decisions for the client or to do anything the latter cannot understand or agree with. Although she acts responsibly for herself, she does not take away responsibility from the client. When not sure of her ground, she admits it; and when she is sure, she knows it is *her* ground and not that of the client, who needs to find his own ground on which to stand firmly.

"Helping the other person to help himself" is something quite in fashion today, but frequently, I fear, it is no more than a rationale to explain away whatever we as interviewers do (Berenson and Carkhuff, 1967b). This goal is by now generally accepted on the cognitive level, but we all do not necessarily hold identical attitudes when referring to it. Therefore, further spelling out of what I have in mind when I use these words is necessary. I mean something quite precise; and so that you may decide what you think and feel about my view, I shall be more specific. My philosophy is not new; to some it may even appear well worn. Nonetheless, I believe it is valid and operationally sound.

Coming right down to it, what do we as interviewers actually bring to the helping interview? Essentially, we bring our knowledge, experience, professional skills, the information we possess, and the resources at our command. Beyond this we bring ourselves: our desire to be of use, our liking and warm regard for our fellow human beings, our background, our prejudices and shortcomings, our own life space, and our own internal frame of reference. (All this, you will recall, I broached in Chapter 1.) Optimally, this is quite a bit, and, therefore, I suppose, we succeed in helping others just often enough to keep going at it and trying harder. Now what does all this mean to the client? Frankly nothing — nothing unless he perceives us and our behavior and attitudes, unless all we are and stand for does not fall on deaf ears, blind eyes, and frozen emotions. Only as we help the client to hear, see, think, and feel is he able to perceive us — after he has first perceived himself and also perhaps after he has perceived our perceiving him. I am certain that he can respond to us only after he has learned to respond to himself.

In other words, I can get through to him when he can and will allow me; only if he is able to get through to himself can he allow others to do so. The therapist or interviewer undoubtedly can aid in this process, but it will always be up to the client to dare or refuse to dare. We can help most, I am sure, by fully respecting the client and his world and by showing him that we do so, not only by our words, but also by our behavior.

Experiencing our attitude, he will become more aware of himself and eventually of us. Feeling respected, he will be able to respect what we may have to contribute. He may not accept this; but even in rejecting it, he may come closer to what will seem right for him — a decision, his decision, albeit reached through us.

An Illustration Cognizant of the risks involved, I shall allow myself to be personal. In our culture, ironically perhaps, we hold the life of the individual to be sacred. Some time ago I received an S.O.S. to go to a hospital to "help" a young man who insisted on doing away with himself. He had recently been blinded and felt, the doctors informed me, that death was the way out. At the hospital we talked — rather, since he absolutely refused at first, I talked. I related what I had been told. He confirmed his intention. Then I told him why I had come. My words are long forgotten, but I recall the attitude. I had been summoned to persuade him to live; however, this was not really the purpose of my coming for I felt that I possessed neither the right nor the power to do so. The decision was his to make. I had come to inform him that should he decide in favor of life, I was prepared to work with him as hard as I knew how so that life might become as meaningful and rewarding for him as possible.

This turned out to be one of those success stories we occasionally encounter. The success was his, though the respect for him and his world was mine. Had he decided differently, I hope I should have respected his decision no less; but, as is now apparent, he would have missed a great deal.

Demonstrating Respect

Respect for the client and her world involves a sincere interest both in her and in it. We show this interest by the manner in which we attend her, by carefully excluding outside interference as much as possible while we are there just with her and for her, and by demonstrating that what is important to her is important to us. When we feel that we require more information or more details, we should not press immediately to obtain them if this involves cutting off or diverting the client's train of expression. For if we do so, she will then think that we are more interested in what appears important to us than what is significant to her and that she must adapt her interest to ours. A thin line divides interest from curiosity. It is intangible, but I know it is there; and I think we all realize that most clients appreciate the former and resent the latter. They are quick to sense that when we are interested, it is for their sake and that when we prod or act curious, it is for our own.

Acceptance: A Matter of Respect

I have become more and more unhappy with the generalizations we all make about acceptance. We must learn to "accept" our lot or our handicap or our fate. We must "accept her as she is" and, naturally, ourselves "as we are." This represents for me a passive and false attitude, whereas I consider genuine acceptance as something very active and honest. It involves striving, coping, changing, and respecting.

After years of pondering, I have arrived at an operational definition of acceptance that includes the following components: a deep respect for those making up humankind — young and old, wise and less wise, rich and poor, black, white, and colored. A deep respect for Julie, this very particular client who has just been sitting with me. A real caring for her as a fellow human being — as Julie, a member of our human family and, perhaps most important, a basic trust in her choices and decisions. Acceptance, as I understand it, is a dynamic concept and it means treating the client as an equal, regarding his thoughts and feelings with sincere respect. It does not mean agreeing; it does not mean thinking or feeling the way he does; it does not mean valuing what he values. It is, rather, the attitude that the client has as much right to his ideas, feelings, and values as I have to mine and that I want to do my utmost to understand his life space in terms of his ideas, feelings, and values rather than in terms of my own. Such an attitude is difficult to maintain and even more difficult to communicate to the client. At times it may be misunderstood and interpreted as agreement, consent, or reassurance. And yet we have no choice but to attempt to be accepting. Otherwise, the client will suspect that we are judging him, asking him to feel and think as we do or, even worse, to think and feel as we believe he ought to be thinking or feeling.

Herman identifies with Max Frisch's antihero, Stiller: it is good to run away from oneself, one's feelings and problems; it is so rewarding that Stiller denies his existence as Stiller utterly — and Herman chooses to do likewise. This way, he maintains, "there is no hurt." And so I learn — slowly, it is true — to accept "Stiller." "Good evening, Mr. Stiller," I say. Herman laughs a little but does not reject the greeting. He knows I tease him a bit and he likes it. He knows I trust that his choice is temporary — and he likes that too. I have the confidence he does not yet possess, that he will change, discard Stiller, and become himself.

Natalie is through with marriage. She has the child she always wanted. Men are all right but husbands are unbearable. Her lifestyle is very different from mine. Once I understand how it works for her I can accept and appreciate it. But I am still troubled by what it and she are doing to the child. She is angry with me and shops around for child-rearing techniques.

"What am I worth?" clients will ask directly or indirectly, implying that worth to be all but nonexistent. They seem to have heard "you are worthless" so often that they finally introject this judgment.

David, when really respected as a human being, feeling cared about, begins to dare new choices involving new behaviors. His pictures are no longer "junk" — just good enough for the drawer. He now displays them in his home and even, when offered a price, sells one or two. He is not so certain now that he really "wastes time" and is beginning to plan for the future.

Vic is a glassblower. Before leaving on a trip abroad he presents me with a very delicate figurine. I admire it and thank him but wonder aloud why he would feel the need to bring me a gift when it is he who is going away. Vic needs more approval and caring from me. This is his way: to give in order to receive in return.

When I accept an idea or feeling, I am telling the client something to this effect: "I hear you" or "So this is how you see it." I endeavor to show her what she has shown me so that she can examine it, become aware of it, reflect upon it — do whatever she likes with it — but, basically, so that the feedback will provide her the opportunity to test whether it expresses her true self or a self she wishes to amend, reject, or modify. In other words, I try to provide the client with feedback that is undistorted by my own person and personality. I return to the sender the communication she transmitted to me. The less distorted it is when it gets back to her, the more I have accepted it and shown respect for her. There is nothing of me in this process except the way I receive her message and transmit it back to her. I am a faithful listener, observer, and reporter. What I return to the client are "facts" she has stated. They may be highly emotional or intellectual; they may be clear to me or not; they may seem "good" to me or "bad" — or even incomprehensible. I report what I receive. I treat whatever she says with respect and treat her as of equal worth with myself.

When Bill exclaims, "My math teacher is a complete fool," I accept this, showing him his low opinion of his math teacher so that he can do with this what he will. He may repeat, modify, enlarge upon it, and so forth. It is probably true that I shall be able to accept Bill's statement more readily if my own opinion coincides with his and less readily if I think the reverse; but this only shows how complicated and difficult accepting really is. I may, of course, stop short of acceptance. I can agree with Bill; I can disagree with him. I may reward or punish him. Or, having accepted how he feels, I may think it necessary to tell him how I feel. However, if I wish simply to accept his feeling about his math teacher, all I can do is provide him with feedback and indicate by my behavior that I have listened with understanding.

Another aspect of acceptance is the ability to treat as a respected equal someone of another culture, race, color, or faith. Here the feedback may become distorted by our own lenses, the nature of the distortion depending upon the type of lenses we wear. Acceptance does not require strong liking, but acceptance is undoubtedly impossible when strong dislike is present. We cannot truly help a person we cannot accept, in my opinion. In such a situation the only path open to us is to deceive neither ourselves nor the client but to help him find someone who can accept him. This is no disaster. On the contrary, if we have honestly tried to accept but to no avail, there may be no better alternative.

Inability to accept someone may occur even when cultural differences are absent. An incompatibility of personalities may exist. Here, too, it is best to allow ourselves to realize what is occurring so that we may extricate the client, as well as ourselves, from an uncomfortable and pointless situation. In short, in the helping interview we must be able to accept ourselves — our ideas and feelings as well — and to act accordingly. Our range of acceptance may or may not broaden with time, but we can help only when we can accept.

Genuine Liking — and Disliking

A genuine liking for people is a gift from heaven. We are either born with it or we are not. Those upon whom the gift was not bestowed are neither better nor worse than other people, but they lack a trait indispensable in the helping professions. If our preferences lead us to machines, plants, animals, abstractions, or whatever, but not people, we should indulge and foster such preferences. Many professions do not demand — some even exclude — a genuine liking for people. However, for those who use the helping interview as one of their tools, it is essential.

He who genuinely likes people tends to be optimistic about them. He feels involved with those about him whether this be person to person or, indirectly, through the media. He tends to be tolerant of human weaknesses and foibles but is convinced that humans have it within them to act heroically and selflessly. He who feels genuine warmth toward humans likes to learn about people and their behavior, examine their motives, and reflect upon their inner lives. Therefore, he tends to delight in literature, poetry, and the human aspects of psychology. He is somewhat detached at times but never distant. If his liking for humanity is indeed genuine, he does not have a particularly strong need to be liked in return. He usually is, because warmth seems to elicit warmth, but this is in spite of, rather than because of, his need.

We find such people in all professions, in all walks of life. We find them in the helping professions as well, luckily, for here they can develop professionally what they seem to have acquired naturally. People who genuinely like others have much to learn before they can be of professional help, but they have a good start (Truax and Carkhuff, 1969).

He who genuinely likes his fellow creatures is, in my experience, a warm, interested, caring, and involved person. From this vantage point he looks about, observes, acts, and reacts. The attitude he expresses toward others, he expresses toward himself as well. He who likes others genuinely, cannot but like himself as well.

No correlation exists, either positive or negative, between my genuine liking or disliking of the client and the outcome of her therapy. My genuine, personal liking of the client is a matter I must confront. It may help push therapy forward but, on the contrary, it may impede it. It is certainly not a necessary ingredient for change, and I feel that it has been overrated or even misunderstood in our field. If I like Helen — as, indeed, I do — it is because she is a fighter and because she appreciates and knows about music and we can talk about it during the chitchat part of our sessions. But this says more about me than about her. I like fighters and music and so we hit it off. As for her therapy, it never got off the ground.

I like fighters and people who are intelligent and cultured. This sounds simplistic but, after all, liking is preferring, and I have my personal preferences, too. I like Gabriel for his sardonic sense of humor and because he has striven hard to overcome his manic-depressive psychosis — also because we can discuss politics when we both need a short respite from the toils of therapy. Gabriel was able to change. We enjoyed our encounter while it lasted. We liked each other.

I try very hard not to let my liking for Herman get in the way of our joint task. I enjoy his wit and his intelligence. We talk music and philosophy. We do not see eye to eye on either. But I must maintain an adequate distance lest I fall into the trap of his defensiveness, his "Stillerism," for then I could not be the therapist he is seeking and badly needs.

Beyond common interests and preferred traits, there is that intangible something called "chemistry" that either develops or doesn't. I just like Gail and don't know why. She works hard to support her four kids without any assistance. She writes bad poetry and finds it difficult to learn Hebrew. She is busy living, but that doesn't explain it either; it is just a matter of "chemistry."

Howard and his entire family are sick. When he and I talk opera all problems are laid aside for a while. I understand his need to drink. Even were he to stop, he would find an alternative escape.

Genuine dislike should be researched and written about more extensively. Should the client genuinely dislike me as a person and not just be put off by some behavioral characteristic of mine (with which he may be willing to put up for the sake of therapy), he will stop coming. If I genuinely dislike a client as a person, this will emerge during our trial period and we will part. This has rarely happened and, when it has, the dislike was mutual. I genuinely dislike certain behaviors of some clients. I try hard not to generalize, but it has happened that I did not stop at disliking the specific behaviors and began to dislike the person as such. No correlation exists here either — positive or negative — between my genuine dislike of client behaviors and the success or failure of therapy. I much prefer working with clients I genuinely like, though at times it is challenging to work with those whose behaviors I find uncongenial.

What I disliked about Jim was his carelessness and bad manners. He never closed the faucets properly and left the light on in the bathroom. He always interrupted and, even when in agreement, could not allow himself to agree without reservation. He frequently overslept and would cancel at the last moment. When he did come, he yawned and stretched as if to emphasize his boredom and lack of motivation.

Roger arrived with his guide dog, who lay quietly on the floor between our feet. Roger was rough with the dog and even brutal at times. I could not always control my anger at his behavior. Roger was not a fighter; he felt people should befriend and help him — after all they could see and he could not. He was passive, totally uninterested and uninteresting. For him it was a great effort even to come and talk. One day he stopped making the effort.

Sharon was voluble and loud. My verbal and nonverbal cues to lower her voice were of no avail. For years she had been convinced that her husband was just about to leave her: she had discovered, been informed, overheard by chance, opened his mail by mistake, turned out his pockets by accident. . . . Certain of his imminent departure, she enjoyed several affairs "just to revenge myself." Her husband has not left her yet — I sometimes wonder why.

Sexual attraction and repulsion exist in therapy as in all other forms of human interaction. In therapy and out I too have been attracted by certain women. Not being a student of Reich, not even of Ferenczi, I do not believe in therapy in bed. I shall not pursue this subject further here, as this is not an autobiography.

Understanding

The knowledge that she was understood is certainly an important aspect of that meaningful experience the client will take with her from the helping interview if the relationship between her and the interviewer was positive. For the client to be understood is essential to the interviewing process, but there are different ways of understanding, some of which help more than others.

Three Ways of Understanding Throughout the ages many great writers have shown and recently numerous psychologists have pointed out that there are three alternative ways in which one person may understand another. One way is to understand about him. I read about him, I hear others talk about him, I hear him discussed at staff conferences − I understand about him. I understand him, so to speak, through the eyes of others, not through my own or his. This is remote understanding and is two stages removed from the person himself.

To take two simple examples: I understand about Louis that he speaks only French. And so when I meet him, I address him in his own language, and we converse. Thus I understood something about him in advance, acted accordingly, and it worked. But it is not always so simple. From a report submitted to me, I understand about Nancy that she is a poor student and that she may well be retarded. When I interview her, I gradually become aware that she is hard of hearing, ashamed of it, and desperately trying to conceal it. This was not too difficult to discover. It merely involved giving up trying to understand about Nancy and starting to understand Nancy. This method is less remote and one step closer to Nancy herself.

The second way of understanding a person, therefore, is to understand her, not through the eyes of others, but through our own. Since this is the method by which we most frequently understand others, it deserves further scrutiny. When I understand you or fail to understand you, I use the resources at my command: my perceptual apparatus, my thinking, my feeling, my knowledge, my skills. I understand you or do not understand you in terms of myself, my life space, my internal frame of reference. If we do not speak the same language − although we may well both be speaking English — I may not understand you at all. If I am suffering from indigestion, I shall understand you differently from the way I should had the one I love just agreed to marry me. And, of course, the same goes for you in your effort to understand me, except that for you it is harder still. You came to me for help; and, therefore, in addition to everything else, you have that something on your mind about which you came to see me.

In brief, when I understand you or when I do not, it is in terms of myself, my background, my experience, my imagination. Very often, I suppose, we cannot do otherwise and at best can only be aware that this is what we are doing. Let me give a few examples to clarify: "I don't understand you. It's so hot in here, and yet you keep complaining that it's cold." This is simple and obvious. I cannot understand that you are cold when I am warm. The inference is, of course, that there must be something wrong with you. "I understand you perfectly. Had I been in your place, I should have acted just the way you did." This example is clear, too, but compare it with this: "I don't understand you. In your place I would have done just the opposite, and I assure you . . ."

There are, undoubtedly, some universal human emotions, but we tend to understand only in terms of ourselves the person expressing them. I understand your expression of joy or sorrow if it is consistent with the joy and sorrow I have experienced, know about, or can imagine. Otherwise, I cannot understand you and, more likely than not, consider you "wrong" or "strange" or "absurd." I may understand Mr. A.'s grief over the loss of his right hand. I cannot understand the grief that Mr. B. expresses over the loss of part of his left pinky. I understand Johnny C., who likes school, but I cannot for the life of me understand Johnny D., who hates it. I can understand taking a drink once in a while. I can even understand Mr. E., who spends part of his welfare check on drinks. But I simply cannot understand Mr. F., who spends his entire monthly check in the local bar within a week of the day he receives it, beats his wife, and blames me for the fact he has no money!

If we do not understand another person, we may well want to find out what is causing the barrier. With time we may accept lack of communication as inevitable under certain circumstances. Then, at least, we can attempt to cope with what we are not understanding. Although the barrier will not have been removed, neither will it have been fortified.

The third way to understand another person is the most meaningful but at the same time the most demanding. It is to understand with another person, as Rogers (1961, Ch. 17) has so well put it. This calls for putting aside everything but our common humanness and with it alone trying to understand with the other person how she thinks, feels, and sees the world about her. It means ridding ourselves of our internal frame of reference and adopting hers. Here the issue is not to disagree or agree with her but to understand what it is like to be her. Seemingly quite simple though in reality difficult to achieve.

All the doctors consulted agree that Mr. Crane must undergo heart surgery. They concur it is a simple operation that is frequently performed with a high percentage of success. I may know something about heart ailments; I may have undergone surgery myself. But here is Mr. Crane steadfastly refusing to consider the operation. I want to understand with him what is going on within him, and so I shall do everything in my power to understand with Mr. Crane what this operation means to him, what lies behind his stubborn opposition. I want to share with him his strong resistance to what is, according to the doctors, a simple matter. I may not succeed, but I want to try as hard as I know how. He may eventually speak of his deep fears. If he does, the two of us can then explore them, and ultimately Mr. Crane may undergo that operation. But if I consider him stubborn or foolish or primitive, if because of his attitude I feel repulsed or rejected, if feeling pressed for time I insist he see things the way I do, I shall most probably get nowhere.

Listening: An Essential Tool Understanding involves the use of an indispensable tool: listening (Barbara, 1974). Genuine listening is hard work; there is little about it that is mechanical. Listening requires, first of all, that we not be preoccupied, for if we are, we cannot fully attend. Secondly, listening involves hearing the way things are being said, the tone used, the expressions and gestures employed. In addition, listening includes the effort to hear what is not being said, what is only hinted at, what is perhaps being held back, what lies beneath or beyond the surface. We hear with our ears, but we listen with our eyes and mind and heart and skin and guts as well (Ekman, 1964).

Our goal is, I presume, to listen with understanding. This has to be learned and practiced. We must become familiar with this tool, see how it functions so that we can make it serve us as well as possible. We must understand what is involved for us in listening before we are able to listen with understanding. A simple test will show us whether we are learning to listen. It has worked for me and for some of my students as well. The test is this: if during the interview you can state in your own words what the client has said and also convey to him in your own words the feelings he has expressed and he then accepts all this as emanating from him, there is an excellent chance that you have listened and understood him.

As we learn more and more to listen with understanding to others, we increasingly learn to listen with understanding to ourselves. The result is that eventually we can listen to the client and ourselves at the same time without one getting in the way of the other. After all, since I am the one who is listening with understanding — trying hard to, at least — my presence is important. I act and react. As I follow the client, I think and feel. Soon I shall say something; and so while attending to her, I must attend to myself as well. This can become complicated at times, for even with the best of intentions I find myself evaluating her and what goes on between us. I find myself approving here, disapproving there; agreeing or disagreeing; confirming or denying. I may express all of this, only a part of it, or nothing. But I must listen to myself as well as to her, for we both are involved, and we both are important.

There is a danger here that should be stated outright. I may listen so carefully and try so hard to understand that I become absorbed into her internal frame of reference with the result that finally I have difficulty telling us apart. If this happens, I shall not be able to help because the form of help the client requires usually goes beyond listening with understanding. I must remain myself — if only to enable her to get closer to herself. While listening with understanding, I may understand something that she as yet does not; I may acquire insights into her situation that she may need to hear in order to change. If I stray too far from myself and draw too close to her, I shall not be there with my own frame of reference to help her on with hers when she may most need me. I may, at long last, feel I understand with Mr. Crane what it is that deters him from the heart operation, but only by communicating this to him, by examining this with him, can I help him to take the step that will lead him to the operation and, I hope, to a healthier and better life.

Listening and Understanding

Above and beyond what I have written about listening with the client in order to understand him, I wish to emphasize two aspects of this process that I have learned to appreciate increasingly over the years: tuning in and tuning out.

When tuning in, I give the client my total attention. I try to be with him, to enter his world, to share his internal frame of reference, to feel what it is like to be him before, ultimately, returning to myself. I try to catch every word, every nuance of his verbal and nonverbal communication. I am completely, undividedly tuned in to him and him alone and I show this by word and act. After Rose's first suicide attempt, we had this interchange:

CL. I'm still terribly angry with my husband — running off like that and shooting himself in the woods. Not caring who found him. I figured that what he could do, I could do just as well and so I tried it . . . but I wasn't good enough at it to succeed.

TH. You wanted to get even with him.

CL. Oh, yes, to get even with him — leaving me like that with two kids and no income and no explanation whatsoever. I hate his guts for that; it's wiped out our entire past.

TH. You insist on remembering that last act only.

CL. Yes. And what do I have to live for?

TH. Now you're angry with yourself for not having succeeded.

CL. You bet. I could kill myself! I'll try again, you'll see. Next time . . .

TH. Next time you'll really show him and everyone else.

CL. (weeps quietly and then hysterically) I've got nothing to live for; you don't want to get that into your head either.

TH. I'm just like all the others.

CL. Yes . . . no . . . I do trust you but you don't really understand that I have nothing to live for.

TH. And the children?

CL. I knew you'd say that. Well, if he didn't care about them, why the hell should I?

TH. When you were crying so bitterly I thought that perhaps it was partly for them.

CL. I don't know — for them, for me, what difference does it make?

TH. I did catch the tremendous anger in that outburst, but I sensed compassion, too. Did you feel that?

CL. Oh, just leave me alone!

Lennie and I worked together for a very short time. The solution he hit upon for his "problem" seemed so obvious to him that he could not fathom his not having found it long before.

CL. It's amazing how beautifully things fall into place now that I've found the key. I always had trouble with my father and so I have trouble with boss after boss. All I have to do is become my own boss and I'll come out on top.

TH. The other way might be to deal with the difficulties you had with your father and are encountering with other authorities . . .

CL. I don't even want to consider that.

TH. I also represent authority for you.

CL. Never thought of that. . . . Perhaps. . . . But that makes no difference. Now that I've found the solution I want to become independent as soon as possible — in business. At home, with Naomi there's no problem.

TH. You prefer circumventing the issue rather than facing it head on.

CL. I think so; if I change my mind I'll let you know.

The second way of listening to understand which I find very effective is, paradoxically, tuning out, or what Sullivan liked to call selective inattention. Here, I try very hard to understand the client without concentrating on his words, because much of his talk is meaningless, misleading, or not really directed at me. I pay attention, however, to how he acts and reacts within himself and, when working with a couple, to what occurs between them beyond the words they exchange. And all this to get at the core; I tune out in order to understand.

Leah and Jack came together just once. As they palavered and argued I could feel the power he still exercised over her, as well as Leah's as yet feeble attempts to resist, fight back, stand up to him. Oppressed for twenty years, she clung to the fact of his betrayal with all her might. He still tried to dominate her with charm and threats. She was struggling to break loose. Beyond the shouting I could hear what was not being said.

He It's over. Forget all this nonsense and come back home and I'll forgive you.

She No, this is my only chance to get out.

He I warn you. If you don't accept my terms, we're through.

She I hope I can be strong enough so that we can be through.

During the latter phase of his therapy, Tom inundated me with lengthy letters. At first I perused them carefully. They contained no new material but consisted of streams of anger, sadness, and misery. Tom never referred to these letters in his sessions. They continued to arrive — a veritable avalanche. I stopped reading them and stacked them, unopened. During our last general cleaning I discovered them, still unopened.

Sol and Erna came together for his first session, which caused me to pay particular attention to the interaction between them. I found it fascinating. She confirmed, corrected, and amplified all of his statements. Sol suggested that she express herself directly.

She demurred, explaining that it was his session and he had come to discuss his problems. He resumed but now always checked out with her. She was wearing not only the pants but the entire suit. When I began to take measurements for a suit that would fit Sol, she withdrew him from therapy.

When in doubt as to whether I have understood the client, I apply two simple and by no means original tests: First, as mentioned previously, if I can restate clearly what the client has said and he accepts my version, I have understood him. With Martha, I almost always failed; with Alexandra and Sandy I did pretty well.

Second, if I can predict the client's behavior, I understand him. I knew that Charles would not participate in the T-group in spite of his grumbling. I knew what Aaron would eventually do, just as I was convinced that Rose would pull through. Tom did surprise me with the way he completed therapy.

Needless to add, understanding does not necessarily involve approval. At times ethical problems arise with which the therapist must deal. I can understand the client's use of drugs and even his decision to peddle them, but that does not imply approbation, and I make it quite clear that it doesn't. I can try hard to understand the client's decision to relinquish her child's upbringing to her parents but that doesn't imply approval either and I say so unambiguously. When Bob, depending on his mood of the moment, either raves about or bemoans his business dealings and sexual adventures, I understand but am far from approving, and this he knows very well.

Suggested Goals in Listening Beginners in the helping interview often inquire what they should seek to understand now that they really wish to listen. No all-encompassing answer, of course, exists, since so many variables are involved. However, it may be important to listen with understanding to some or all of the following:

1. How the client thinks and feels about himself; how he perceives himself.
2. What the client thinks and feels about others in his world, especially significant others; what he thinks and feels about people in general.

3. How the client perceives others relating to her; how in her eyes others think and feel about her, especially significant others in her life.
4. How he perceives the material that he, the therapist, or both wish to discuss; what he thinks and how he feels about what is involved.
5. What her aspirations, ambitions, and goals are.
6. What defense mechanisms she employs.
7. What coping mechanisms he uses or may be able to use.
8. What values he holds; what his philosophy of life is.

Needless to say, this is no "licensed guide"; it is merely something for us, when beginning, to cling to — like a hand in the dark. With a bit of light, we shall drop the hand.

Achieving Empathy

Now a little story. In one of Israel's kibbutzim, or collective settlements, there was a donkey. It was a special donkey indeed, with long silky ears and large shiny eyes, and all the children loved him dearly. And so when he disappeared one day, all the children were very upset. He had been the favorite attraction of the children's farm. During the morning the children used to come in twos and threes or in entire groups with their teachers to visit the donkey. The little ones would even take short rides on his back. In the afternoon the children would drag their parents to the children's farm to see Shlomo, the donkey. But now he was missing, and the children were downcast. The sadness proved to be contagious; and before the day was out, all the kibbutz members had assembled in the large dining hall and, with concern written on all their faces, were trying to decide what to do next. They had looked everywhere, but Shlomo, the donkey, had not been found.

On this same kibbutz lived an old man, the father of one of the earliest settlers. He had become somewhat senile of late, and the children sometimes made fun of him quite openly, although the adults were a bit more circumspect. Well, when the entire kibbutz population was gathered in the large new dining hall wondering what to do next, in walked the old man dragging Shlomo, the donkey, behind him. The jubilation was great, the astonishment even greater. While the children surrounded the donkey, the adults gathered about the old man. "How is it," they asked him, "that you of all people have found the donkey? What did you do?"

Well, you can imagine the embarrassment of the old man and his joy, too, for never had he been paid so much attention. He scratched his bald pate, looked at the ceiling and then at the floor, smiled, and said: "It was simple. I just asked myself, 'Shlomo' [for that was the old man's name as well], 'if you were Shlomo, the donkey, where would you go off to?' So I went there and found him and brought him back." Incidentally, Fenlason (Fenlason, Ferguson, and Abrahamson, 1962) tells a similar tale. I can vouch only for my own.

This story exemplifies empathy (Berenson and Carkhuff, 1967a), another important aspect of the helping interview, as I perceive it. It means feeling yourself into, or participating in, the inner world of another while remaining yourself. The old man found the donkey because he tried to feel where the donkey must have wanted to go as if in a way he were the donkey for a moment. He knew he was not, however, for he went and brought him back. Empathy in the helping interview is similar to the third way of understanding — understanding with — discussed above. The empathic therapist tries as much as she possibly can to feel her way into the internal frame of reference of the client and to see the world through the latter's eyes as if that world were her own world. The words *as if* are crucial, for although the therapist is empathic, she never loses sight of the fact that she remains her own self. Knowing all the time that she is distinct from the client, she tries to feel her way about in the internal world of thought and feeling of the other in order to come as close to him as possible, to understand with him as much as possible.

The empathic therapist explores with the client the latter's internal world of thought and feeling so that the client may come closer to his own world, his own self. The empathic therapist so cares for the self of the client and so wants him to learn to care that she is willing to abandon temporarily her own life space and try to think and act and feel as if the life space of the other were her very own. Being there, she may be able to understand with the client; but it is only when she returns to herself, to her own life space, that she is able to help. Now she can share in the thoughts and feelings of the client as if they were her own because she has understood these with him. The client will have sensed this. He will have felt that the therapist really cares about him because she has tried so hard to understand; now the client will want the therapist's reactions to what he found so that this understanding of himself will become part of the interaction.

Let us return for a moment to Mr. Crane, who, you will remember, needs an operation but refuses to consider it. After several talks, the therapist now understands what lies at the root of this refusal. During the talks he had tried to think and feel as if he were Mr. Crane. He had felt the other's anguish at having lost a dearly beloved brother a few months previously as the result of an operation — of an entirely different sort. He had been confused as to the meaning of surgery. Was it not all equally dangerous? He had thought — as if he were Mr. Crane — of the lot of his wife and children were he to die, and had wanted to get well so that he could support them once again in the accustomed way. And right along he had let Mr. Crane know by his attitude and words that he was understanding with him. Then it was over. Mr. Crane felt understood; the therapist reverted to his own frame of reference. He, having understood, wished to help now more than ever; and Mr. Crane, having been understood, was ready to listen. Only now could Mr. Crane hear and understand what the doctors had actually said concerning his operation. A short time after it took place and Mr. Crane recovered.

Empathy is not a synonym for sympathy. Sympathy involves sharing common feelings, interests, loyalties. When related to social patterns and mores, sympathy may run the gamut from pity and charity to sincere compassion for another. Sympathy is important and necessary at times, but it is not empathy and, furthermore, is not always therapeutic in the helping relationship.

Nor should empathy be confused with identification. When I identify with another, I wish to be like him — to think as he does, to feel and act as he does. I wish to be like him at the expense of my own self. I wish to erase myself and to substitute the self of the other. Empathy always involves two distinctly separate selves; identification results in one. When the therapist identifies with the client, he becomes the client. Thus it may happen at times that the therapist becomes so troubled by the misfortunes of the other, so overwhelmed by the seemingly crushing problems of the other, that by the end of the interview both may be reduced to despondent ineffectiveness. Then the client will need another person who can understand with her but who will remain his own self and consequently be able to give of that self in order to help the other confront her troubles and problems.

Here is another story, related by one of the participants of a workshop at which I facilitated. It, too, illustrates what empathy is all about.

Once upon a time in a small town in Poland, there lived a Chassidic rabbi renowned for his wisdom and good deeds. He had as his helper a very devoted sexton who assisted him as much as possible, since the rabbi was busy for long hours every day. Besides assiduously studying the Holy Scriptures, he saw streams of supplicants who came from great distances, as well as from his own parish, in order to seek the wise rabbi's advice.

One day, after a long period of hesitation, the sexton finally dared to ask, "Rabbi, how is it that you perspire so profusely, summer or winter, when receiving those who come to see you? There are a great many of them, I know, but after all you only sit and talk." To this the rabbi replied, "True, we only sit and talk but just consider what I must do each time I see a visitor: I must take off my clothes and put on his so as to understand him properly. Then, very quickly, because so many are waiting their turn, I must put on my own clothes again in order to give my advice. As you know, I see about four supplicants an hour. Therefore, I must take off my clothes, put on theirs, and then change back to my own four times in just one hour — and you are surprised that I perspire so profusely?"

The more specific the client can learn to become, the better the chance the therapist has to be truly empathic, to familiarize himself with and to feel at home in the internal world of the client. The more we model specificity, the more our clients will adopt it. Empathy is a state of total immersion. As long as this state lasts, I am the client and wish to be so as much as I possibly can. Eventually, I leave him and return to myself and perceive him from my own internal frame of reference — but with one difference; I was he for a while and I know what it is like and I do not forget.

The hospital was on the line; Rose had tried again — and failed again. Aside from a broken leg and some cuts and bruises, she was fine and would be all right. She had driven her car over the mountainside. The car had turned over several times and was completely wrecked. Rose would be released from the hospital within three weeks. Knowing Rose, I was certain that she would not try suicide again. Still limping a bit, she came in to see me:

> CL. Yes, they told me they had spoken to you. I know you're glad; you certainly don't try to disguise it. Well, I'm not glad. I really and truly meant to go through with it, but I botched the job again. I've nothing to live for and it looks as if I haven't anything to die for either. I won't try again because I'm too much of a coward. Fate or whatever it is won't even let me rest.

> TH. Of course I'm glad. I know you well enough to know you have lots to live for, but you are still too angry and upset to admit it.

> CL. When I approached that cliff I was determined to die but then, just for a second something flashed through my mind that shouted "Live." I suppressed it damn fast and plunged on.

> TH. It's that flash, that tiny flicker I'm counting on.

> CL. I feel so tired; all I want is to sleep and never wake up.

I felt such strong empathy for Rose, was so familiar with her internal world that I could allow myself to say to her what I expressed above. With Eric, matters stood very differently. He was losing his sight fast now and had just been relieved of his position. He had not been dismissed outright and Personnel was looking for a more suitable post for him. Meanwhile, he was asked not to come in, but to wait at home. Eric was convinced that no post would be found. He felt his life was over. He came to consult only because his wife brought him — he no longer had any will left. I was kept at arm's length. There was no tiny flicker of hope to cling to. Eric hanged himself at his place of work; this was his way of getting even.

From the first, Aaron was prepared to let me enter his private world but with one strict proviso: not to try to change him. Persuaded to come by Judy, who for a while participated, Aaron enjoyed our sessions — he loved to talk. Father of three sons, a former paratrooper, Aaron was the personification of the Israeli he-man stereotype. Judy had insisted they come because their marriage was foundering.

When Aaron realized that I truly respected his proviso, he opened up. He was an alcoholic and would go on drinking; drink enabled him to keep functioning. He drank less at home for the sake of Judy and the boys, but his entire day revolved around alcohol; when to procure it, where to consume it unnoticed. At his plant he still managed to hold onto his responsible job, but he didn't know how long this would last. As for Judy, he well understood her unhappiness and frustration. He did not enjoy the sexual act with women, hadn't touched her in months and could not bring himself to make more of an effort than he was already making. Truth to tell, he preferred boys. He did not allow himself to carry out his desires but confined himself to masturbation while looking at pictures. His hobby was serving as a volunteer firefighter. Racing to a fire stirred a great excitement in him. During his stints of army reserve duty he volunteered for daring missions. He liked to roughhouse with his own boys.

Aaron called his life a bluff, albeit till now a successful bluff. He felt like a juggler balancing a stack of plates on his head; one false move and the entire structure would collapse. He had achieved a sort of workable balance. Change he would not. Should more be demanded of him, he knew the way out. Without meaning to, Judy was rocking the boat too hard. In addition, his drinking was no longer the well-kept secret it had been. Aaron's world lay before us like an open book. However, neither of us dared touch it. When Aaron finally put an end to his misery, he was found in the fetal position.

Albert had just returned from a long trip abroad. He phoned, asking that we meet "sort of on a friendly basis . . . not to work, therapy or anything like that." Albert could just about let me glance into a tiny corner of his private world. He could allow himself hardly more than that:

CL. You want me to talk about things I don't want to talk about.

TH. Even before Freud's time people talked about sex.

CL. Well, I find it very difficult. Let's wait a little longer.

TH. It's up to you but you always put it off.

CL. I don't want people to think I'm abnormal.

TH. Do you think so?

CL. I most certainly do not, I mean . . .

TH. What do you mean, Albert?

CL. I suspect I may possibly have homosexual tendencies.

TH. Tell me more about your concern.

CL. No, I've already said too much. I told you, I can't talk about these things.

And Albert really couldn't. He admits to having a male friend ("the best thing that ever happened to me and there isn't anything dirty about it I want you to know.") Albert is thirty years old. He is a promising artist in whose life, so far, sex is taboo.

Sam has just left with his family on an extended and challenging business venture. The challenge appeared so tremendous that he returned to therapy to work on the ensuing anxiety. After a few sessions he had recovered from his anxiety attack and most symptoms had disappeared. He reminisced about our work in the past:

CL. I still remember our early sessions years ago and the long lists I used to bring to every session. You said that was to avoid confronting the real problems. Even today I've brought a list but now it's different; now it's just to make sure I cover everything. My God, was I dependent on you for a while!

TH. Yes. I wasn't always sure you would ever stand on your own two feet again.

CL. When you told me that then, I began really to trust you. It was only then that I allowed myself to talk about the homosexuality.

TH. I was very surprised.

CL. So would lots of people be if they knew — but no one knows who matters. I've got it down to an art. No one in the family has even an inkling. I'm really a good father and husband and sex with Miriam is fine. The other thing is fine, too, but I don't mix up the two. I used to be scared to death that Miriam might find out. Today I don't know. I'm not going to tell her but I don't believe it would break up our marriage. And now with this AIDS business, I'm doubly careful. You know, I really feel fine.

TH. You sure sound it. . . .

Both the phenomenological and the sociological aspects of marginality require empathic understanding. Those who consider themselves to be marginal, are seen as such by society and accept their fate, do not as a rule seek therapy. Those who try to drag themselves out of the marginal condition but fail do come to us at times. Those who feel themselves to be marginal but are not regarded as such by others present a favorable prognosis for therapy.

Ben had a way of rhapsodizing about his marginality:

CL. I even tried work a couple of times. How silly that was! I didn't earn any more than I do now, on the dole. True, there are philosophical, existential questions — am I entitled to the dole? Does society owe me a living? Do my parents have to support me? Now that I have all the time in the world, I think and write about such matters.

TH. Yes, I read the notebook you left with me last time. You wax eloquent about being marginal.

CL. Yes, I've gotten used to it and it's a way out for me. I take the barest minimum from society. In return, I bother no one, threaten no one and commit no crime. Other "marginals" cost society much more. They steal and rape and murder. Law enforcement and jails cost society large sums of money.

TH. When I try to see things from your point of view, I almost admire you for the poverty and chastity you practice;

only the prayer is missing, perhaps. But when I look at you from my frame of reference, I feel sorry for your barren and wasted existence.

CL. I do, too, sometimes but then I think of the alternative, of the conformity required and am glad about my choice. I really feel free now except that I must remember not to stand at street corners and stare, so they won't charge me with vagrancy again. I fulfill my obligations to my parents and visit them every week so they can see I am alive and well. My frugality — they're getting used to it. I live very nicely for a whole month on the fee for a single session that they pay you. I don't mind coming to talk to you even though that breaks into my routine, but it's really pointless.

TH. You're showing kindness to your parents by coming to see me.

CL. That's it exactly.

Ben had tried and failed and had already stopped trying before we met. Henry fought me every inch of the way:

CL. Before I met you I held down an ordinary job and was lonely after work. Now I have a miserable job and am just as lonely after work. So I've gained nothing and lost a lot.

TH. You're doing a good job at the switchboard, whereas in your former job —

CL. But I hate it and I was pretty good at the other job, too. I've still got nothing to keep me busy after work and so we continue to fight at home. They get in my way on purpose.

TH. If you were home less all this would change.

CL. I know what you're hinting at but I won't do it! I don't want to associate with the blind even if I could be their leader. I've nothing in common with them. I'd rather have no friend than a blind one, and I will not date a blind girl. I make enough money so I can afford a sighted prostitute once in a while.

TH. You won't accept the blind as just people who can't see, even though they might be ready to help you and be helped by you.

CL. I won't have anything to do with them. In the office, the girls look at me as if I were queer or something. I made a date with one of the operators I talk with but she doesn't want to go out with me again. I just can't go on like this. (weeps)

TH. You feel lost and angry at yourself and me.

Evelyn has tried for a long time to move more into the center of things, only to find herself thrown back onto the sidelines. Now in her fifties, she still tries steadfastly to escape her marginality, but the odds are against her. I admire her courage while she bemoans her fate. Wherever she looks she sees families with children and grandchildren. In some of these households she is welcome occasionally but knows she does not fit in. Women who live alone, as she does, do not interest her as a rule. They are busy bemoaning their own fate, and Evelyn prefers crying alone. There are no men in her life. And so she dreams of the past, blames her parents now and again, and is frightened of the future. She'll try another sabbatical year abroad; perhaps this time . . . She craves companionship, but all she has are "four walls to look at, talk to, and drink with."

Those who, despite society's acceptance, regard themselves as marginal can profit from the empathic listening and understanding. Seeing in the therapist society's representative and slowly grasping his respect and acceptance, they dare to expand their individuality. Requiring fewer defenses since they feel attacked less, they gradually abandon their fringe position.

David was always reserved but even he found it hard to exclude the pleasure from his voice:

CL. I am playing with the idea of a one-man exhibition of my paintings. Sometimes I still feel that I should be like everyone else and hold down a job and bring home a regular salary but I'm slowly getting over that. Mornings I can look at myself in the mirror without reproach. Now that I encourage it, people ask to see my pictures — some even want to buy. Perhaps I'm not a social misfit after all.

TH. I can practically hear you shouting with joy.

CL. Let's not exaggerate — but it is a good feeling; very good!

TH. It's good not to feel an outsider any more.

Esther considered herself marginal for a long time after she began working outside the kibbutz. She felt people looked down on her and gossiped behind her back. Today she is proud of the salary she brings home to the kibbutz and of the position she holds in her profession. Respecting herself, she can feel others respect her and ignore those who do not. Fighting marginality is an endless war for some; Esther persists in fighting and she is coming out on top.

Our Own Behavior

We have not quite finished with our discussion. As a matter of fact, we have now reached what I believe to be its central focus: ourselves in the helping interview. Let us assume that we wish to behave in the manner proposed in this chapter. The question will soon arise: How can we communicate all this to the client? How can we let her know that we truly respect her, that we are really interested, that we are listening carefully to her, that we are trying to understand her just as hard as we can, that we accept her and her world for what they are, and that we wish to empathize as much as it is in us to do? For we may ask ourselves what point there is in all this unless the client senses our interest, our genuine liking, and our honest desire to help.

I cannot evade this basic line of questioning. I have an answer. It may not satisfy; it may seem threatening or arouse a sigh of relief. Whatever the effect it may produce on you, for me, at least, it is an answer. The answer is: by our own behavior in the interview, both verbal and nonverbal. Only this will communicate to the client what we are really feeling and thinking. We are involved in this relationship as much as he is, and what we do or leave undone, what we say or leave unsaid, will get across to the client. He will sense and respond to our warmth or coldness, our real involvement or our façade, our immediacy or remoteness. He will respond to us as a thinking and feeling person if we can allow ourselves to emerge as such. He will respond to anything of ourselves that we present — or to nothing of ourselves if that is what we are giving him.

The question then comes down to this: How ought the therapist behave in the helping interview? I very much wish to present my answer because I feel it is basically correct. So strongly do I feel about this that I may perhaps sound dogmatic.

Humanness the Essence

I believe with the existentialists (Beck, 1966 [see especially the chapter by Dreyfus]; Buber, 1970; Bugental, 1965; Jourard, 1971; May, 1969) that, above and beyond every other consideration, the interviewer ought to behave as a human being in the interview, exposing as much of his humanness as possible. He should behave neither like a puppet nor like a technician. He should cast aside any mask, façade, or other "professional equipment" that creates barriers between the client and himself. He should bring himself into the helping interview in so open a manner that the client may easily find him and through him come closer to herself and to others. The interviewer should not be afraid of revealing himself. He wants the client to reveal herself and hopes that the latter may learn something from him, be helped in some way. Does he wish the client to learn from his behavior that she, the client, must not reveal herself, that this is dangerous, undesirable, unseemly? If the interviewer is remote and cold, can the client be expected to come close and be warm? When the interviewer is cautious and wary, can the client be unguarded? Will the latter be free to express openly her thoughts and feelings to someone barricaded behind a wall of professionalism? If the interviewer attempts to understand with her her thoughts and feelings, will not the client want and be in need of these thoughts about her thoughts, these feelings about her feelings?

Being human in the helping interview refers to — beyond what has been said about respect, interest, listening, understanding, acceptance, genuine liking, and empathy — that something about our own behavior which gives substance to those very attitudes. First of all, we must be prepared to show the client who we are without holding back so that he will feel encouraged to look at who he is without reservation. We must be sincere, genuine, congruent (Rogers, 1961) — not act so, but be so. As long as the client entertains any doubts about us as human beings, he will not allow himself to trust us. He will feel that it is unwise, unsafe, and unacceptable to trust others and himself. If he senses that we are genuine in what we do and say by the way we express our thoughts and feelings, our ambivalences and uncertainties, he may learn that it is safe to expose himself through his. If he hears us and senses no contradictory message behind our words, he may learn to listen genuinely to himself without censorship.

We must learn to become ever more sensitive to what takes place in the helping interview; to listen with that "third ear" that Reik (1977) describes and let the client know that we are indeed sensitive and aware, not by telling her we are, but by behaving in such a way that she sees we are. We must allow ourselves to be free and spontaneous; we must not hold back in an attempt to conform with the pattern of a "model" interviewer lest the client learn to react to him rather than to us. We shall never reach perfection in interviewing, but I am firmly convinced that we can approach the humanness that constitutes its essence.

The interviewer, being merely human, cannot be more than human. If he is not less, the client will benefit. But now I wish to leave generalities and be more specific about my own behavior. This can be hazardous, as talking about ourselves often is; we may be accused of boasting or of false modesty. But I shall take the risk — and rather lightheartedly at that — since I intend to be descriptive and not evaluative.

Like most of us, I want to be and also to be perceived as being genuine and warm. To be myself, I must be physically comfortable. I receive clients in slippers — without socks during the hot months. I never wear tie and jacket but prefer open-necked shirts with the addition of a sweater on wintry days. During the cool seasons I wear long trousers but change to shorts as soon as it gets warm. Even here in Israel where informal dress is still in vogue, this is considered somewhat idiosyncratic. How I would fare elsewhere, I cannot say.

As to the work style I attempt to adopt, it specifically involves creating rapport with the client and using as many of the client-centered leads and responses as possible, thus enabling him to delve deep within himself. Once beyond our trial period, I use whatever methods and techniques that enable the client to change in his chosen direction and that seem to me legitimate and ethical. Throughout this book I describe my style. All I can add at this point is that I consider therapy really hard work; it is fun, too, at times. We need that to carry us over the hurdle.

During my hospitalization and convalescence from a heart attack, all sessions were, naturally, canceled. Some clients visited me in the hospital, others sent flowers and greetings, still others simply stayed away. When I was permitted to return home, I was strictly instructed to rest fully for at least two months. I obeyed, but not immediately. I insisted on meeting every client once in order to explain my condition and immediate plans and to hear his. I also met once with the therapy group I was working with at the time. In this way I intended to minimize misunderstandings, to prove to each client that I was still alive and to enable her to express whatever feelings and fantasies she might have about my coronary, the unplanned break in our sessions, and whatever else was on her mind. One client never returned; she already felt so rejected by the world that my involuntary rejection proved too much for her. Naturally, I did not seek my physician's approval for this plan — he surely would have withheld it. In retrospect I am still glad I went through with it, believing that it aided both clients and my own recovery.

I have stopped smoking. Some of my clients are heavy smokers, but because I realize that breathing in others' smoke is as harmful as breathing one's own, I politely but firmly forbid smoking in my workroom and have even gone so far as to remove the ashtrays. So far, even the heavy smokers have found it possible to comply. Those who feel like smoking during the break in long sessions retreat to the waiting room or the garden.

At times I feel it advisable to suggest breaking off therapy. I am opposed to wasting either time or money and favor avoiding frustration as much as possible. With the very best of intentions, client and therapist do not always make it. Even when good rapport has been achieved, the client sometimes cannot profit at all or profit further from the therapeutic encounter. Glenn saw himself as too "polite and docile" to initiate conclusion of our meetings, but when I suggested the possibility he grabbed at the chance. Olga's reaction was superficially different:

TH. I notice, Olga, that even your note-taking has ceased. I've been wondering whether it's worth your while to continue in therapy. You've often expressed doubts, and frankly I've come around to this opinion. Perhaps you want to think it over.

CL. I'm very surprised you suggest stopping just when I feel we are making progress. I want to talk about what happened last night when we were all having supper together. . . .

Two weeks later Olga herself suggested we stop. She knows that my door remains open should she wish to return and try again.

When, after three months, Alexandra's symptoms had practically disappeared and she felt much stronger and much less weepy, we were ready to stop — or so I thought. Alexandra began to weigh the desirability of "doing a more basic job."

TH. Perhaps you find it difficult for us to part.

CL. No, I don't think that's it. I just thought that, perhaps, since I'm so much better we should go on and get at the root of things.

TH. Do you feel ready for such an undertaking?

CL. Frankly, no, but I thought . . . What do you think?

TH. I think you should first enjoy your regained health and good spirits and, if after a while, you should consider . . .

A job well done with objectives reached should satisfy. Alexandra, as I see her, is not cut out for prolonged deep therapy. Incidentally, she called not long ago to relate that she was feeling very well; not a word about the "basic job."

Claire and Jim had gone as far as they would ever get in therapy, I thought. They were just repeating themselves and getting upset instead of applying their learnings from therapy to everyday life. I told them so. At first they both objected — and for the same reason. Both felt that the other had not yet changed enough. Claire wanted Jim to continue alone. He refused, maintaining that he saw no point in coming alone. Finally they both agreed to stop therapy for the time being — or for good.

Sid and Diane were prepared to stop, but each wanted the other to accept the blame for the therapy's failure:

She. There's really no point going on here since you say that I don't attract you any more.

He. I did say that but I said more, too; that you won't do anything to change the situation.

TH. Here we go again.

He. I don't think that only I'm to blame. I was never particularly attracted to Diane but we managed pretty well.

She. Sure, till you started with that woman who —

He. But that wasn't a cause; it was an effect and you don't want to get that into your thick skull.

She. My parents always said I shouldn't marry you.

TH. I see we're going over familiar ground.

At times, I myself do not know if it would be wise for the client to stop. What both of us realize is that she is stuck. Nothing is happening; no new material is presented; no movement takes place. The client has reached a standstill, knows that she has, and is fully aware of the fact that the therapist cannot solve her dilemma.

I can easily recall four clients who looked for help from me, not because they were particularly disturbed or burdened by painful symptoms but because they required a "third ear" and found it only in therapy. All were conflicted about their marriages. Each had had a lover for a long time and none could break free from either the legal spouse or the lover. With each one I examined the conflict carefully; we weighed pros and cons, pluses and minuses. Each client asserted that he could not go on "like this" but that is exactly what each one ultimately did. Just as there are persons whom therapy cannot help, so there exist situations in which therapy is powerless.

Herman has been stuck now for a very long time. I think he rather enjoys this state. He disagrees but admits that, for the time being at least, it is preferable to any alternative. Although he continues to cling to the Stiller syndrome, I have recently detected a slightly derisive laugh when he mentions Stiller — as if to say "I know I'll want to give it up one of these days but it's still too convenient. There's plenty of time and meanwhile I can enjoy the fun." Herman knows we are stuck but doesn't even consider stopping therapy. We both know he will eventually break out of his fortress. Meanwhile we wait patiently.

Friendships Lost and Gained

Those who came to therapy looking for a friendship are bound to be disappointed. True, therapy contains certain aspects of friendship such as caring, listening, interest, and respect, but essential elements are missing: mutuality, reciprocity, spontaneity, and informality — to name a few. Friendships develop at work, at play, at school, on trips, in childhood, and in adulthood. Therapist and client have not met, generally speaking, before therapy begins and they will not meet again, usually, upon its completion. Therapy is one-sided; friendship cannot survive if it is that. Therapy is education, paid for; friendship is never that. Friendship involves mutual sharing; therapy certainly does not. We choose our friends but not our clients and seldom even our therapist. Friendships, one hopes, endure; therapy does not.

And yet, Helen came looking for friendship. I understand her need and happen to like and respect her. She rejected therapy, as we have seen. As it happens, we have mutual friends and, at the moment, volunteer at the same institution. If we meet again, something may develop but it won't be therapy.

Evelyn looks desperately for friends but has no illusions about me in that respect. She used to fantasize about visiting and going out together with my wife and me — no erotica involved here — sharing meals, chatting, but this stopped long ago. Now she comes when she needs a pep-shot; there are elements of friendship in this, too, but the kind therapy can tolerate.

Clients do fantasize about their therapist, of course. They want to possess him, to be parented by him, to be loved and admired. They want also to hate and torture him and to get revenge for all the pain he has supposedly inflicted. They take him to bed, on a trip, to a concert or museum. They show him off at a party. They seldom fantasize about having him just as a friend.

Careful bookkeeping reveals that through therapy I have lost one friend and gained two. As to the loss, I took a calculated risk. A very good friend found herself in an awful marital imbroglio and seriously contemplated a "final solution." I sent her immediately to a therapist I trusted. They did not hit it off and she was soon back. With great hesitation I agreed to see her and her husband. The therapy was short and successful but the price was our friendship.

Luckily, my friendship with Ely did not affect the work Shosh and I decided upon; on the contrary, I believed it helped. As for Esther, there was a time I saw her so frequently and she telephoned so often that she seemed almost part of the family. We saw Abe and the children socially, together with our own children, and when Abe developed cancer we were never far away. Esther is still almost part of the family.

Leah divorced Jack and is now happily remarried. It just so happens that we knew her present husband even before she did and now meet them socially from time to time. No one is in the least embarrassed by our original connection.

And yet, when all is said and done, the best policy would still seem to be not to mix clienthood with friendship. The client-therapist relationship is a unique one, and we do best to respect it as such and leave it at that. The other day a friend called desperately for help. I suggested a therapist; they clicked at once. Had they not, I would have suggested another therapist and, if necessary, a third one.

Professional and Personal Ethics

I cannot leave this discussion of our attitudes and behavior in the helping interview without some reference to the values we hold as professional persons. These are bound to affect, if not to control, our attitudes and behavior toward our clients, professional colleagues, the law, society at large and, of course, ourselves. Ethics and prose have this in common: we use both constantly but are rarely aware of the fact. We speak English all the time with people who also speak English, but this obtrudes upon our attention only when we meet someone who does not know English at all, or when we are required to learn a foreign tongue. It is pretty much the same with values. Unless confronted by values different from our own, unless called upon to defend and justify ours, we tend to take them for granted and their propriety as obvious.

Our clients in the helping interview do not leave our values unchallenged. By examining their own, they may be challenging ours. While insisting that we define for them what is right and wrong, they may be groping for their own ethical standards. It is impossible to tell them that we hold no values, for we do. Neither can we legitimately claim that our values are of no concern to them. We may prefer not to disclose them outright, thus leaving our clients to ponder and guess. Alternatively, we may state our values, assuming they will be adopted by our clients, and feel hurt and resentful when they are rejected. Or we may insist that values have no place in the helping interview and suggest we get on with the business at hand.

At this point it is useful to recall why our client has come. Generally it is so that we may help her to function more adequately and to make decisions that will be meaningful — yes, let me say it, right for her. The ethical burden this imposes on us may seem unbearable unless we remember that she is here so that we may help her to decide rather than to decide in her stead and, furthermore, that she is also influenced by others in her environment. Ultimately the client will have to choose in which direction to go, what values to adopt, and what values to discard. Perhaps she can learn from her encounter with us how to look at values, how to relate to them, how to examine them before making her choice. Perhaps she can learn from her contact with us that values are not necessarily — certainly not all of them — static. Perhaps she can look upon values as a part of life and upon life as an ongoing process of being and becoming, of standing and moving, of stabilizing and changing.

I believe that we should not hide our own values when these are relevant to our client's quest. I believe that we should state these simply and frankly as being ours, here and now, in order that he may examine his own here, now, and later — often much later. If we have succeeded in creating the sort of relationship I have been stressing all along, we shall not hold back this part of ourselves, but neither shall we try to impose our own values upon him. We shall allow ourselves to function as a resource person for our client so that he can use the helping interview to really help himself by examining ever more deeply his frustrations, anxieties, and inner struggles.

There are, of course, limitations. For me there are two crucial ones. First is the matter of confidentiality. Questions of right and wrong are always connected with attitudes and often with specific behavior as well. We cannot, morally, encourage disclosure about values, attitudes, and behavior unless we are certain that we can guarantee confidentiality. If we cannot, it is essential to state this clearly, for the client has every right to know what will be kept confidential, what may be kept so, and what will not. Given this information, he will decide how to proceed. Here again, the relationship that has been established may determine his decision.

Second, I may find it impossible not only to share the client's values but even to grasp them. The lifestyle she advocates and demonstrates may clash so deeply with the values I hold that we shall have to consider whether I can be of help to her at all. Whether she is "with" the counterculture and I am not, or I am "with" it and she is not, if I cannot empathize with the client, if I am unprepared or unsuccessful in trying to see and feel her inner world, I had better say so openly and help her to find someone who can. Just because there is so much social upheaval all about us, there is no reason to add unnecessary emotional upheaval to our clients or to ourselves. There are limits to our capacity for humanness.

Those engaged in the helping interview are bound to interact with other professionals. This interaction will, at times, raise ethical issues. These issues tend to be minimal if I work privately in my own office. Here my contacts are with my own professional supervisor and my professional peers upon whom I can — I hope — rely, as they are bound by the same ethical professional code as I. When working in an institutional setting, I am bound by that code of ethics prevailing in the institution. If it clashes drastically with my own, I must try to change it or else move on to another position. Of course, I may decide to compromise for one reason or another and shall have to rationalize as best I can. Whatever the case may be, the client is entitled to know to what extent his privacy and our confidentiality are limited. This will not always trouble him, but we must make it our concern to inform him.

I may be a member of an interdisciplinary team composed of professional and paraprofessional persons. My own work on such teams has been most rewarding when ethical standards were clearly set, implicitly or explicitly, and when the need of self-aggrandizement at the expense of the client on the part of team members was at a minimum. To reveal everything that is absolutely necessary and absolutely nothing that is not is the rule that has worked for me. Frequently the client knows and is glad that we are in contact with other professional persons. We may discuss with her what to divulge to whom and for what specific reason. We should never do so unless she consents or unless she is aware of the limits imposed upon privacy and confidentiality by the institutional setting in which the helping interview is carried on. The client deserves to know where she stands, and we must be discreet. Mutual trust is hard to arrive at but is all too easily lost.

We of the helping professions rarely come into conflict with the law on professional grounds (see special issue of the *Personnel and Guidance Journal* on ethics, 1971). At present, in democratic states at least, the law protects the privacy and confidentiality of our clients and our right, nay our duty, to act accordingly. There are, however, nuances. For one thing, we must know just what the law says regarding our professional ethical rights and obligations. For another, we are not always equal before that law because our professional affiliations differ and, within the various professions, there are different ethical standards and procedures for certification. Should legal difficulties arise concerning, for example, privileged communication (*Personnel and Guidance Journal*, 1971), there are lawyers to consult, legal advisors to our profession and, should it come so far, a judge. Our basic rule must remain to protect our client and to reveal only with his consent. The law, I believe, will protect us both. The more basic ethical dilemma lies elsewhere, in our relation to society at large and to ourselves.

As members of society at large we are constantly confronted with the following question: What are my values; what is my ethical stand on this issue or that? With social turmoil all about us, innumerable groups fighting for what they consider their rights, increased use of drugs, rapidly changing sexual mores, and so on, do we have a stand on such issues, and how do we communicate it to our clients? How do we help those who shout *No!* to culture and establishment but who, shouting aside, come to us for understanding, empathy, guidance? And what about the "generation gap" between our clients and ourselves, our clients and their parents, our clients and their children? How do our fellow professionals, team members, supervisors, employers, look upon our stand? Do we appear to them as unregenerate reactionaries or as potential and therefore suspect revolutionaries? Or do we bury our head in the sand with the hope that when we re-emerge into the sunlight the upheaval about us will have vanished?

Some of us may find temporary assuagement in the belief that, imminently, computerized counseling will ease our burden. Others will make a mockery of privacy, confidentiality, and of the helping interview itself. Difficult as these issues are, we cope with them, each in her own way, in our personal and professional lives.

This is my way of coping with some of these issues. I submit it for your examination because we dare not work by questions alone. I am uncompromising in my refusal to change the intimate setting of the helping interview. It belongs to, is a part of, the client and of me. Technology must not come between us. It may assist, when mutually agreed upon, but no more than that. I attempt to keep myself open to change and to remain curious as to what is going on around me. I want to stay in touch with change and with reliable information concerning it. I find this somewhat difficult at times due to the constant burgeoning of newly developed methodology, theory, and evidence. Finally, I continue to be optimistic about human nature, for I wholeheartedly believe in our potential for good in spite of witnessing frequently our capacity for evil.

4 • RECORDING AND RECALLING THE INTERVIEW

Note-taking

Note-taking is an integral part of the interviewing process. We need notes to refresh our memory, to remind us to carry out our part of an agreed plan of action, to discuss the interview with professional colleagues. The most meaningful reason for keeping records may be to enable us to follow our own growth and development, to show us what we have done or left undone, how we have behaved in a given situation or with different clients under various circumstances. Recording can be a bridge from past to present to future performance on our part as we gain experience in interviewing.

Many Different Approaches

There are probably as many ways of recording the interview as there are interviewers. I believe it to be true that if the client can relate to the interviewer, he will be able to relate to the interviewer's style of note-taking. If either the interviewer or her recording gets in the way of the helping interview, the relationship is bound to suffer. If the therapist is comfortable with herself and her method, chances are that the client will quickly learn to accept both.

In our culture, when note-taking is discriminately handled, it is not resented. On the contrary, its absence may be looked upon as negligence or lack of interest. Usually no explanation of our recording practice is required. However, should an explanation be requisite because of the needs of either or both partners in the interview, it can be easily provided. I know a teacher who when interviewing a pupil generally explains: "I won't write down anything while we are talking now because I want to pay attention to you and me. But after you leave, I'll jot down some notes so I can better remember what we talked about. If you wish to do likewise, we could even compare notes afterward."

During the first interview with a new client a rehabilitation worker of my acquaintance says something to this effect: "I hope you won't mind my writing things in my notebook now and then while we talk. I just don't trust my memory; and if I don't jot things down, I may get uneasy and lose track of what's going on. I can listen to you best this way."

I know interviewers and therapists who feel that no explanation is necessary and behave in such a way that none is. There are those who note down straight information only. Others also record plans of action and decisions mutually arrived at. Some therapists write down ideas and feelings expressed by the client; still others note in brief their own responses as well. A friend of mine used to take copious notes. Over the years he made several attempts to cut down. During one such attempt the client, whom he had seen a few times previously, perceived his effort and remarked, "You'd better write more; it'll relax you."

I have also known of instances in which the client took notes and the therapist did not. This situation may be a bit uncomfortable at first. The shoe seems to be on the wrong foot, but why, actually, should we think it is? Perhaps we still equate note-taking with being in charge.

Some "Don'ts"

Nevertheless, several "don'ts" deserve stressing. Don't turn note-taking into cross-examination: "Now let's see if I wrote down correctly what your feelings about your wife are." Don't let note-taking interfere with the flow of the interview: "Please don't talk quite so fast, I just can't keep up." If you allow yourself to become more involved with recording than with the client, you are not giving him the attention he deserves and needs. Recording should always be subordinate to the interviewing process, never the reverse.

Don't hide behind or escape into note-taking: "Now let me see . . . yes, my records here indicate that at our meeting last week your attitude toward managing on the budget we agreed upon was much more cheerful." A client once complained about her counselor: "He uses his notes the way my husband uses his newspaper. I can't get through to either one."

Don't be secretive about the taking of notes, lest this arouse the anxiety or curiosity of the client. Finally, when taking notes in the presence of the client, don't write things you are not prepared to have him see. A therapist was once called out of his office during an interview. Upon his return the man he was interviewing said, "I saw what you wrote there about me being uncooperative and aggressive!" If we consider it legitimate and necessary to note comments meant for ourselves alone and not for the client — such as evaluations, assessments, conclusions — we ought not to write these in his presence. And they must, of course, be kept from him during future interviews if these occur.

In short, just as everyone develops his own style of interviewing, so everyone develops his own style of recording the interview. Both undergo changes as we gain experience and become more comfortable with ourselves and the client. I have found in my own career that as time goes on, note-taking decreases in quantity, and a style conducive to good interviewing and commensurate with personal needs is acquired.

The Ethics of Note-taking

Now that we have our notes, which we took either during the interview or as soon as possible after its termination, what do we do with them? Within the context of present social norms interviewing wears an inherently ethical aspect. The helping interview is assumed to be confidential and is often openly stated to be so. The client comes to us taking for granted that here she need not hold back since the professional setting itself ensures against prattling or, for that matter, against any disclosure whatsoever without her specific consent. Unless she can trust that what she divulges remains confidential, and will certainly at no time be used against her, she may not be able to confide. This trust must be kept.

Our notes, the record of the interview, may be in the form of a résumé, a running account, brief points that serve as reminders, or a combination of all these with possibly a summing up and an evaluation. The tangible remains of the interview, these notes are confidential as well. They should be kept where we alone have access to them and must not be left lying about even temporarily, lest those for whom they are not intended happen upon them. They may be properly shared only with professional persons whose task is to help us to be as effective as possible — for example, our supervisors and those who work with us on a professional team dedicated to helping the client. Although therapists and interviewers do not always clearly state this, many of them keep certain confidential information wholly to themselves, share most information with supervisors and team members, and report only the necessary minimum to administrators. I know therapists who keep separate files on the same client for these different purposes.

Honesty Essential

Whatever the best procedure may be, I am certain of one thing: we must be honest. If the notes taken are to be used for the purpose of research, we should state this at the outset. In the event that the information gathered cannot be kept confidential, we should frankly indicate this, too. Above all, we should not promise confidentiality if we are not certain that we can provide it. The question "If I tell you what happened, do you promise not to tell my teacher?" should not be answered in the affirmative unless the therapist fully intends to keep the promise. It need not be answered positively, however, for I, the therapist, may not be prepared to promise something about which I know nothing. I can reply: "Well, I'd rather not promise without knowing; but tell me what's on your mind, and then we'll try to figure out together what this is all about" or "I can't promise without knowing; but I do promise that if you tell me about it, I won't do anything without first letting you know what it is and discussing it with you." After trust has been established, the client may no longer require us to keep information confidential, but will rely upon our professional judgment.

Two more examples. A woman may address a probation officer in this way: "I want you to promise not to tell my boy that I came in to see you." An honest rejoinder would be, "Perhaps you'd like to tell me what you want us to talk about, and we'll see about this as we go along." And, finally, a child may say to her teacher, "You'll tell the principal anyway so why should I talk to you?" There may be no point in the teacher's promising not to tell the principal because she may be obliged to do so or may wish to discuss the matter with him. One way to express this would be, "I may want to tell the principal something, but I won't tell him anything except what we agree upon at the end of our talk."

Tape Recording

In this increasingly technical age something must be said of the audiotape recorder and the more recently developed videotape (see below). A tape of an interview cannot be considered as merely notes. It is a complete record of what has been said and in the case of videotape is also a visual record of what has taken place. Such a record can serve many good purposes, but it is not note-taking. Because of the cost and space factors involved, tape interviews cannot generally be preserved over long periods of time, and one can hardly refer to tapes as readily as to written notes. Tapes may be transcribed, of course, but this involves additional time and a specialized secretarial staff, which, more often than not, is unavailable.

The primary use of the taped interview is learning or research. Here we shall consider the former only. I know of no better device for showing the therapist objectively how and what he is doing. The use of tapes may be threatening at first; but as one gets accustomed to them, they can be most rewarding.

"Did I really talk that much?"

"I don't recall her having said that at all. I wonder where I was."

"Boy, I sure interrupted him over and over again. I wonder if he noticed it as much as I do now."

"I was much better today. I listened well, and I think I understood what went on and expressed it. But I'm still a bit too fast on the pickup for my taste."

To me this is meaningful learning. Instead of falling back on my memory, which is bound to be selective, I can check and see. In addition, I can carry on this sort of learning by myself at my own convenience and leisure.

Most clients accept my explanation of the tape-recording equipment in the room and of the ethics of recording without comment or protest. Once the fact of recording is taken for granted, the actual taping is forgotten and ignored. On occasion, I have run into clients who not only fear it but suspect the existence of hidden equipment that records without their knowledge and permission:

CL. (in tone of pretended jest) I'd better be careful here. I'll bet everything is photographed and recorded.

TH. Neither is happening at this moment. I'll want to tape some of our sessions, but only if you agree. I can lend them to you if you'd like to listen to them afterwards.

CL. If you record, I won't be able to talk. I think I hear . . . Are you sure?

TH. You're very uneasy about it. I promise nothing will be taped without your knowledge and consent.

CL. I believe you, but I still think I hear something.

This particular client never returned. Renee, on the other hand, asked permission to examine the machine and even wanted to learn to operate it on her own. I never attempted to record any of our sessions — Renee was far too tense for that — but there was no question here of suspicion or lack of trust.

Therapy did not begin with the electronic age. I often use my own "recording devices" that assist me in recalling. I practice listening so that I can pretty much restate what client and I have said. I train my memory to retain essential passages and points that require delving into. Walking up and down in the garden between sessions seems to sharpen my powers of concentration and to keep me close to clients.

Still, keeping records is most useful. Natalie was so ambivalent about her son that, when favorably inclined toward him, she would totally forget her resentments and frustrations — to the extent that she doubted my veracity when I pointed these out to her. Only when she heard herself on the tape did she become convinced.

Vic thought little of my equipment; his was far superior. He recorded long monologues and brought them in for us to analyze. Once he produced a recording of one of our discussions that he had taped on a pocket machine of whose presence I had been totally unaware.

Shirley fought for her rights as a woman and as a feminist. Toward the end of sessions, she would repeat and note down the main points she had made that day concerning her daughters, her husband, Dan, and the state of their marriage. She would bring Dan's comments on her notes and her own responses to these comments to the next session. Finally she brought Dan himself. Note-taking served her therapy well.

Joy and Andy found it very difficult to listen to each other. Andy would frequently deny having said what Joy claimed he had — and vice versa. They would argue simultaneously, making it impossible for either to be understood. One day Joy suggested they play back the tape that was recording the session:

She. Then we wouldn't be able to argue as to who said what.

He. I think that's great — but only if you'll really listen.

She. We haven't even begun and you're already at it. Why me? Who says that you're such a great listener?

TH. Do you want to hear that last exchange?

From then on, whenever Joy or Andy made a point he or she thought the other had missed, we would play back the tape. Both partners really learned to listen. This in itself did not solve all their difficulties, of course, but it certainly improved their communication tremendously.

Sandy never came without her miniature tape recorder. She always "studied" the last tape before the next interview. There were periods during her therapy when she could not come every week. She maintains that the tapes helped her bridge over the time gap. Sandy always came "prepared." A slow starter, studying the tapes helped her decide just where she wished to begin. Recording did not help Sandy only cognitively; it served as an encounter with herself, thus enabling honest self-expression. Her sister Peggy also came for therapy for a while. Imitating Sandy, she brought a tape recorder as well. But Peggy was not Sandy. She started recording, but turned the tape off and continued without it. She could not learn to feel at ease with it.

Very few clients have taken advantage of my offer to let them listen to our recorded tapes. Olga took her own notes during sessions, as we have seen, and so did Herman for a while. He wrote copious notes at home and brought them in to read to me. When I suggested he might be hiding behind them, he gradually stopped the practice. He still remains Stiller but there is no longer a barrier of notes between us.

Natalie kept a journal. She brought it with her but did not always refer to it. I enjoyed her style of writing. In the journal she allowed herself to be much more definite, specific, and assertive than she did orally. But Natalie did not persist in keeping her journal. She found it too much of an effort to keep up anything for very long.

Some clients need structure. They feel and function better when arriving at sessions with a set of notes — an outline, a number of points to be discussed, topics and subtopics, all depending on the client's make-up. Pedantic Isaac, who could not decide whether to leave his wife or his mistress, brought up-to-date "balance sheets." The points in favor of staying or leaving shifted, but Isaac himself remained immobilized.

Sam was always subdued and courteous, but his notes, without which he never appeared, were loaded. Thus, totally out of context, he asked:

CL. Will I ever be completely cured again?

TH. What a surprising question! I don't know if anyone is ever completely well. Can you be more specific?

CL. Will my symptoms recur? Will I always be a little anxious? Will I have to come running to you again?

TH. I can't say for sure but, should you again be under great pressure, you might possibly want to come back. . . .

CL. Not that I mind coming to you if I have to: I was just hoping that, perhaps . . .

TH. You would not need me again. Look, Sam, some people have bad teeth and others a weak stomach; nearly everyone has something wrong with him. You have this tendency to anxiety with accompanying symptoms. As you admit yourself, you manage extremely well most of the time, but now and then you need a little help. What's wrong with that? I have to make a living, too . . .

Once I dared to lead with:

TH. Sam, is there an item on your list that you make very sure we never get to?

CL. There is — death — I'd like for us to discuss it but I'm just too scared. I can't even talk about an ordinary illness without feeling slightly faint. I was present at the birth of our last child and that was hard for me, but I forced myself to do it. As for death, I postpone the subject from week to week; just the thought of it is enough — but everything else on the list I do bring up so I feel I'm doing quite well.

It is my belief that, as a matter of ethics, the fact the interview is being taped should not be concealed. If I tell the client that it is my custom to record interviews to learn from them afterward and that the tape will be kept confidential, he will usually not object. In fact, after the first few minutes, he will not react to it at all, for he will no longer notice it. The client will not be uneasy unless he feels that I am. If I can say that he, too, may listen to the tapes to learn, so much the better. If after all this the client still objects, it is probably best to respect his feelings. Some people are simply afraid or suspicious. In areas or cultures in which the tape recorder is seldom used or seen, for the therapist to insist might prove harmful indeed. When one finds she is working with suspicious people, the wise thing to do is to get at the suspiciousness and leave the tape recorder alone for the time being.

I am very impressed with the benefit clients can derive from listening to their own tapes. This is true for children, adolescents, and adults. At first, interest may center on the technical aspects. It may then shift to the sound of one's own voice — something we use so much and about which we know so little that often we are unable to recognize it. Later, interest usually focuses on what actually took place in the interview. The interview is a serious, purposeful conversation carried on between two people. By listening to his own interview, the client often acquires a deeper appreciation of its seriousness, clarifies for himself his purpose in it, and obtains much significant insight. As far as I know, we tend to use taped interviews solely to promote our own learning. They can, I am suggesting, promote learning on the part of the client as well.

Videotape

Videotape has added such a momentous new dimension to our subject that it warrants consideration under a separate heading. Human beings are rather conservative creatures and it takes us time to assimilate and to apply methodologically the many inventions technology has put at our disposal. The videotape has taken its place among the standard equipment for training, treatment, and research in schools, clinics, and universities (Berger, 1978; Geertsma and Mackie, 1969).

Picture has now been added to sound, sight to hearing, seeing to listening. The television screen has supplemented the audiotape recorder. We are no longer limited to the spoken word. While retaining it, we have access as well to movement, to gesture, to the rich and ever changing world of body language — in short, we have access to our entire range of behavior. We can observe it over and over, if we so choose. We can attempt to replicate, reinforce, or change any aspect of behavior we are intent upon studying.

Seeing ourselves behave is exciting, challenging, and, to most of us, threatening at first. Till now, we have examined our behavior through feedback from others and through our own acquired insights. Now it literally unfolds before our eyes. We are shown indisputably how, in fact, we behave.

"When he said that I leaned forward as if I wanted to eat him alive. . . . No wonder he looks scared."

"Look how his fists are clenched!"

To me, the most exciting and, I admit, the most threatening aspect of videotape is that it enables us to study simultaneously both our verbal and nonverbal communication. We can judge for ourselves to what extent our words match our actions. The mouth speaks and so does the rest of our body. Now we can compare and contrast the two. We can see ourselves as the client may see us. Does our behavior, there on the screen, form a whole? Are we in fact the words and feelings we express or do we notice a clash somewhere, a slight discrepancy perhaps, between word and gesture, which may well arouse doubt in the client as to our sincerity? Most important of all, do we only sound genuine or do we look genuine as well? Let me quote from practicum sessions of trainees in interviewing:

"That constant smile . . . I must learn to wipe it off my face. I didn't feel as if I were smiling all the time. I must have been even more anxious than I realized. I want to smile only when there is really something to smile about."

"Good heavens! I'm perspiring as if I were doing heavy physical labor. I hope I can get over that before I begin to interview in earnest."

"I'm frowning much too much. It is because I am concentrating on what to say next but it makes me look angry. I wouldn't want to be interviewed by someone who looks as fierce as I do on that screen."

Videotaping is not, as a rule, practical in day-to-day interviewing; as standard equipment it is still too cumbersome. However, for teaching-learning purposes, it is an ideal tool. In simulation and role-playing, for example, I learn not merely about my behavior, but am actually confronted by it as I view it on the screen. Now, I can study my behavior not only through others' comments but by my own observation. The choice challenges me directly: is this the way I want to behave? What in my behavior do I wish to leave as is? What would I like to change and in what direction? I can experiment repeatedly with various facets of my conscious behavior.

Now that videotaping is accessible to almost any training program, we need no longer come to the helping interview without a clear picture of how we function. We can observe ourselves in action and can, at long last, really and truly learn by seeing. Videotape will not make genuine interviewers of us all. It will definitely assist those who are ready to tackle the never-ending task of trying to be what it is within them to become.

> "That pat on the shoulder was just right. It expressed exactly how I felt at that moment."

> "This time, I did not recoil the way I used to, when verbally attacked. I can take these assaults better now."

> "I was really getting impatient with her at that point. The tap-tap of my left foot shows it. I'm glad I was able to say it to her in words as well. It sure helped the interview along."

Supervision

In the area of supervision I find the tape to be the most useful teaching-learning tool. The more experienced we become, the more we are requested to train and supervise neophytes. This involves teaching new therapists to improve their skills and become increasingly independent. To the extent that we succeed in this, their clients, it is assumed, will benefit. In this sense, our efforts are indirectly therapy and deserve further attention.

At work, both new and experienced therapists are alone. Even when engaged with a client, we are alone. This is felt particularly by the neophyte: teachers are absent, books and notebooks out of reach, supervision will take place only the day after tomorrow. It is impossible to turn to the client for help. There is a feeling of loneliness and isolation. It is my belief that, though a difficult experience, it is an invaluable and essential one for the beginning therapist. Confidence is a result of wavering; experience the consequence of daring, and coping the gradual abandoning of familiar but unnecessary defenses.

I well realize that I am espousing an old-fashioned — some would even say outdated — position. Old-fashioned I may well be; the fashion now considered old was once young, when I was. Nowadays, the telephone will ring on the neophyte's desk if the supervisor listening in and observing through the one-way screen feels that he is in difficulties. I consider this harmful for the therapist and client alike. When the supervisor actually enters the room where the client and neophyte are sitting to "save the situation" I am completely flabbergasted. This I consider actually destructive of the rapport between therapist and client.

I want those whom I supervise to know from the start that in our profession they must stand on their own feet, that the sooner they begin, the better it will be for them and, in the long run, the easier. I explain that I am a minimalist when it comes to supervision and that our goals are bound to be limited: to help them become ever more aware of what is taking place within themselves as well as between clients and themselves. In order to achieve this goal I suggest that they bring to supervision their notes, their tapes, and their own readiness to learn and grow.

Even the best notes taken during and immediately after sessions are bound to be impressionistic. From them we can seldom tell what actually took place, but only what the therapist perceived. This is important, but the neophyte's tapes tell us more and tell it objectively.

Bea remarked perceptively:

N.* I suppose my clients will mind less than I will. After all whatever they say is legitimate. They won't be criticized though I may be.

S. That's true perhaps, but you want to become an experienced therapist, whereas what they want is to finish as quickly as possible.

N. I think I'll tape first the client with whom I feel most comfortable. (slight laugh) He'll be supporting me without knowing it.

---

*N stands for neophyte; S stands for supervisor.

S. Whatever works best for you — as long as we get tapes to work on.

It was rough going at first: her notes were so complete that taping was superfluous; the tape recorder at her clinic was unavailable; she got the machine but pressed the wrong button; she worked the tape right but the voices were practically inaudible. . . . Gradually, Bea began to bring well-recorded tapes that we could analyze. Once she had fully grasped that her responses and leads weren't as stupid or insensitive as she had feared, Bea began to enjoy supervision. She became much more aware of what she wished to change in her style and with what she was pleased. Her voice sounded stronger, more assertive and, for all that, warmer. Her slight stammer disappeared and she interrupted less frequently. Feeling more relaxed herself, she could help the client express his deeper feelings and examine them. She became adept at terminating sessions. The tape had become a meaningful tool for her.

One day Bea came in with an idea; she did not want us to talk about Itamar any more. There was nothing more to be said. She just couldn't get him to talk. The tape she had brought of their last session was practically soundless. She thought she understood his defensiveness, the aggression hidden behind his pacifism and kindness to animals, his fears regarding women, but still . . . He had already hinted at stopping therapy as he was "not good at it." She wanted us to role-play a session and tape it. She would be Itamar and I was to be Bea, the therapist:

TH. You've talked about your latest stint of reserve duty in Lebanon and I've been kind of puzzling things over. You say you are a pacifist and yet as an army medic — a job you volunteered for — you expose yourself to the sights and risks of war. True, you throw yourself into battles not to kill but, rather, to save lives, but you seem to enjoy what you are doing. Is there a discrepancy somewhere?

CL. I don't know. . . . Maybe. . . . I hate war but if I can save lives I'll do it and I don't mind carrying stretchers under fire. It even makes me feel good.

TH. Sort of a thrilling feeling.

CL. Yes. I don't run away from danger.

TH. You seem to enjoy it. That reminded me, somehow, of your behavior in that accident. You gave first aid to the wounded; you helped them even though you had to hurt them — and I sort of had the feeling you enjoyed that as well.

CL. I don't think I'm a sadist.

TH. I was wondering whether perhaps you might not have ambivalent feelings — sort of hating and yet liking certain activities, aspects of life, like having to hurt in order to save but enjoying the hurting too — a way of allowing yourself to be aggressive.

CL. (long silence) You're probably thinking of the big knife I showed you. I've never hurt anyone with it, but I might just need it in self-defense.

TH. It's interesting that you should mention that knife just now.

CL. Perhaps. . . . When I think of Jiffy . . . He's really a powerful dog and when I run with that animal I feel terrific.

TH. He makes you feel safe and powerful too.

CL. Not the way I feel in class when I try to keep the seat on either side of me free so that I can concentrate. Then I feel very vulnerable — especially if a woman manages to sit down next to me.

Bea stopped the role-play at this point. She had long since gone beyond what Itamar would or could say in such a short time, but she had found herself more at home in his world, felt much more empathic toward him, and could go back to him surer of herself and their joint task.*

We all make mistakes. In our profession, unfortunately, we make them with people. One of the goals of supervision is to render these mistakes as few and as harmless as possible for both client and neophyte. I have never forgotten the lesson I learned

---

*Shortly after this episode, for purely technical reasons, Itamar and I began working together.

through supervision when I just started out. I was working in a rehabilitation agency at the time and had been strictly advised not to provide clients with my private address and phone number. Clients belonged to the agency, my supervisor explained, and could always contact me through it. This seemed sound policy and I obeyed. But one client, cleverer and more experienced than I, managed to wangle my phone number out of me on a pretext I long ago "forgot." I do recall the feeling, however: rules are made to be broken and I was smart enough to know when to do this; here was a client who really had to speak to someone now and then and he had chosen me. I wasn't going to let him down. He lived alone, had no close friends, and all he wanted . . . I felt very virtuous because of my high-minded generosity. From that day on, I knew no peace for months until the client finally relented — or found another inexperienced worker. My supervisor said nothing — but that was enough.

Another incident from those early days has remained vivid in my mind, but for very different reasons. One of my colleagues, also a beginner, encountered problems of adjustment and needed someone to confide in. We would go out to lunch together, stay after work occasionally, and talk. We did not consider this a professional relationship and neither of us even wished to see it as such. But my supervisor, who somehow had found out about our talks, thought it necessary to point out that the agency was ready to offer counseling services to staff members also and that I had overstepped the bounds of my role. He insisted that I should have referred my colleague to the service!

I was once requested to supervise the staff of a residential school for disturbed children. After meeting with the members of the staff individually and in a group, it became clear that supervision was not what was needed. The entire institution was so strife-ridden, the staff members so hostile to each other, the administration so ineffectual, that the best course to follow was to transfer the children to other frameworks and close down the school. It was a drastic solution but I dared to suggest it and, when my views were accepted, helped to carry it out.

More experienced therapists, myself among them, derive great benefit from reciprocal peer supervision. A small group of therapists meets on a more or less regular, if informal, basis. They share each other's difficulties, doubts, and learnings. They discuss clients, analyze tapes and notes, and speak of current professional literature, as well as anything else that concerns them professionally. They must not necessarily belong to the same "school" of therapy, but an important requirement is a basic congeniality.

I find the last supervisory meeting almost as exciting as the last therapy session. Bea and I had reached that point. She felt both sad and happy but was confident that she had received from me just about as much as I had to offer. In the future, she might seek out another supervisor with a different approach but, right now, we agreed, she was ripe to go on independently. She was surer of herself and ready to take the plunge. Now and then, she knew, she would hesitate, make mistakes, and change her mind, just as every therapist does. It had been good to work together and now it was good to part.

5 • THE QUESTION

Ruth, thoughtfully: "I don't ask you any questions because the answers I seek are my own, not yours."

Sam, bewildered: "I always come with questions and you always turn things around so that I have to try to answer them for myself."

The Need to Inquire and the Need to Divulge

Recognizing and accepting our basic need to ask and to be asked, I wish in this chapter to examine the question, our main tool for this objective, and point out its limitations and inherent pitfalls. In and out of therapy, most of us feel a need to inquire and to be inquired of. This occurs on both a social and a professional level.

We inquire in order to show interest and concern; to assuage our curiosity; to gather information; to remind the other that we recall what she has previously told us. We wish to be inquired of for the very same reasons; we want to be cared about, remembered, taken seriously, considered worthwhile. On the professional level the client's expectations remain the same and, if anything, are heightened.

Because of his prior experiences the client expects questions and waits for them. It would seem that the fulfillment of these expectations proves to him that we care, show interest, and know our business:

> CL. Are you waiting for me? Is it up to me to start?

> TH. I guess it is. I really can't know what to ask you at this point as I don't know you or even what brought you here. So why don't you just tell me what brought you here?

For most clients this response legitimizes their desire to begin, but others still hesitate:

> CL. I just don't know where to begin. It would help me if you were to ask something.

> TH. All right. What would you like to discuss first?

Strange as it may seem, this simple restatement is helpful to many. The need to be questioned is so ingrained that it looks for justification in the oddest way, as it were, right under our noses.

The pressures of social and professional expectations work on the therapist as well: if I refrain from asking won't I seem unprofessional? If I do not inquire about his health or the important party she talked about last time, won't I come across as rather callous and uncaring — not even bothering to remember what the client brings to therapy? If I do not lead by inquiring, won't he simply wait in silence till I do, so that he can follow as he has learned to do in the "outside world"? How will I ever understand her if I do not pose questions?

What is taking place within me? Perhaps I really should inquire more. Why should the poor client struggle when I could so easily facilitate his task? And wouldn't it really help both of us if I possessed more information about him, his family, his work, his past? We are on the brink of treading on dangerous ground. We feel this in our professional bones and hold back, and so we must, I still believe.

It is absolutely essential, in therapy, to demonstrate to the client from the first moment on that this encounter is meant to be a very special experience for her. It is about her and for her and centers on her. I want to show from the outset that she is in charge and that she must be so if we are to deal with the matters that have brought her to me. I do and shall want to help her push ahead in her self-exploration. I may well pose a question occasionally to facilitate her search, but I do not wish to get in the way and will do all in my power not to circumscribe her life space. I want her to feel, here with me, free as is humanly possible to pursue her goals in her way, using her own style. I hope my attitude will convey concern, interest, caring, and respect — but by other means than that of the standard pattern of questions and answers. As I am also part of the present equation, I will usually suggest during the first session:

> *TH.* There may be things you'll want to know about me. Feel free to ask. I may not always be able to reply, but if not, I'll try to explain my reasons. Anything on your mind right now?

I generally make it clear that I won't be asking questions merely out of "politeness." Neither shall I refer to our last session, though assuredly I shall try to remember its essentials. Time has elapsed since our last meeting. What was important to the client then may seem trivial now, and if not, he will return to it of his own accord. He may prefer to express feelings and thoughts that concern him right now and about which I still know very little. I shall gladly follow the direction in which he heads and will not hesitate to let him know when and what I do not understand. Should more information prove necessary, we can go into that as well. As we have seen, some clients will insist on more leads from the therapist, and we shall have no choice but to provide them, but only after our first efforts have failed. Our primary goal is to push ahead. If questions turn out to be really essential for the client, we must surely ask them but as sparingly as possible and as open-ended as well. We must be patient, steadfast, and undogmatic in our approach.

Some clients may be so accustomed to being asked before speaking out that it is hard for them to change, and they may see in our injunctions more hindrance than help. So we shall have to come to their assistance in order to bridge over uncomfortable silences and to push ahead when they seem to be stuck.

> TH. You're finding it hard to continue. Would you like to say more about the difficulty you encounter with men?

> CL. I had a really bad experience a few years ago and I think I never got over it.

Sometimes a bit of encouragement proves beneficial:

> TH. You're not finding it easy to talk of yourself without being questioned, but I'm beginning to get a rough picture of the things you want us to discuss. I was just wondering how your wife's breakdown affects the kids and yourself.

> CL. Yes, but first I have to tell you that my wife and I were on the verge of separating when she got sick and today I feel as if I were to blame . . . that we could have avoided . . .

At times, even this will not suffice and then we must let the client show us the way although leading questions from us may prove unavoidable. Some people just are and will remain followers.

Fortunately, one factor operates in our favor — the client's need and, therefore, his desire to divulge. Most clients have much to tell; they fairly brim over with thoughts and emotions they are bursting to relate. It is up to us to make them secure and comfortable enough to overcome their initial fear and hesitation. Once they appreciate that speaking, divulging, opening up in the way best for them is legitimate — is in fact what the "talking cure" calls for — they will be on their way. Once Laura had grasped that fact she could say:

> CL. I feel that now I can call the shots. If you had asked about my husband or daughter, I would have replied, but perfunctorily. I mentioned them in the first place and, naturally, was prepared for you to ask, but because you didn't I could concentrate on myself. Otherwise I wouldn't have dared to do that for quite a while — it just wouldn't have seemed the right thing to do.

Gabriel put it differently:

> CL. Whenever anyone talked to me in the hospital, it was to
> get information, and I gladly answered questions because it
> made me feel good when someone seemed to care. But I found
> no one there who would listen to me just because I wanted
> to talk, because I had things to get off my chest. So I gave up
> on that angle till I came here. But you make it hard for me,
> too; you don't ask questions so it's all up to me now.

When the client realizes that she can talk about whatever she
chooses, that the word *appropriate* does not exist in her encounter
with us, she will generally open up — the way we do when we
talk to complete strangers: I need not hold back; I will not see
this person ever again; he does not know me. We will go our separate ways — I, having unburdened myself; he, having enabled me
to speak. Although in therapy we do meet again and do not remain strangers, the legitimacy and the appropriateness of self-
revelation are essentially identical.

Divulging involves cleansing. I speak, I reveal, I "come clean."
Long ago, the Greeks knew of this cleansing of the soul and called
it catharsis.

After a good deal of circumlocution, Carl revealed his "secret."
It has been weighing on him for a quarter of a century. Very few
are in the know, having either discovered it by chance or else
having been told in bare outline by Carl himself in a moment of
weakness. In that memorable session, he finally allowed himself
to treat it openly. It still comes up now and again in his ongoing
therapy:

> CL. After revealing my secret to you, I have been thinking of
> it more, rather than less, but when I think of it now it hurts
> and disturbs me less. I am still repelled by what I did over
> twenty years ago, but somehow it is part of my past and so
> belongs to me. I'm not going to shout about it from the roof-
> tops but I can speak more easily to myself about it.
>
> TH. You can kind of accept it as part of you.

The guilt we find it hard to bear leads us to confess — be it in
church, at the police station, or in the nonjudgmental presence of

the therapist. It is as if confession — with or without ensuing punishment — frees us. The human contact confession provides lightens the burden.

Bob continues his self-destructive behavior. But we both notice a slight shift in orientation. He initiates more sessions and often begins them by saying, "You'll hang me for this but . . ." or "I know I shouldn't run away but I'm going to." Now Bob wants me to stop him. He fights me, he argues — but he runs away much less. He brings his outlandish plans to therapy before carrying them out, as if to say: "For heaven's sake stop me. I shouldn't do this but I can't help myself yet. I am weak but you are strong. I don't want to listen to you being reasonable, and yet I do. Please stop me from destroying what I am trying to build."

Questioning the Question

In this connection I shall also question the question, that is, the use of the question. I wish to consider the various types of questions and the different purposes they may serve. If you examine random interviews, you will find most of them so studded with questions that you may begin to think the only thing the interviewer can do or feels comfortable in doing is asking questions. Her questions seem to keep her afloat; take them away from her and she will sink.

Yes, I have many reservations about the use of questions in the interview. I feel certain that we ask too many questions, often meaningless ones. We ask questions that confuse the client, that interrupt him. We ask questions the client cannot possibly answer. We even ask questions we don't want the answers to, and consequently, we do not hear the answers when forthcoming.

However, my greatest objection to the use of questions as such lies deeper. It brings us back to philosophy for a moment — but sometimes one must retrace one's steps a bit before going on. If we begin the helping interview by asking questions and getting answers, asking more questions and getting more answers, we are setting up a pattern from which neither we nor surely the client will be able to extricate himself. By offering him no alternative we shall be teaching him that in this situation it is up to us to ask the questions and up to him to answer them. What is worse, having already become accustomed to this pattern from previous experience, he may readily adapt himself to it. Here again he will perceive himself as an object, an object who answers when asked and otherwise keeps his mouth closed — and undoubtedly his mind and heart as well. By initiating the question-answer pattern we are telling the client as plainly as if we put it into words that we are the authority, the expert, and that only we know what is important and relevant for him.

Underlying this sort of behavior is an unstated assumption on the part of the therapist and client that also needs to be openly stated here, namely, that the client submits to this humiliating treatment only because she expects you to come up with a solution to her problem or because she feels that this is the only way you have of helping her. As for you, the therapist, you have asked your questions and gotten your answers; now show your tricks. If you do not have the solution up your sleeve, if you cannot help after the long third degree, what right had you to ask? What are you good for? The client may feel all this; but whether she does or not, you will. Having asked the questions and obtained the answers, you will feel obligated to formulate a solution, to provide "the" answer, to pronounce your "verdict." Well, if this is what you want and the client is ready to put up with it, no more need be said except, perhaps, that our two philosophies fundamentally differ. I am convinced that the question-answer pattern does not create the atmosphere in which a warm, positive relationship can develop; in which the client may find a valuable experience; in which she may discover more about herself and her strengths and weaknesses; in which she has an opportunity to grow.

"Shall we then," I hear you asking, "eliminate all questions?" Obviously we must pose questions at times, but — and this is a very large "but" — it seems to me that:

1. We should be aware of the fact that we are asking questions.
2. We should challenge the questions we are about to ask and weigh carefully the desirability of asking them.
3. We should examine carefully the various sorts of questions available to us and the types of questions we personally tend to use.
4. We should consider alternatives to the asking of questions.
5. We should become sensitive to the questions the client is asking, whether he is asking them outright or not.

The ultimate test, of course, is this: Will the question I am about to ask further or inhibit the flow of the interview?

Open Versus Closed Questions

Let us then delve more deeply into the matter of questions in the interview. First of all, we shall consider the open question as opposed to the closed one. The open question is broad, the closed question narrow. The open question allows the client full scope; the closed question limits her to a specific answer. The open question invites her to widen her perceptual field; the closed question curtails it. The open question solicits her views, opinions, thoughts, and feelings; the closed question usually demands cold facts only. The open question may widen and deepen the contact; the closed question may circumscribe it. In short, the former may open wide the door to good rapport; the latter usually keeps it shut. It is easy enough to differentiate between broad and narrow questions. For example:

"How did you feel after the game?"
"You felt great after the game, didn't you?"

"What's the matter with you today?"
"You don't seem your usual self today. Anything happen?"

"Do you want to learn shoemaking?"
"Learning shoemaking is a possibility. Do you have any thoughts or feelings about that?"

"You like school, don't you?"
"Do you like school?"
"Some people like school; others don't. How about you?"

"I'm sure you love your new sister. She is adorable, isn't she?"
"Your little sister looks adorable to me, but then I'm not her brother. How do you feel about her?"

You can make up your own list and then perhaps ask yourself to which type of question you would prefer responding.

We should not proceed without mentioning the question that includes the answer. This type of question is more than a merely rhetorical one because it assumes that the answer provided by the questioner is the answer the client would provide had he really been asked. It is more closed than the closed question, which at least requires an answer unknown in advance to the asker. But here there is no alternative to the answer given or suggested by the question itself.

"No one would steal unless he knew why, would he?"

"It's perfectly clear that this is how she would feel after what you said, isn't it?"

"You'd better keep away from people like that. Everyone knows what they're up to — that's obvious, isn't it?"

Similar but slightly different in implication is the question that does require an answer but which the therapist or interviewer asks so that you will agree with him, if you know what's good for you. You have no choice unless you are prepared to risk the therapist's wrath, displeasure, punishment, or total bewilderment.

"You didn't mean to do this, did you? It was because you were upset and tired that you hit him the way you did, wasn't it?"

"You don't really want to leave us yet, do you? Just because you're angry right now, you wouldn't want to endanger your health, would you?"

"You didn't mean what you said about your father, did you? He really does love you, and you know it very well, don't you?"

"You don't really dislike all blacks the way you said you do, do you? We are all brothers under the skin; you do believe that, don't you?"

Questions such as these may sound ludicrous, and yet they are frequently posed, unwittingly at times, even by those who find them so.

Direct Versus Indirect Questions

Next, a distinction must be made between direct and indirect questions. As indicated by their name, direct questions are straight queries, whereas indirect questions inquire without seeming to do so. All the above-cited open questions are direct. We can make them more open still by stating them indirectly. The indirect question usually has no question mark at the end, and yet it is evident that a question is being posed and an answer sought. Below are some open questions followed by indirect versions:

> "How does it feel to do your homework with all these little kids about?"
> "I wonder how it feels to do your homework with all these little kids about."

> "How does the new job seem to you?"
> "I wonder how the new job seems to you."

> "You've been here a week now. What do you have to say for yourself?"
> "You've been here a week now. There must be a lot you want to talk about."

> "What do you think of our new grading system?"
> "You must have many thoughts about our new grading system."

> "How do the new braces feel?"
> "I'd sure like to hear about the new braces."

Perhaps you will contend that some or all of these indirect questions are not questions at all. If they do not feel like questions, then so much the better. There are those who maintain that these indirect questions are questions nonetheless, and I am prepared to agree with them. I like them because they do not always seem like questions although they do show interest. They tend to leave the field wide open for the client; they let him carry the ball.

Double Questions

Now we come to a kind of question that, as far as I am concerned, is never helpful in the helping interview, or anywhere else, for that matter. I am referring to the double question. At best, it limits the client to one choice out of two; at worst, it confuses both her and the interviewer. The client does not know to which of the two questions to reply, and after she has finally answered, we do not know to which question she has responded. Nevertheless, we all use double questions now and then. I do too, and every time it happens, I could kick myself. The way out, I suppose, is to accept ourselves as human beings, who must err at times, and then to make the best of the situation. For me this involves retracing my steps and untangling the two questions so that both the client and I may know to which she actually responded.

First, here are a few examples of the "either-or" double question, which limits the poor client to one choice out of two. He might prefer both or neither or a third; but here he is, forced to choose from what we are pleased to offer him.

"Do you wish to come in tomorrow or on the day after?"

"Do you want to sit near Jane or near Judy?"

"Do you wish to study the violin or the cello?"

"Do you wish to live with your mother or your father?"

"Do you want to sew or to knit this morning?"

"Do you prefer to study carpentry or to study housepainting?"

The only excuse I can accept for this sort of question is that the interviewer has no other alternatives at her disposal or that she knows the client so well that she is certain both choices are relevant. In either case, however, the excuse is flimsy. Other alternatives could perhaps be made available; possibly the client has changed his mind or may want to do so. The interviewer, therefore, might say:

"All we can offer you at the moment is either carpentry or housepainting. I'm wondering if one of these appeals to you. If not, we can think further."

"You've been either sewing or knitting lately, Mrs. Smith. There are lots of other things you can do here, such as basketry, rug weaving, jewelry making, mosaics. Would you like to try something different this morning?"

As for the double question that simply confuses both partners in the interview, the less said the better. A few examples will help to show us just how confusing this technique can be and thus make us more aware of the importance of avoiding it.

> *TH.* Did you get up on time by using the alarm clock, or did your mother wake you?
>
> *CL.* Oh . . . I just managed to catch the train.

> *TH.* Did you watch TV again last night and leave your homework for last, or did your mother force you to sit down and study?
>
> *CL.* Mother went out to the movies last night.

> *TH.* Are you managing better with the crutches now, and how about your glasses? Do they fit?
>
> *CL.* Oh, yes.

> *TH.* Was there an organized activity last night, and did you participate?
>
> *CL.* Some of the kids decided to go swimming.

> *TH.* Did you study French in school, and do your folks still speak it at home?
>
> *CL.* I have a cousin living in France. She took up English in school and invited me to spend the summer with her.

> *TH.* How's your Dad coming along, and how is Mother's job?
>
> *CL.* My brother Jack is home on leave right now. He told me that there's a new ruling and I may be able to enlist in the fall.

Perhaps I have belabored the point; but since we can never obtain a single, meaningful reply that answers two questions, it is best to ask them separately, that is, if they need to be asked at all. Otherwise, the client may give up and answer neither, thereby taking things into his own hands — as we can see he has done in the examples above.

Bombarding

Before passing on to another aspect of the question, I cannot resist pursuing the frequent absurdities of the double question to an even greater absurdity. I am referring to what is known as "bombarding" with questions. Here the tool becomes a weapon wielded against the client, if not in a deadly manner, at least in one that can hardly inspire trust, make for rapport, or create an atmosphere in which the partners in the interview can mutually examine the matter at hand. Instead, the client finds himself caught in a hailstorm of questions; and if he runs to the nearest shelter, we can only admire his urge to survive. I shall give one example without further comment, as it speaks for itself:

> Well, why don't you answer? Do you need more time to think? Isn't there anything you can say? Didn't I make myself clear enough? Do you think that I don't know what has been going on or that I don't care? Would you rather I stop asking? Would you rather I leave you alone for a while?

Until she heard her own tape, this interviewer claimed that she had tried to get the client to talk and that he had refused.

I seem to hear someone raising the objection that this example is too extreme and that I am being facetious. Be this as it may, bombarding and probing are no less present in the following excerpt, though not so obvious at first glance or at first hearing:

> IER. Hello, Jack, come right in. I'm the placement officer at the center. I understand you'll be leaving us soon. What would you like to do when you get out?
>
> CL. I don't exactly know. You see —
>
> IER. What have you done in the past?
>
> CL. Well, I tried my hand at several things, but then I got sick and —

IER. Yes, I know. Did you ever learn a trade or go to trade school?

CL. I started welding but —

IER. Right. That's out now. Is there something you're interested in now?

CL. I was thinking that perhaps merchandising —

IER. What did the vocational counselor suggest? Did he discuss your test results with you?

CL. He thought merchandising might be all right, but he said I'd need more education than I've had.

IER. How much have you had?

CL. Eight years.

IER. How old are you now?

CL. Going on twenty.

IER. Are both of your parents alive? Will you be staying with them when you leave us?

CL. I sure hope so because . . . at first . . . I'll need help . . . and . . .

IER. Do you think you'd like to go back to school for a while?

CL. I suppose so, but I don't know whether financially —

IER. Just what is your financial situation at the moment?

CL. Well, it isn't very good.

IER. What appeals to you about merchandising?

CL. Contact with people and goods, I suppose.

IER. Did you have anything else in mind?

CL. I like the law.

IER. Were you thinking of becoming a lawyer?

CL. I don't know. I think Dad would like me to help him around the farm if I could . . . I mean, if the doctors agree.

IER. What kind of farm does your Dad have?

CL. Practically everything but no cows.

IER. Anything else besides merchandising and the law interest you?

CL. Well, I used to do some photography?

IER. That sounds interesting. What did you used to do?

This, I think, is probing with the best of intentions. The placement officer means to help, and Jack seems ready for and in need of help. But so much bombarding is going on that neither can really help the other. They can hardly keep up with what is being said, let alone explore Jack's thoughts and feelings. No attempt is made to enable him to express himself fully. No wonder, then, if he should feel it is up to the placement officer to find the solution. Nothing has been done to encourage him to arrive at one or to make him feel that he may be capable of doing so. Unhappily, this example is not extreme. I wish it were.

The Shoe on the Other Foot

Now let us put the shoe on the other foot. What shall I do with the questions the client addresses to me? What if he probes or bombards me with questions? I have no comprehensive answer to this, but there is, I believe, a positive approach, which I wish to share with you.

I feel certain that we ought not to reply to every question. At times ethics may even prevent us because by so doing we might betray the confidence of someone else. On the other hand, we should, I feel, respond to every question we are asked and treat each question just as we do everything the client says — by listening to it with as much understanding as possible and being as helpful as we can in our response. Not every question calls for an answer, but every question demands respectful listening and usually a personal reaction on our part.

It is interesting to note in passing that although therapists and interviewers are quite prepared to use questions freely — very often too freely — they are unprepared for and more or less wary of questions directed at them. Perhaps these are the two sides of the same coin. If we can learn to threaten less with our questions and to feel less threatened by questions directed at us, we shall be better practitioners of the helping interview. Once we see the question as one of the ways in which the client expresses herself, we may not be perturbed by her asking. We may not be jolted into a defensive attitude based on the reasoning, "I must have done something wrong if she's beginning to cross-examine me." This attitude will almost inevitably communicate itself to the client: "I'm supposed to ask the questions around here. Who do you think you are, questioning me?"

Examining our "danger" a bit closer, I think that the client may conceivably question us about three areas of interest to him: others, ourselves, and himself. (I am not taking into account rhetorical questions, to which no one really expects an answer. We must simply learn to identify these and remain silent.)

There is a fourth area — that of seeking information — but it is more apparent than real. Usually it is a cover for or extension of one of the three above-mentioned areas; and should we fail to understand this, we may miss a great deal of the ongoing interaction. I am not suggesting that questions which obviously request information should not be treated at face value. I am suggesting that we be careful and always verify that there is nothing hidden beneath the surface that warrants a response as well. "What time is it?" sounds innocent enough. However, in the interview it may mean: "How much longer must I take this?" or "I wish this would go on, but I know it won't" or "I hope you won't keep me much longer; I'm missing all of my gym period." If feelings such as these are hidden behind the questions, our providing information alone would indicate that we are not sufficiently sensitive to what is taking place. A sensitive response to the feelings behind the question might be: "I wonder what your feelings are about our talk this morning" or "Time seems to fly today, but we'll have to stop soon" or "Are you wondering how much longer I shall be keeping you? What subject are you missing now?"

Thus we ought to supply the information requested when it is feasible and appropriate to do so, but we should always be open to the possibility that there is something behind and beyond the question which is worth getting at. I am not speaking of probing such as that in the following example (it is no secret by now what I think of probing): "It's nine thirty-five. I've told you the time;

now why don't you tell me what you really wanted to ask. Come on, don't be afraid; I won't bite."

Particularly with these straightforward requests for information we must keep our "third ear" working; for although ostensibly asking a question, the client may be communicating something else. I recall that once I was asked my name early in an interview. I supplied it, thinking the client might well have known what it was. I added this and wondered aloud whether he had any feelings about the name. He had — very strong ones — and the interview was on its way. I do not mean to make a mountain of a molehill. Nothing may be concealed behind the client's question, but it is worthwhile to examine it sensitively just in case there is.

When the client questions us more specifically in any of the three areas mentioned, I believe the approach should be the same: to respond at all times in a manner helpful to the client, and to be sensitive and honest when we answer the question and also on those occasions when we do not answer it. If we can relate our response back to the client's frame of reference, we shall generally not go wrong.

The Client's Questions About Others

Let us consider now the client's questions about others. For example: "The woman who left just as I came in seemed quite upset. Did you give her a hard time?" What shall we do with this? Surely not ignore it and just as surely not answer it directly. After all, her interview was confidential, just as his is now. Perhaps he is concerned about himself and the hard time he fears I may give him. Therefore, I might honestly respond, "I can't tell you about her, of course, just as I couldn't tell her about you; but I'm wondering whether you're uneasy about our meeting, feeling I might give you a hard time." An alternative way would be to ignore entirely the reference to the woman, as if it were understood that she would not be discussed, and to say, "I suppose you're wondering how you and I are going to get along."

Many possibilities exist in this area in which the client questions us about others. I wish to touch briefly upon only these: (a) when the other person has been known to both the interviewer and the client prior to their present contact; (b) when the person is known to the client only; (c) when as a result of the helping relationship the interviewer meets the other person, known previously to the client only.

In the first instance the client may say to us: "Well, now I've told you the way that doctor treated me. What do you think of him?" We may wish to express our opinion of him. Whether we do or not, it is usually best to revert to the client's frame of reference. "I personally like him very much, but I understand you feel he has treated you pretty coldly, sort of like a number instead of a person."

When the other is unknown to us, it is all the easier to shift back to the client's life space: "I don't know Dr. L., but I get the feeling that you like him so much you are just a bit sorry he helped you to get well so fast and brought you to the point that you are ready to leave the hospital the day after tomorrow."

When the client knows we have become acquainted with the other person (who may be close to him), a situation can arise that interviewers will handle in different ways. The client may say: "So now you've met my mother. She must have told you plenty about me. What did she say? Come on, don't pretend she didn't." Although the following responses by interviewers are dissimilar, they have three things in common: the interviewer is honest about what he reveals or does not reveal, he expresses his thoughts and feelings sincerely when doing so at all, and he ends up by reverting to the life space of the client.

> "You know, June, I can't tell you what she said, just as I couldn't tell her what we've been talking about. We had a good long talk, and as a consequence I think I better understand your relationship with your mother and hers with you."

> "Your mother asked me not to discuss our talk with you. She'd rather you ask her directly what she said to me. I wonder how you feel about that."

> "Your mother did say things about you that you may consider 'bad' of her to think or feel. I got the impression that she really thinks and feels as she says. She just sees things differently from the way you do. For example, she really feels you stay out too late at night and that as a result your studies suffer. She very much wants us to discuss this further. Have you done any more thinking about what we said last week?"

The Client's Questions About Us

The second area is the one in which the client directly questions us about ourselves. Here again I can suggest only an approach. Answer directly when appropriate, do not take over the stage for long, and revert to her as soon as possible.

> CL. You're a wonderful person to be able to listen to me the way you do. Isn't it hard on your nerves though?

> TH. I'm glad you like me, Hank. I was getting a bit nervous, and I'm glad you brought it up. You've been smoking one cigarette after the other this evening. I think I just got nervous watching you being nervous. There's something you want to talk about but haven't been able to yet, isn't there?

> CL. You've got on a different dress again today. How many dresses do you own?

> TH. Not all that many, really; I just alternate a lot. You pay lots of attention to my clothes. How does it feel to wear the uniforms you have to wear around here?

> CL. Do you have any children of your own?

> TH. Yes I do, two boys. The elder one is Jimmy's age. I wonder if you got around to talking to Jimmy's teacher about the lunches.

> CL. Have you ever been divorced?

> TH. No I haven't. Are you perhaps saying that no one who hasn't been through what you have will be able to understand?

> CL. How do you feel about being blind?

> TH. Well, can't say that I like it. I think I'm trying to do what you are, which is to manage as well as possible. I've been at it longer, though, and so it may be easier. You know, you've never really spoken of your feelings about blindness or about anything else, for that matter, since we started our talks. I wonder if the ice is beginning to melt some.

The Client's Questions About Himself

The last area consists of questions that the client poses about himself. Without repeating what has already been said, I shall cite some examples that reflect the same approach:

> CL. Should I major in French or Spanish?
>
> IER. That's what we want to decide together. So far, I know that you could master either, that you like both, but that . . .

> CL. Do I look sick to you today?
>
> IER. Do you feel sick today?

> CL. Have you made up your mind yet as to the "type" I am?
>
> TH. Frankly my mind doesn't run along those lines. I don't see you as a "type." I'm trying to see you as you, as Paul. I think you may need to classify people and so perhaps you think I do so.

> CL. Do you think I should take that job?
>
> TH. I see that it is very hard for you to decide. I can't tell you whether you should take it or not, but I can try to summarize the pros and cons as I understand them from your point of view. Well. . . . Now I'll add some that I have been thinking about. . . . It's not an easy decision to make, and I want to help you as much as I can to make up your own mind one way or the other.

> CL. Look at me! Would any boy ever want to get close to something like me?
>
> TH. I think you're asking me if you will ever have a boyfriend or perhaps if any man will ever want to marry you. Honestly, I don't know. At first I found it hard to look at you, but I don't any more. I don't know, either, what can still be done in a medical way. But you know, Judy, I find it much easier these days to look at you than to listen to you. I'm not criticizing, only telling you how I feel. You sound hard — you sound so hard I get the feeling that if any boy were to try

to get near you, you would push him away just to prove to yourself that no one wants to get close.

I have a slight suspicion that this section somewhat resembles a cookbook. My intention was to suggest possible ways of approaching the stove without getting burned. How to respond to the client's questions, when and whether to reply, are such personal matters for the individual interviewer and depend so much on the individual client that I am not certain I have succeeded in what I set out to do — to offer an approach that I find helpful. I trust you will find your own whatever you may decide to do with the above.

"Why"

The single word that symbolizes inquiry more than any other and is most frequently employed in asking questions is the little word *why*. At the outset of this discussion I want to confess that I have an aversion to the way the word is generally used, if not to the word itself. A legitimate basis for the use of this word in our language undoubtedly exists, but I maintain that *why* has so often been misused that its original meaning has become distorted. It was once a word employed in the search for information. It signified the investigation of cause or reason. When employed in this manner even today, it is appropriate, and I know of no other to take its place. Unfortunately, this is generally not the way it is used at present.

Today the word *why* connotes disapproval, displeasure. Thus, when used by the interviewer or therapist, it communicates that the client has done "wrong" or has behaved "badly." Even when that is not the meaning intended by the interviewer, that is generally how the word will be understood. The effect upon the client will be predictably negative, for he will most probably have grown up in an environment in which "why" implied blame and condemnation. Naturally enough, he will react to the word in the interview the way he has learned to react to it over the years, even though the interviewer may have used it simply in the sense of genuine inquiry. Thus, whenever the client hears the word *why*, he may feel the need to defend himself, to withdraw and avoid the situation, or to attack.

In their early years children use the word frequently — often to our distraction. For them it is a key to unlock the secrets of the world about them; it enables them to explore and discover. They ask for information without implying moral judgment, approval, or disapproval. But they learn. They learn that the adults surrounding them use the word differently — to put them on the spot, to show them they are behaving in an unacceptable manner. Slowly but surely the children stop using the word for the purpose of inquiry and begin to employ it against others the way it has been used against them. The child's ears ring with the questions: "Why did you muddy my clean floor?" "Why are you barefoot?" "Why don't you use your knife and fork properly?" "Why did you break that dish?" etc., etc. He learns to imitate his elders. Soon enough he will say to his friend, "Why did you take my bike?" to show that he disapproves of the act and not because he is interested in obtaining a bit of useful information. He will say to his mother, "Why must I go to the store?" not because he wants a reason but because he doesn't wish to go. This is his way of saying, "No, I am against it."

At the same time children discover a way to defend themselves against the threatening word. In countries where English is spoken they will answer *because* when asked *why*. In Israel the word for *why* is *lama*, and the answer the children supply is *kova*. This means literally "hat" and is as senseless, of course, as they perceive the question itself to be. Such replies are more than a defensive maneuver, however. They indicate that the children are learning to play the game according to adult rules. They have discovered that there is no meaningful reply to the question and that none is, in fact, anticipated. Whenever they hear the word *why*, they now know that what is really meant is, "Change your behavior; act the way the adults, the strong ones, want you to act." And they respond accordingly.

Later on they learn an additional lesson. Day in and day out in school they hear: "Why are you late?" "Why didn't you do your homework?" "Why can't you listen?" "Why don't you answer?" When they attempt a reply, either they are not listened to or, even worse, they are punished twice over. So they learn not to reply at all. They may or may not change their behavior; they may submit or revolt; they may succeed or fail in adapting themselves to their adult environment. Whatever the outcome, the little word *why* has become anathema.

This is the main reason for my strong aversion to the use of *why* in the helping interview. Regardless of the interviewer's intended meaning, *why* is too often perceived as "Don't do that" or "I consider this bad" or "You ought to be ashamed." Consequently, the client will withdraw into herself, attack, or rationalize, but she will not come closer to us or to herself. She will not feel free to explore and examine but, feeling threatened, will need to defend herself as best she can. Here are some examples:

Teacher. Why did you talk to Bill in class today?

Student. I didn't. . . . I didn't talk to Bill.

Teacher. But I saw you talking to him during math class.

Student. Oh, that was nothing. I won't do it any more. I just asked him . . .

Teacher. But, Charlie, I don't mean to scold you. I just wanted to know why. You know, you boys have been ignoring him ever since he came into our class, and I was glad to see that at last . . .

The intentions were good, and the harm done was probably not great. But it could have been avoided so easily had the teacher told Charlie at the outset that she had noticed him talking to Bill and wished to find out from him what was going on between them, whether there was really a change.

TH. Mary, could you tell me why your mother came to see you last night?

CL. I'm sorry, Miss Jones. I know parents aren't supposed to stay after nine, but . . . it was important . . . it won't happen again.

TH. But, Mary, I wasn't finding fault. I didn't even know she was here after nine. I noticed that both of you looked quite concerned and. . . .

Again no real harm was done, but this misunderstanding as well could easily have been avoided. Both Charlie's teacher and Miss Jones were honest and interested and not out to find fault. However, they were perceived in another light by Charlie and Mary, who assumed from past experience that the way they were being questioned meant they had done wrong. Only after this misconception had been rectified could both interviews progress in a manner helpful to all concerned. In interviewing, the less clearing up we have to do, the better, because trust and respect do not stand up well under the strain.

Unfortunately, I cannot yet rest my case. Even assuming that the negative connotations associated with the word *why* have been exaggerated here or that they can be rectified by the interviewer, I should still object to the misuse of the word. More often than not, clients perceive it as probing, and all too frequently interviewers resort to it to express their frustrations with the client, themselves, or both. The *why* seems to demand of the client an answer that he may not possess, one that is unclear to him, or one that he is not willing to share — at least not yet, perhaps because of the way the interviewer is going about obtaining it. Often a tug-of-war will result to test who can hold out longer. Whatever the outcome may prove to be, in my opinion it does not justify the method.

I may sincerely want to know the *why* of someone's behavior: the cause, the reason, the need, the motivation, the explanation. And so I ask, "Why?" It is easier for me to ask than for the client to reply. For one thing, she may not really know why; she herself may be puzzled by her conduct. Or she may be groping for the answer and finding several possibilities. Different, even contradictory, forces may be impelling her or holding her back. She may even know or, at least, think she knows but not wish to reveal it. She may be confused, ashamed, or even amused — she may simply decide to keep this "self" secret to herself. Whatever the reason, this kind of probing and pushing is distinctly unhelpful. We may extract an answer of sorts, but, more likely than not, it will be one produced to satisfy us, one the client feels we want to hear, rather than a true, significant step forward for her in her understanding of herself.

Often we shall have our answer but at too high a price. We may cause the client to close up rather than open up, defend rather

than look within, rationalize rather than cope with his own truth.
A few common examples will illustrate what I have in mind:

IER. Why were you late again this morning, Jean?

CL. The bus didn't stop again. Too crowded.

This answer may or may not satisfy the teacher, but Jean knows
there is more to it than that. She can't, she won't, put it into
words. Another quarrel at home this morning — screaming and
crying — and it didn't seem worthwhile getting up. It was safer
under the covers, pretending she was still asleep. But she won't
tell her teacher that; she will hardly admit it to herself. The
crowded bus story sounds as good as any other. Let the teacher do
with it what she will. Jean might have allowed herself to be more
honest with herself and the teacher had the interview begun
differently, had the teacher said something like this: "I've
noticed, Jean, that you've been coming in late these past few days.
I wonder if there's something wrong and if we here at the school
can help. I can stay after class today. Perhaps we can get together
then and talk about it. What do you think?"
Here are some other examples:

"Now, why didn't you take that job, Joe? We agreed you
would. Other people would have jumped at the chance. Why
didn't you go out there? There aren't that many jobs around,
you know, and I was sure you would try it. You said you
would. Why didn't you?" The client remained speechless. He
himself didn't know why. Mr. Gates was right, but he
couldn't tell him so. He couldn't tell himself. It had something to do with that hand. He thought he was over that. He
knew Mr. Gates thought he was over that. He had taken the
subway out to the place. He had repeatedly told himself that
this time he would see it through. And, then, he had felt
that hand in his pocket — or rather the lack of it — and before he knew where he was, he was back home again. He remained silent, confused, ashamed. Only much later did he
understand all this; only much later could he feel how he
had felt and verbalize it. Right now he hated himself and
Mr. Gates, who became increasingly impatient. Joe finally

produced an answer, "I couldn't find the place." Mr. Gates retorted: "You couldn't find the place . . . after all the explanations! Well, something else turned up today. It's right in your neighborhood. I'm sure you can do the work. Want to try it?" Mr. Gates had calmed down. He had received his answer.

"Why didn't you take those pills I prescribed? Didn't I tell you how important it is for you to take them?" Mrs. Bell tried hard not to cry. She knew the doctor meant well. She also knew how busy he was and how long it would take her, her of all people, if she tried to tell him why. She knew exactly why, too. She didn't know if she was right or not, but she didn't care about that. She knew she didn't care if she got well again. As a matter of fact, she got more attention being sick than being healthy. She knew lots of things — about her kids and their kids and the way they had gotten her into that home. And about the home . . . she knew plenty about that, too. But the doctor wanted to know why she hadn't been taking those pills, and so she thought fast, "I'll take them from now on, Doctor; you'll see." The doctor was pleased. He smiled, held out his hand, and ushered her out of the office. He really didn't want to know why. He just wanted her to take the medicine. He liked the old lady but was too busy to waste time.

"Why did you do so badly on those college entrance exams, a bright fellow like you?" Jack replied, "I really don't know; I can't figure it out." The counselor prodded: "But you must know; you must have some idea, at least. After all, you took them, not I. Why did you do so poorly?" Jack really didn't know — at least he wasn't aware of the fact that perhaps he did. He felt the counselor was annoyed with him and seemed to care more about why he had done so badly than about the fact that he had. Not knowing what to say, he said nothing.

I hope I have made my point. All the clients cited above felt threatened, prodded, pushed. They did not feel that the interviewer cared about them, respected them, really wanted to help them. They were not enabled to express what they thought and felt. They perceived themselves as rejected, misunderstood, imposed upon. Hence they withdrew, prevaricated, or hit back even if the only weapon with which they could hit back was silence.

Should the word *why*, then, never be used? I know I wish I myself would employ it less, for in spite of all my reservations and objections to its use, it keeps on cropping up. I try to avoid it and am glad when I succeed, but often enough there it is to be dealt with again. The little word, however, does have a justifiable place, and this is the one additional point I want to make here. If the client perceives that our attitude is unthreatening and if we use *why* simply to obtain factual information that the client possesses and we feel we need, then our use of the word should not cause undue damage. Perhaps I am saying this to comfort and solace ourselves as we continue asking *why*, but I hope this point is indeed legitimate.

For all the reasons given above, I feel that we should use *why* as sparingly as possible and that when we do use it, we should do so to get at facts rather than feelings, at thoughts rather than emotions. In our culture facts and thoughts are more readily accessible, more easily disclosed, than feelings and emotions. In a nonthreatening atmosphere in which trust and respect are present, I think one might inquire:

"Why did you move to our city?"

"Why do you wish to register your child at this school?"

"Why are you planning to come back to work after all those years you spent at home?"

If, in spite of our precautions, we sense that our question has placed the client in an awkward position, we can still retreat and rephrase it. As careful as we may be, we never know for certain how someone else will perceive a question that we regard as entirely innocuous or factual. We can only be as sensitive as we are and strive to become as sensitive as it is within us to become.

Concluding Reflections

How to Use Questions

H. S. Sullivan, the noted American psychiatrist who, incidentally, wrote an entire book on the psychiatric interview (1970), knew how to listen to his patients. He would listen with great concentration, trying to understand. Then suddenly he might come out

with something like this: "Well, isn't that interesting?" as if to
imply: "So what? Where do we go from here?" A comment like
this is what I seem to be hearing now. I did not intend to kill the
question in this long tirade. It has its place in the helping interview — such an important place indeed that I had no choice but
to go into the matter at length. The question is a useful tool when
used delicately and sparingly. Too often, I fear, it is employed like
a hammer. When used indiscriminately, it hampers progress.
When used threateningly, it is dangerous. I do not retract a word
of what I have written, but I feel I cannot be let off so lightly. The
issue still remains: How and when can the question be used to
advantage in the helping interview? I think I have answered this
implicitly in the preceding pages, but to round off the discussion
I shall now be explicit.

Let's consider the how. Except when our questions are for the
purpose of filling out forms or obtaining needed specific information
(when the closed question may prove unavoidable) they ought to
be, I am convinced, as wide open as possible. They should be
single questions, not double or multiple ones. They should be
stated as succinctly as possible and still remain clear and understandable. If they can be indirect rather than direct, so much the
better. The fewer direct questions we ask, the more likely it is
that we shall not create an atmosphere of "I'm here to ask questions, and you're here to answer them." I strongly favor eliminat-
ing the *why* questions as much as possible. One final point. After
we have asked the question, we ought to stop right there and wait
for and listen to the answer. If we do not, this ought to tell us
something about the questions we are asking. We may discover
that they are not nearly as important and meaningful as we may
have believed. Listening with understanding to our own tapes can
be most revealing in this respect.

When to Use Questions

Next the when. One situation that calls for questions is that in
which we have been unable to hear, listen, or understand for one
reason or another. I think it is better and more honest to inquire
rather than to substitute for missed words those we surmise were
spoken. We may go about this without asking a question directly,
but the effect will be the same:

"I'm sorry. I missed that last part. What did you say?"

"I didn't catch your question about Joe. I was too engrossed in noting how nervous you seem."

"It's too bad about this interruption, but I just couldn't prevent it. Where were we when I was called out?"

Such questions may reveal some of our shortcomings but will not, I believe, push the client away. In showing her our concern, our interest, our human fallibility, they may well bring her closer.

A second situation relates to whether we have been understood by the client. At times we talk more than we intend or express ourselves clumsily; then we wonder whether we have gotten our intent across. Occasionally we may say little, and the little we say seems to us unambiguous; yet we wonder whether we have been understood correctly. Sometimes we simply feel the need for feedback from the client to be certain that he has perceived us as we meant to be perceived. Whatever the case, I feel it is preferable for us to voice our doubts rather than to remain silent and keep wondering. Otherwise, the uncertainty may increase and blemish the relationship that has been built up.

"I'm afraid I've been rambling on. What did you understand me to say?"

"I haven't made this very clear, have I? What sense, if any, did it make to you?"

"Well, that's it. I felt you really wanted my honest view on this matter. Now I should very much like your honest view of mine. What do you think of it all?"

"I have the feeling we've been talking at cross purposes for the past few minutes. I think it would be helpful to hear more from you about your suggestion so that we may understand each other better."

Third, I may want to phrase a question to assist the client in clarifying or exploring further a thought or feeling he has been expressing. It may be just to let him know that I am with him, listening and trying to understand; or sensing that a little structuring may help him carry on, I may phrase a question to provide this. My intent is not to divert him from his course but, on the contrary, to keep him on it. I have in mind questions or statements such as:

"You mentioned many children. What did you mean?"

"That feeling in your chest, can you describe it more fully?"

"It sounds as if you really hated it. Did you?"

"I wonder how you felt when she called you on the carpet."

"The way you talk about 'the old people up there' I get the idea that at times you count yourself in and at other times out. Is that how it is — sometimes in and sometimes out?"

"I see you're seriously considering leaving home. Any ideas as to what you'll do then, assuming you don't get that job?"

Statements or questions like the above may fall into this category or into the one that follows. Sometimes we are the one who needs clarification (although we may impute this need to the client) while at other times both of us may require it. In either case a question may help clear up ambiguities.

Still another situation may arise, one in which we need further information — not to appease curiosity, but to understand more fully. We may feel that we need to hear more from the client in order to understand and relate to her frame of reference. The amount of questioning we engage in here will depend on our sensitivity to and our grasp of the situation. Unless we are very aware of what we are doing, our own needs may get in the way of the client's. Much depends on how we word our inquiry and whether or not we interrupt her stream of talk, thought, or feeling. Knowing that I am not the most patient human being, I try to follow the rule of interjecting a question only if lack of comprehension of what has gone before would hamper my understanding of what is to come.

"How long has your father been paralyzed?"

"I didn't quite understand what led you to change your job. Could you tell me a bit more about that?"

"I think I understand what your feelings were about Mary, but how does Phil come into it?"

"I wonder how you felt when Jim came home after the accident."

"Have you ever undergone surgery before?"

"Can I just stop you for a moment to ask whether you spoke with the principal?"

Finally, I may feel it necessary to ask something that may assist a client who finds it hard to continue talking although he seems to have more to say. This can be tricky. The client may simply be catching his verbal breath, and by questioning him I may get him off the track. Undoubtedly, risks are involved, but the right question at the right time may help the client bridge an awkward gap or break a long and heavy silence.

"Is there anything else you'd like to discuss today?"

"I see you find it difficult to continue. Perhaps we could talk a bit more about your stay in the hospital. Would you like to do that?"

"I understand you went to the ball game but left in the middle. What happened?"

"Now that you have the results of those tests you took, I wonder whether they have affected your vocational plans."

"I don't know what to make of this silence, do you?"

"You said something about difficulties in the workshop when you came in. Are you interested in talking about that now?"

The Question in Retrospect

In summing up, I am still convinced that the fewer questions we ask, the better and, above all, of the necessity to avoid the question-and-answer pattern. If we must say anything at all to get the client started and if we feel we must inquire, our question should be as neutral as possible — for example, "How are things?" To inquire about his health, to display interest or concern by questions at the outset of the interview, may well deter the client from bringing up what is uppermost in his mind at the moment. This is not as far-fetched as it sounds; it often happens. The greatest concern we can show the client is not to get in his way.

If we do not shut them off, clients will continue to inquire of themselves. My custom used to be to reply to questions as briefly and factually as possible and to reflect them back to the client. Today I find that I allow myself more leeway and freedom. I try not to be overly expansive, but I believe I am less brusque and more at ease in replying than I used to be. Helen's question deserved a serious reply:

> *CL.* Tell me the truth. Have you been able to help people as uptight as I am to loosen up?
>
> *TH.* Without generalizing, Helen, I would say that this depended more on them than on me. I remain pretty much the same person in the equation. It depends on their motivation, belief in therapy and in me, as well as the amount of time they are willing to devote to the process. Trying to loosen up can take a long time and it most definitely demands much patience — and patience, quite frankly, I am not sure you sufficiently possess. It's a frustrating business, too, at first. Your pattern, as I see matters, has been to run away from frustrations into that fortress you've constructed and that, of course, is what you have been doing here as well.

I suggested to Helen that we proceed very gradually, setting for ourselves very limited goals at first but, as I feared she might, she refused, thanked me, and left.

Jane was very much in awe of her father and spoke of him only in superlatives. As we progressed, she became aware of and began hesitantly to express negative feelings toward him:

> *CL.* I don't like talking this way about my father to you, since you know him.
>
> *TH.* Yes, Jane, it's true I know your father but only very slightly. I never meet him socially and, it goes without saying, we never discuss you. What you may find a bit difficult

is to face some of those negative feelings toward him that you were just on the verge of expressing.

Aaron never cared to know what I thought of him and his behavior, but one day he asked me a question that I've never forgotten. He inquired whether I would be prepared to discuss him with Judy and the children, should they want me to one day. He was very uncommunicative and extremely tense. I decided neither to reflect nor to interpret and not to turn the question back to him. I replied that should this occur, I would agree. Judy and I did, in fact, talk about Aaron several times. She handled the children herself.

Despite the way I feel about the little word *why*, there are times when I use it in a rather provocative manner. I return to it over and over again, *ad absurdum*, hoping thereby to stimulate the expression of thoughts and feelings. In this context, the use of *why* turns into a kind of game, of which both sides are aware. Peggy felt she just had to reach a decision that very day and begged me to do all in my power to help her reach it. I promised to try:

CL. I've got to reach two crucial decisions today — about my marriage and my career. I can't postpone it any longer.

TH. Why can't you — you've been doing just that for years.

CL. That's the reason; I've waited too long already and registration ends this week and my husband refuses to budge.

TH. He still doesn't want you to have a career of your own.

CL. No. A job, yes, but no more than that. He is the provider and I'm the homemaker and mother. I agreed to that arrangement when we got married and for him that still holds today.

TH. Well, why not?

CL. Because I've changed and because I don't love him any more and because I've found a profession I enjoy and am good at.

TH. So why is there a problem?

CL. Because I'm scared and spoiled. I'm not sure I can really make it on my own and I am used to all kinds of little luxuries. I also don't know how the children would cope. But I am going to sign up for my last year of graphology and if that means leaving the house, I'll leave.

TH. Why leave the house?

CL. Because I won't have a moment's peace there. I'm approaching forty and I've just got to stand on my own feet. But I'm scared and spoiled and don't know where to begin. I can live with my sister at first; she's invited me. I'll take the two little ones with me — the older kids will prefer to stay with him, I think. He thinks only of the damn business and says I could help him if I really must work. I'll show him that it isn't too late for me and that graphology isn't crap, as he calls it. I think I've just about decided to pick up and go.

TH. Why take such a drastic step?

CL. Because! You know better than to ask! I'm really scared but I see I've already decided without having been fully aware of it. I'll call to let you know. . . .

In spite of our scruples regarding questions, we all continue to ask them and, I suppose, must resign ourselves to this. If we do not hamper the client in his quest for autonomy, self-expression, and self-awareness; if our questions remain relatively neutral and if through them we can help him to open and expand his life space, we shall have done rather well.

What follows is a rather long excerpt from a session with Barbara, a young woman who could not decide whether to leave her husband or her lover:

TH. Well, Barbara, how are things?

CL. No change. I've got nothing to say.

TH. So it will be pretty silent around here.

CL. Perhaps you'll start for once.

TH. O.K. What is uppermost in your mind at this moment?

CL. That I really can't go on like this. I'm living with two men and I'm not cut out for that. Of my own choice I had a baby. I hoped that this would bring me back to my husband, somehow, but it just isn't happening and with the other man nothing is moving either. He is still with his family, though he says he's prepared to leave the moment I say the word and leave mine. But he doesn't believe I will — and he may well be right.

TH. Where do you yourself fit into all of this?

CL. I don't. I'm just mixed up. I'm not prepared to renounce either of them but know the situation can't continue because I don't have the energy to go on much longer. I'm not my old self any more at all.

TH. This crisis is wearing you down.

CL. And how! I used to be sensible and calm. I used to be able to concentrate on reading and preparing my lectures but now . . .

TH. So the affair is losing its glow.

CL. Maybe. Both men still want me, but that can't go on for long either. And I just cannot decide. My sister came to visit the other evening. She says I look and sound a wreck. She's sure I should stick to my husband and kids and give up the other man entirely. I've tried that, but it lasted all of three months. I'm sure I wasn't neurotic before all this started, but now I wonder.

TH. This thing is getting the better of you.

CL. I know you can't decide for me, but still . . .

TH. You want to hold onto the best of both worlds but are finding yourself more and more torn apart in the process.

CL. I'll go off my head, yet. Who would have thought that this could happen to me, sensible, cool Barbara!

TH. What happened to Barbara?

CL. After having chosen a career and a husband, set up a home and had two kids, she suddenly returned to her adolescence and fell in love and, being stubborn as she is, wants both worlds simultaneously and finds she can't have it that way. So she tries one thing or another but it's all no good. I don't really blame either man. If I could make up my mind and stick to my decision, everything would fall into place.

TH. But you want both worlds just a little longer.

CL. I probably married too early — didn't have enough experience. I always wanted a man who would resemble my father and chose my husband accordingly. The other man is just the opposite of him and that's why I don't entirely trust him. But my husband bores me to death. No surprises with him. Everything in order, everything in place, just the way I used to like it.

TH. You seem to be rebelling against your father rather late in the game.

CL. I only know I can't take it much longer. (begins to cry softly)

TH. Is there any way I can help right now?

CL. I wish you could but no one can. I know I have to decide and I even know what I must decide because I'll never have it as good as I could have it now with my own family — but I just can't bring myself to take the step!

My battle with the question is over. I meant to dethrone it but not to drive it out of the palace. I intended to stimulate you to think about questions and their place in the helping interview. I feel very strongly on the issue and, I suppose, show it. Putting my ideas down on paper has been helpful to me. I hope it may prove helpful to you as well — whether you agree, disagree, or withhold judgment. If as a result of reading this chapter, you have become more aware of the questions you ask, communication has taken place.

6 • COMMUNICATION AND FACILITATION

In this chapter we shall discuss communication and facilitation. Let us begin with the former. In a sense we have been discussing it right along. Without communication there would be no interview. However, as we well know, there are interviews — even helping interviews — in which the communication is far from optimal. The interviewer's goal is to facilitate communication, but obstacles that impede, distort, or complicate it often arise. There are, obviously, various factors that can help or hinder communication. I have already stated some and hinted at others. I intend here to arrange these factors within a framework that may render them more meaningful. Like much else in this book, such an approach is not original with me. However, I find it congenial, clear, and simple. It has worked better for me than any other framework I have tried; pragmatically speaking, I have found it to be true. This framework includes two basic concepts: defenses and values.

Defenses and Values

The less defensive we as therapists or interviewers can become,
the more we shall help our clients discard their defenses. Communication between us will improve as a consequence. The more
we become aware of what our values are and the less we need to
impose them on the client, the more we may help him become
aware of his own values and retain, adapt, or reject them as he
sees fit. Knowing my own values, I can state them. If I can accept
them as a changing part of my changing self, I may be able to
accept his as a changing part of his changing self. Some of these
values of mine may remain constant for me, and some may for
him; but I shall not be afraid to expose mine, nor shall I fear being
exposed to his. He, in turn, may learn not to fear exposing his
values or being exposed to mine because he will know that he is
not being threatened. In such an atmosphere he may learn to describe his values without fear of being judged. He will not need to
defend because he will not feel attacked. Perceiving no necessity
to adjust to the interviewer's values, he may discover those he
really believes in.

Some time ago I spoke with a young man who, looking back
upon his school years, had this to say about one of his teachers:

"He was my teacher for three years in junior high school, and
I gave him hell. I was a devil then and hated the guy. That's
what I thought then, but it wasn't only hate. He didn't let
me get away with a thing in class, and lots of times he'd keep
me in after school to talk things over. He told me exactly
how he felt, and I remember I told him lots of things. . . . I
don't know why exactly . . . I think, because I trusted him.
Now that I think of it, that teacher never told me he was
right and I was wrong. He said there were things I was doing
he couldn't allow, or something like that, and he told me
why. I told him how I felt about the kids in the class and
how boring school was. He listened to it. We never got to see
eye to eye on lots of things, but we knew where we stood. I
know now that I learned more from him in those talks than I
did during four years in high school. I didn't know it then,
but he taught me to think and to see what I was doing. After
a while he had enough, I guess, and I don't blame him. He

gave me up for lost, I suppose, and he'll never know how much he helped me. It took me years to find it out."

Whenever the interviewer says directly or indirectly to the client, "You may not say this," she is using her value system to block communication. Whenever she states or implies, "I can't listen to this," she is telling the client not to communicate, to be ashamed of himself, to keep silent. If the interviewer will not listen, who will? Whenever the client says to himself, "I can't come out with this" or "She won't want to hear this," obstacles to good communication exist. They may be largely of his own making, but they may also reflect the interviewer's behavior. It is quite another matter if the client can say to himself, "I know she won't like hearing this one bit, but I also know she can take it." We can never be certain, of course, just how the client perceives us, whom he sees in us, or of whom we remind him. The only choice open to us, it would seem, is to be as genuinely ourselves as possible and to behave as nondefensively as possible in the hope that eventually he will see us as we are.

Rogers (1961, Ch. 17) has pointed out that our own need to evaluate, to confirm, or to deny constitutes a major obstacle to good communication. I am convinced that this is so. For example, if when the client tells me that everyone at the meeting turned against him, I show interest in how he perceived the situation, I shall be opening the gates to communication. On the other hand, if I tell him that it surely wasn't so terrible, that he is exaggerating, or that he was probably at fault if people turned against him, I shall be closing those gates. In the former case my response will lead him to explore the situation as it appears to him. I may then be able to help him examine it further and clarify his role as well as his perceptions of others and theirs of him. In the latter case, my reply tells him in essence that he has misjudged the situation and that the fault may well have been his. He may consequently feel the necessity to defend himself against my judgment and thus fail to come to grips with the situation itself.

To take another example, if the client tells me she liked a certain book and I tell her I did not, she will either refrain from examining just what she liked about the book or feel the need to defend her liking of it. On the other hand, if I exhibit an interest in her view, she may feel encouraged to discuss the book and explore what she liked about it. Consequently, she may begin to learn something about herself, her likes and dislikes, her values. Having been respectfully listened to, she may wish to hear my views because she has become genuinely interested in my values — but as mine, not hers. Our respective values may or may not be modified as a result, but at least we shall have learned how we both feel about the book.

Communication is not essentially better if I simply agree with the client when she states that she likes a certain novel. We have really described nothing and learned nothing about each other's values. We do not know, in other words, what led each one to like the same book. One may have liked it because of the plot; the other because of the vivid characterization. Reasons for liking the same thing can be very diverse. Regarding communication, the fact of our mutual liking is far less significant than the fact that we have been enabled to express the reasons for it.

There exists a real possibility that as the result of such mutual describing, the perception of one or both partners will undergo change. For some people this offers a challenge; they regard it as a part of growing. For others it spells danger; for them change is threatening, and they cannot allow communication to be clear and direct. They will obstinately defend themselves against change. Their values will prove a reliable shield in warding off the threat.

Many therapists and interviewers who have learned not to fear revealing themselves have discovered that clients absorb this lesson from their example. The therapist can allow herself to describe how she perceives the client's behavior without making the latter feel that he is being evaluated or categorized. The therapist may say, for example, "I feel bored with that old story" or "The way you talk about it makes me feel that there is more to it than that" or "I feel slightly annoyed by those smiles; I wonder how you really and truly feel about me" or "I feel that you want me to tell you what is right for you, but I can't."

Authority as a Defense

At times the therapist or any interviewer employs his authority as a defense, a barricade. "Teachers are never wrong," "The doctor knows best," and "Adults have more experience" are often convenient defenses. They won't solve the problem confronting the client but serve to protect the interviewer from "attack" in the form of an honest search by the client, a real coping with his situation. Confronted by a façade of superiority, the client must defend himself as best he can. If he perceives it as the expression of the interviewer's values, he may either submit or emerge with a shield to defend his own values. Two formidable obstacles to communication will then prevail: the interviewer's use of authority and the client's use of weapons to combat it.

I am not suggesting that our role — our function in society and in the life of the client — has no relation to authority; it has. The issue is how we apply that authority in the helping interview and to what ends. While the interview is proceeding, are we indicating, implying, or stating "This is not to be discussed," "That is a professional secret," "You'll just have to take my word for it," "I know best," or "This is final; there is nothing to add"? When the client is confronted with such attitudes, it is not surprising if she feels that she is being hemmed in and treated like an object. She may submit, learning thereby to depend on authority. She may rebel, resorting to a defense of her own. What will be absent is a free, open expression and exchange of ideas and feelings. Communication will have been obstructed.

The alternative is an atmosphere in which a sense of equality prevails — not equality of knowledge, experience, or professional skill, naturally, but equality of worth and dignity, with each human being fully respecting the other. Here no defensive shield is available to us, the interviewer; we are vulnerable. With nowhere to hide, we may come to light as a real person trying to help another real person. The client will soon discover that we are neither all-powerful, all-wise, nor the embodiment of human virtue. The sooner he does, the better for him and our relationship. Seeing that we are not a closed book, he may permit himself to turn the pages of his own. He will find that the shields he brought with him as a result of habit and experience are not needed here. Since he will be confronting a true other, he will find that he can express his true self. For him, too, there will be no place to hide, but he will not be alone. Another will be there as he begins to cope with his own self.

Do we really possess the answers? Are we certain we are right? Are our conclusions necessarily correct just because they are ours? In an atmosphere in which equal meets equal our certainty may well have to give way to a mutual attitude of "Let's see" or "Let's try." This may be no more than provisional, but it will be understood by both, hence meaningful to both. Deprived of defensive shields, we have no alternative but to be flexible, to look at and respond to all aspects of a given situation. We may help the client reach a decision. We may even be making it for her in a manner of speaking. But whatever we do, we shall be doing it with her, not to her. She will consider herself an equal, allowing herself to take from us what she chooses and to reject what is not for her.

Test Results as a Defense

Interviewers and therapists tend to use another defensive shield. Hiding behind diagnoses and test results, we lose sight of the person and in his stead see the category into which he has been placed. However, I think we are appreciating increasingly that diagnoses may err and that tests results give only a part of the picture. Although more psychological and psychometric tests are available today than ever before, most are still in an experimental stage and can seldom if ever be relied on as conclusive. Even worse for us and our clients, equally qualified experts may arrive at different diagnoses, for test interpretations largely depend on the make-up of the psychologist interpreting them. This is a shaky shield indeed — which may explain why it is held onto with such tenacity at times. Whether we like it or not, the fact remains that even in medicine, which holds diagnosis nearly sacrosanct, specialists concurring in the diagnosis will frequently suggest opposite courses of treatment. In addition, medical opinion seems agreed today that unless the patient wishes to get well, little can be done for him. As in all effective helping relationships, the patient is at the center; we must reach him and reach out to him. Diagnoses and test results may keep the client from himself. An honest, open, human confrontation will not.

Judging as a Defense

A final defense must be mentioned: judging the client. It, too, constitutes an obstacle to open communication in that it encourages us to rationalize our behavior rather than come to grips with it. We judge the client to be "uncooperative," "a troublemaker," "aggressive," "submissive," "eccentric," and so forth. Consequently, we see her as such, and, more often than not, she will tend to see herself as such. But is this her real self, all of it or even a part? Or is this our perception of her, our perception at a given time and place and under given circumstances? Are we perhaps in error? Even if we are right, if we have "judged" her correctly, have we "judged" ourselves as well? May she not be acting this way because of us — because of her perception of us or her reaction to our perception of her?

Students who are attempting to listen to their taped interviews as nondefensively as possible often wonder whether they have judged the client correctly or whether their judging was meaningful at all. Clients as well, hearing their own tapes, frequently begin to wonder if they have perceived the interviewer correctly and judged her fairly. It is amazing how much closer to each other the two partners in an interview can draw when they both remove their defensive armor. Then real coping occurs; and arguing, so frequently found in interviews, tends to disappear. By arguing I do not mean honest disagreement or an open clash of values. I mean misunderstandings, confusion, trying to get the upper hand, making a point regardless of whether it is being listened to, saying something for the record and not to the other.

I have found that the more obstacles to communication there are, the more arguing shows up. This should not surprise us, for arguing is bound to result from these obstacles. Each side holds for dear life to its own; it is give or take, not give and take. Gradually the interview comes to a halt. The session isn't really over, but it seems as if nothing more can be said or done. Client and interviewer appear to be saying to each other: "This arguing isn't getting us anywhere, so we may just as well stop. You can't listen to me, and I can't listen to you, so what's the use." It is useless, in fact. But even at this point if we can be honest enough to realize what has been going on and to express it, we may yet save the situation. "We've been kind of yelling at each other, and now it looks as if there is nothing more to say. I suppose we've gotten things off our chests, but I'm not sure whether we've gotten across to each other. Frankly, as the argument got hotter and hotter, I heard less and less of what you were saying; and I suppose it

was the same with you. Why don't we just assume we've made a
bad job of it and try again?"

The Therapist as Facilitator

The other night I had a dream. I dreamed that I was programming
a computer "therapist" for facilitation. He was to be able to lower
his defenses in order to enable the client to lower hers; he was to
be aware of his own values without imposing them on his clients;
he was not to interrupt the client; he was to talk just the right
amount — not too much lest he overwhelm the client and not
too little lest he be perceived as distant or indifferent. In short, he
was not to be allowed to hinder the client — ever. I awoke with a
start. Despite all our shortcomings, I prefer us the way we are.
Our human failings do at times hinder and impede, but they are
failings the client can understand since they belong to her, as
well. Our encounter, imperfect as it is, is human.

Our client suffers. It is our intention to help relieve this suffering by aiding him to lower his defenses, so that he can face reality
more effectively and formulate values which will give his life
more meaning. We do not aim to juxtapose our defenses with his
or to insinuate our own values into his value system, but this, in
fact, is what occasionally happens and is what we must continuously fight against. We err because we are human. By erring less
we shall help the client more.

Might I possibly have helped Roger more? Perhaps he wasn't as
cruel to his guide dog as I believed. True, he was not a fighter —
but lots of people aren't. Must he be a fighter just because I like
fighters? Yes, he was, indeed, extremely passive, but did I myself
make every effort to draw him out — to show him that I cared?
Or didn't I, in fact, really care? Did my own value system get in
our way? Did I somehow make him feel, without being aware of
it, that if he wouldn't fight I wouldn't help? I'd hate to think that,
and yet . . . At least we both realized that he needed a different
therapist.

Did my defenses get in the way so that Glenn, definitely cognitive in his orientation, could not express more emotion? Did he
cause me to feel insecure and as a result be dogmatic? Did his
keen analytic mind overwhelm me — as it must have overwhelmed others — so that I could not sense the feelings hidden
beneath?

Despite all my explanations, which I do not see as rationaliza-
tions, was I really patient enough with Martha? Or did her aggression and resistance perhaps trigger off defense mechanisms
in myself which made it impossible for us to proceed effectively
together?

I think of Bertha and her son. As long as she could not listen to
him, they barely communicated. As long as she imposed her will,
friction ensued. Every trivial incident added fuel to the fire. The
more she demanded, the more he dug in his heels. I, from my
vantage point looking on, found it easy to see what had gone
wrong and what now was needed. The view from within often
blurs one's vision. As long as Bertha used her authority as Mother,
the struggle continued. When she could allow herself to emerge
from behind that mask, useful communication was restored.

Administering the "talking cure" as I do, and being verbal myself, I can achieve rapport more easily with verbal clients than
with silent ones. I always looked forward to sessions with David,
knowing that he would bring material to discuss and appreciating
the skill with which he did so. I dreaded the early sessions with
Dick. He just could not or would not talk. How could I be of
help? I tried talking, remaining silent, asking questions — I was
even reduced to replying to some of them myself. For a long time,
nothing moved. I anticipated with apprehension his arrival but
sensed his inner struggle, and that, perhaps, helped me not to become defensive myself. In contrast to Martha, I did not find Dick
hostile to me. I still recall the first complete sentence Dick uttered, "You have a new picture on the wall, but I liked the old
one better — I got used to looking at it."

Reality testing is as important for the therapist as it is for
everyone else. Some clients do not talk because they choose not
to; they do not even wish to be considered clients. Working with
couples, we often encounter the phenomenon whereby one partner just will not speak. In Dalia's presence, Simon refused to talk;
alone, he could reveal that for him the marriage was over and
that he intended to leave Dalia. While regretting his uncooperative attitude, there was no choice but to accept his decision.

Clients who consider themselves as having been pushed into
therapy will either get into the swing of it or else leave rather
quickly. Eventually, every client interested in therapy will talk.
Nowadays, Dick can be quite voluble. Dora still requires a little
encouragement now and again but nearly always initiates.

As for the amount of my own talking I believe that with the passing of the years I have tended to talk less — in and out of therapy. But even formerly, my natural pattern was to follow the client. Loquacity seemed to loosen my tongue; when faced with the avoidance of speech, I seemed to retreat from it as well. What continues to amaze me to this day, however, is the insistence on the part of many clients that I never talk!

I have already shown that I deal with interruptions of the therapeutic process briefly and firmly. I will myself on occasion interrupt the client but, to the best of my knowledge, with no disastrous effect. I may suggest to Carl that he not launch out on a new subject as our time for today is just about up. If something was expressed incoherently or too quickly, I may ask that it be repeated. When Esther could not stop perseverating, I would break in suggesting that we pursue a different subject. When the client has obviously misunderstood me or others, I may interrupt in order to set the record straight. As a rule, I tend to interrupt more when I am impatient, upset, or exhilarated. At those times I endeavor particularly to restrain myself.

The relating of dreams and early memories are techniques that facilitate communication. When the client is anxious to push ahead but cannot focus on relevant material to discuss, these techniques are generally very helpful. I myself work with dreams sparingly and can offer nothing startlingly new on the subject. The manner in which the Gestaltists work with dreams fits in well with my own approach, and many of my clients have profited from it.

At one point in his therapy, Tom felt that we were getting nowhere; we were simply moving in circles. In a soft voice, he appealed for help. I suggested that he relate the earliest memory he could recall. After awhile he said:

> CL. I must have been about three years old. It was bedtime and I asked for Mother. Father said she would come soon and told me to go to sleep. For a long time I lay there just pretending to sleep. She never came.

His second memory was of himself in a playground. A bigger child had snatched his toy. He was furious but petrified with fear. The other boy just laughed and flung the toy at his feet. Tom's third early memory concerned a scene in the country. He was alone gathering flowers and leaves. He caught a butterfly and tore off its wings and then ran away sobbing. Now Tom and I had material to work on for many sessions.

Our earliest memories often reveal much of how we perceive the world today. This technique, developed by the Adlerian school of psychotherapy, enabled Dick to look back upon his childhood. He saw himself, in his first memory-picture, sitting on a nursemaid's lap, eating an apple. In the second, he was returning home from first grade. He collected the housekey from the next-door neighbor and waited, all alone, for someone to come home. It took a long time till he could recall the third early memory. In it he was already eight or nine years old. For his last birthday he had received a puzzle consisting of many pieces to assemble in order to replicate the picture on the boxtop. Dick remembered sitting for hours obstinately refusing to eat or do his homework because he had decided that on that very day he would complete the puzzle. He succeeded. Transparent as they may appear to us, for the client, relating such memories facilitates exploration and understanding.

Providing information the therapist possesses and the client needs may also prove very facilitating. After Leah and Jack had left, Leah retraced her steps and sat down again:

CL. I don't believe Jack will want to come again. What do you think?

TH. From the way he stormed out, I would say you're right.

CL. If I wanted to, could I come back alone? I mean, do you see people individually, too?

TH. If you want to come alone we can arrange that. I don't meet with couples only.

CL. I've never been in therapy or anything like that, but I think I'm going to need help. I've always leaned on Jack. . . . I'll have to learn to manage on my own, I suppose. If I decide to come, do you have morning hours available?

TH. We could arrange something for Tuesday or Thursday.

CL. Thanks. I'll be in touch.

Joy and Andy had been referred to me by a child therapist who was still seeing their small daughter, Iris. Even though she herself had referred them to me, they felt the therapist was vexed, now that they were coming. They even feared that the situation might negatively affect their daughter's therapy. Although I thought this most unlikely, I promised to look into the matter. I spoke with Joan, the therapist. She was glad that Joy and Andy were seeing me, but admitted that it had taken her a little time to adjust herself to the new arrangement. She had been seeing Iris's parents occasionally but, realizing that this was inadequate for their present needs, had referred them. I passed this on to Joy and Andy, who informed me that Joan had told them the same thing. Now we could proceed to tackle their marriage.

Claire and Jim came together several times. It was plain that each thought the other was in need of therapy. We finally decided that I would meet individually with each of them and that once or twice monthly the three of us would get together for a long session to examine what was happening to their marriage. I had informed them previously of the one condition I attached to our arrangement, namely, that in our joint sessions I could utilize at my discretion material gathered in individual sessions.

At times, behind a simple request there hides movement in therapy — in the form of information the client himself provides, almost as an aside:

> CL. After vacation, could we change our hours?
>
> TH. Do you have anything specific in mind?
>
> CL. I'd like to come earlier in the afternoon. I've decided not to hang around any longer and wait till someone drives me here. I'll come on my own by bus; perhaps I'll even drive alone again.
>
> TH. Dora, that sounds great to me. We'll find the hours that will be convenient for you.

A controversial issue that requires consideration concerns "others" in the lives of our clients. What if the client wants us to meet them? What if they themselves insist on being seen? Would it not facilitate our task in therapy were we to meet those others the client talks of: parents, siblings, friends, lovers, teachers, bosses . . . the list is endless. Should we sit by and observe how the client behaves with his children, spouse, parents, and so forth and so on?

I have become increasingly convinced that the answer should be negative. Some of those "meaningful others" could not even be reached. They may be dead, far away, or not at all interested. And where would I draw the line? Would I see them with the client or alone? Would they come with his consent or without? And, were they to come, what would we discuss? The client and his "problems" or the visitor or nothing in particular? And afterward, would we be any the wiser or become better facilitators? I am not, of course, referring to family therapy, where the family is essentially the client, or marital therapy, where the couple is the unit. I am referring to the client who is in a dyadic relationship with me.

What does facilitate, I believe, is not the physical presence of those "others" but the exploration of their effect on the client; how she perceives them, how these perceptions become modified, how she defends herself against or copes with them, how she measures herself against them, her deeper feelings toward them, and how, if at all, these feelings undergo change. How does she interact with them and how might she interact with them differently? How is she behaving toward me right here in therapy and what can this teach us about her behavior with "others"? Do her perceptions of those "others" change as her perceptions of herself do so? And so on, *ad infinitum*. At long last I have arrived at a rule that, of course, does not solve everything but at the least makes my life much easier: never to invite an "other" to satisfy his, the client's, or my own curiosity. Tom's father may wish to meet me to see what makes me tick — and Tom might enjoy the interaction. I myself might be curious to meet Tom's father, about whom I have heard so much. Our curiosity might be assuaged, but we may well have impeded the course of therapy. How can Tom, for example, continue to rage and rant about his father now that we have met and I have seen how very nice he really is? And if he is a despicable man, what then? No, the therapist will facilitate most by working with the client. If others from his life must be brought in, the reason must be convincing to all involved and the ensuing contact as brief as possible.

From the first moment on, Anne had wanted me to invite Bert.
His behavior, she claimed, was to blame for most of her troubles.
His careerism, his lack of consideration for her thoughts and feelings, as well as her own professional future; the lack of genuine
interest in the upbringing of the children — all this and more had
led to her "physical and mental collapse." It would be very easy
to arrange a meeting, as he did not always send the driver but
sometimes came to pick her up himself. The Ministry could do
without him for an hour. As time progressed, Anne voiced this
request less frequently, till one day she said:

> CL. I'm really glad now that Bert never came in. He wouldn't
> have felt comfortable and we would have gotten nowhere. As
> it is, I tell him about our sessions and do not hide my anger
> and disappointment from him. We talk more than we used to
> and he is much more attentive to me and spends more time
> with the children. He is sometimes very angry with you and
> thinks you are too much on my side but he's never even
> suggested coming in to meet you.

For a while I toyed with the idea of meeting with Natalie's and
Dora's mothers. Both young women were still terribly dependent
upon their mothers; perhaps even at this late stage something
could still be accomplished. The mother-child relationship had
been so symbiotic that its effects were still being felt. In the final
analysis, I rejected the idea. Dora and Natalie will just have to
learn for themselves to stand on their own two feet as best they
can.

The female member of an estranged couple with whom I was
working insisted that I meet her parents for one session only.
They were at their wits' end and simply had to see me. I objected,
but when her husband pleaded too, I reluctantly succumbed to
the pressure. The parents came and poured out their grief. It was
a sad and fruitless session. I could not, in good conscience, reveal
what they wished to know; I could not even console them effectively.

Very different was the story of Shirley and Dan. Toward the
end of her therapy, Shirley spoke a great deal of Dan and of their
marriage. She wanted a more equal sharing of household chores
and more time for her professional and personal development

whereas he . . . She had spoken to him and he was ready to join her in therapy. I met once with Dan and from then on Shirley and he came as a couple. In this indirect fashion, Shirley had terminated her own therapy and the couple had become the client.

Couples in Therapy

Over the past decade many couples have knocked at my door. Some soon decide not to return, while others remain to work on their difficulties. Leah and Jack did not return together. They, quite obviously, had nothing more to say to each other than "goodbye." Leah did return, as we have seen, to work on her own personal growth, but the couple, Leah and Jack, needed not a therapist but a lawyer. With Dalia and Simon the story repeated itself. All Simon wanted was a divorce and for that I was not needed. They became so hostile to each other that for a while they were unable even to discuss the children and, here again, consulted a lawyer. As for Dalia, she too turned to therapy to try to understand what had befallen her and to learn to cope as a single parent.

Marital therapy has a chance to succeed when both parties, for the moment at least, definitely wish to remain together. They come to therapy because they feel that they are drifting apart, because they want to improve the communication between them, because they want to discuss disagreements about their children's upbringing, or because, having gone through a marital crisis, they want to try to mend what was almost destroyed. Basically, what makes work in therapy possible is the mutual decision — for whatever reasons — to continue together. The motivation for therapy may not be identical for both partners, but there exists enough hope for the future of their relationship and enough mutual belief in the possibilities of therapy to make the undertaking worthwhile.

The guidelines I lay down for our joint enterprise are few and simple: to meet no less than once a week — if possible for a full hour; and that whatever is communicated to me, by phone, letter, or in individual sessions, may be used at my discretion in our joint meetings. Individual sessions with either partner can be initiated by him or by myself but must be made known to and approved by the other partner.

Alice and Don came together but, in fact, Alice had "brought" Don — who had agreed to participate only because he realized that Alice was suffering. He was prepared to cooperate if there was a chance that therapy would help them. We soon agreed that I should see Alice alone for a few sessions to hear her complaints. I met with Don once, but he had little to add to what he had already said. Alice was a talkative, active, and dominant personality and made her grievances known in no uncertain terms: Don devoted too much time to his business, let his partners take advantage of him, and often seemed to prefer their company to Alice's. She did not really believe that he was having an affair with one of the women partners, but he was so swayed and bamboozled by her that her family profited at the expense of Alice and their four children. Alice was extremely tense and suspicious at first but gradually calmed down and relaxed and could enjoy family life once more. Therapy had helped her and she was ready to terminate. We decided to invite Don to join us for what we assumed would be the last session. At this point Alice received a shock. No, Don did not wish to quit. In fact, he hadn't even begun yet. Having undertaken the step, he wanted to do a thorough job and not just "clean off the surface." Alice had been unfair and suspicious, demanding, and cantankerous for years and now it was time to "put all the cards on the table with no aces up the sleeve." It was the perfect opportunity to really work at improving their marriage once and for all. Alice could not but agree. Obviously, the presence of the therapist, a third, neutral person, gave Don the strength and courage to do what he could not have attempted to do on his own.

It always amazes me how, often, two people who have been living together for years hesitate or do not dare ask of the other what to the outsider seems a simple act — and one that obviously would improve the relationship. For instance, it has occurred more than once in my experience that one of the partners has been put off by the bad breath of the other, especially in intimate situations, but has not dared to say so lest it "offend" — as if by not mentioning it, he could hide his repugnance. When complaints of this sort that are so easily remediable are, at long last, uttered, the marriage improves "miraculously" and therapy may be speedily terminated. I refuse, of course, to serve as intermediary in such situations but encourage the couple to interact and communicate freely and openly in our joint sessions.

Claire and I met years ago when her first husband, still in his twenties, died of cancer. Since then she had married Jim and borne five children. Recently she returned to therapy, this time with Jim. They were both over forty by now. Claire was very busy studying again and tried to spend her free time with the children. Jim admitted he was jealous; he felt like a "second class citizen." First came the children, then Claire's studies, then her work — he for sure came last and he resented it. He needed and wanted her attention, devotion, and love and felt he wasn't getting his fair share of them. Even sex wasn't important to her any more, especially since he could no longer "perform" the way he used to.

Claire saw them as a middle-aged couple surrounded by children, busy with their respective jobs, studies, and hobbies. Jim, she claimed, acted as though he were one of the children. He envied them, fought them, and resented their constant presence and the attention they received from her. All he got, he retorted, were scoldings, reprimands, and innuendos about his "impotence."

We met together and in dyads. Jim really tried to change, to be more cooperative and to act more grown up. But, he complained, Claire refused to budge from her own behavior. She insisted that there was no reason she should — now that he was really behaving in a more adult manner and was willing to cooperate, their marriage had indeed improved. We agreed they had reached a deadlock and at that point they left. The children, I presume, will keep them together for the time being, but I would not be at all surprised were they to return to therapy one day. Intelligent and well-intentioned, they will want more than they have achieved, and they may even progress on their own.

Dan, Shirley's husband, first joined us as an absentee partner. Once Shirley had succeeded in "putting her own house in order," as she expressed it, she turned to Dan and their life together. They loved each other and the children. Their marriage, by ordinary standards, would be considered a very successful one, but Shirley was far from satisfied. She was a modern woman who held feminist views and did not feel that Dan shared equally the burdens of the household and child rearing.

Since his shadow now appeared in every session, I suggested that it was time for him to appear in person. Dan agreed to join Shirley. The absentee partner was now present. He accepted without any problem the fact that Shirley and I already knew each other well and made it clear that though he was not interested in therapy for himself, he was certainly ready to work on their marriage and matters concerning the family. It often takes an absent partner who turns into a present one some time to adjust. Not so with Dan; he fitted into the framework of our sessions as if he had been physically with us from the beginning. He was well aware of Shirley's grievances but felt he was more than doing his share around the house aside from putting in long hours as plant manager in a large and successful factory.

She. I don't see why, if one of the kids gets sick, it is I who have to stay home and give up my work in my art studio. My work is no less important than yours.

He. I agree that it isn't less important, but someone has to stay home and I've got to be at the plant. I am essential there, as you well know, and we need my salary so that, for one thing, you can have your studio.

She. And there's your male chauvinism again! I had to wait to open the studio till the children were old enough to go to nursery school. Before that I had to carry each of them nine long months, neglecting and postponing my career while you went right ahead advancing in yours and now, after all that, I must hear that I'm still not making money and that you're subsidizing me. Well, I won't have it!

He. Oh come off it, Shirley, I've even stayed home occasionally, but that can only be the exception, not the rule. I have a very responsible job and you know it. I'm happy at it and earning well too and we can afford all the babysitters needed. After work, I think I do more than most husbands and fathers.

She. What the others do or don't do interests me very little. You do the general marketing once a week, feed and bathe the kids at night and want a pat on the back for that. What I insist on is for you to take on the responsibility for the entire household two weeks out of four. You shouldn't just shop from a list I prepare. Two weeks out of four you should make up your own list; see what's needed and get it, take care of the bills and see to the babysitters and whatever else is needed so that I have equal time for my career. But that you refuse to do with the lame excuse that you're not a house-wife. Well, I wasn't one either, but I had to learn and you can do the same.

He. You're going a little too far here. When I get home it's usually after nine or ten hours of hard work. I am willing to help but not to carry the entire household on my shoulders half the month. You can rest every afternoon when the kids do and yet you expect me to get up at night when one of them cries — just because you are with them more than I am during the day. Don't you realize that the artificial division of labor you demand would wear me out and ruin our marriage? Where would you be then with your art and your studio?

She. There we have it! My art doesn't really count, isn't worth very much. When I try to tell you even a tiny bit of what I go through during the day in the studio or even at home, you fall asleep on me — and you never tell me about your day.

He. How can I? You never give me a chance. Mostly I hear complaints and resentment and anger. Listen, Shirley, I didn't create the world; I take it as I find it and try to make the best of it.

She. Of course you do, because it's your world, a man's world. It took me a long time to wake up but now that I have, I insist on my rights, too. I don't enjoy fighting all the time.

He. Well, if you don't, just stop because I'm beginning to get fed up. I used to love to come home but now I take my time about it because as soon as I come in, you lecture me and find fault.

TH. It sounds to me as if you two had not really discussed these issues at home as calmly and clearly as you are doing now.

He. That's right. At home we begin to yell and then she cries and I go about my assigned tasks for the evening!

She. Yes, you do your tasks but not out of conviction and only because you have no choice. But you do have a choice — you can get up and leave. (cries) I didn't mean that.

He. I know you don't mean it, and I don't want to leave. I just want us to find sensible, workable solutions. I don't even claim that justice and equality and all the other things you talk about exist.

Shirley and Dan have come a long way since that stormy session. Neither is completely satisfied even today, but together they make a happy and well-functioning couple that has learned to give and take, listen and understand, and live from day to day in an imperfect world.

The joint work with Tamar and George began after both had been in individual therapy with me. Tamar had first come as a recently bereaved war widow who had to learn to rearrange her life from top to bottom. She wanted her children to grow up cherishing the memory of their father and wished the same for herself. At the same time, she wanted, eventually, albeit with feelings of guilt and remorse, to try to establish a new permanent relationship with another man. She was young, her children small, and she knew that this was the course her husband himself would have prescribed for her. Yet she felt she was betraying him, failing him in an important way, and consequently, she broke off every potentially serious relationship before it developed. Not surprisingly, the children were ambivalent as well; they wanted a new daddy as the house felt incomplete without one; however, surrounded as they were by photographs and mementos of their own father, they found fault with every man Tamar brought home. When Tamar had passed her initial period of mourning, she resumed her work with energy and soon afterward felt strong enough to conclude therapy.

Two years later, George appeared. He had lived with Tamar for a few months. He and his two small children had moved in with her and her own youngsters. They tried to be a family, but soon discovered that life together was too complicated and replete with friction. George had moved back to his own apartment and now wished to work on his behavior toward his children. He knew he was too rigid, too strict and unbending with them. He loved them dearly but felt he was not bringing them up satisfactorily. They weren't happy kids. They could barely recall their own mother, who had passed away when they were very small, and they were sorely in need of a feminine, nurturing figure in their household, but Tamar had not filled this need. She was so wrapped up in the relationship with her own children that she had little time and even less affection — not to speak of love — left for them.

George chose to seek me out knowing that Tamar had previously been in therapy with me. Even though he had left her and they had broken off their relationship, he still hoped they might get together again as they really loved one another but just could not manage with the difficulties living together had entailed. Soon after this, Tamar contacted him wishing to resume their relationship and, consequently, joined our sessions.

Therapy may involve but does not consist only of problem solving. Tamar and George did not, in fact, solve their problem. In therapy they were able to examine the issues and to weigh the advantages and disadvantages of living together. George insisted that they again live under one roof and have their own child as soon as possible. Tamar refused to renew the "trauma" of their living together as a family. Right or wrong, she did not love his children. The four children did not get along together and must be brought up in separate households. As for themselves, Tamar did love George but felt they would have to wait. Once the children were bigger, she and he would be able to really live and "grow old together." Till then they could meet evenings and spend occasional weekends and vacations together, but no more than that. George refused to go along with these "delaying tactics," as he put it. He wanted a woman in his home, a mother to his children as well as a companion for himself. When it became clear to all of us that nothing new was being expressed or suggested and that both Tamar and George remained adamant, we decided to bring our sessions to a close.

Separation

When are my responses as therapist really helpful to the client? This is the central issue we have been dealing with in this chapter. I wish to explore it more specifically now, concentrating on the problems of separation, a topic with which we, as therapists, must so often deal. To be separated forever from a loved one is surely one of the deepest tragedies of life, and many clients resort to therapy to help them mourn, cope with their grief, and make the best of what remains to them.

In general terms, we know what must be done. We must listen in silence, respect the client's tears — thus facilitating catharsis; allow him to talk as much as he requires till he has talked himself out. Aside from the therapist, there is by now no one to whom the client can bare his heart. Others are either engrossed in their own private grief or else occupied with the business of dealing with everyday life. So we become the priest, the Wailing Wall. Inevitably, there remains the client's unfinished business with the departed to work through and the coming to terms with the irreversibility of separation. Gently, we always try to push him into the direction of life, of what still remains, what is worth living and struggling for.

Separation Through the Death of a Mate

Fanny came in soon after her husband, Gus, had died, the victim of a car crash. They had been married for twenty years; there were no children. At first Fanny talked much of Gus and their life together. From session to session she mentioned him less and, instead, spoke of the children in her kindergarten class. She spoke quietly, almost in an undertone, and for a long time seemed the personification of sadness. But as she spoke of the children, she gradually became more animated and even vivacious at times. She talked of child development and of parent-child relationships. She asked for my professional opinion but ignored any suggestion that she refocus on Gus and herself. Fanny led and made me follow her lead. This process may not have worked for everyone — for Fanny it did.

Peter, on the other hand, would talk of nothing and no one but Charlotte. She had died of cancer and had suffered so much toward the end that death seemed a merciful release. Aside from the children, he spoke of Charlotte only with me. Externally, his life proceeded normally. He could not bring himself to speak freely of Charlotte to anyone without feeling he was imposing or causing embarrassment. He did not need therapy, he told me, but only the chance to talk himself out with someone whose role it was to listen. Peter was an engineer and far from used to expressing his feelings. He spoke in fits and starts, memories tumbling over each other. He had no illusions about himself and was sure he would remarry, sooner rather than later. From me he seemed to expect silence and an occasional sign that I had listened and understood.

As the reader may already have guessed, Rose's tale had a happy ending. Gradually, she devoted more time to her children and showed renewed interest in her work. Her appearance once again became important to her. She bought new clothes and went out to meet people. Her anger was dissipating and the mourning process was approaching its close. We prepared to terminate therapy, but for a while Rose always found a good excuse for yet another meeting, until one morning she came in and said abruptly:

> CL. This will be our last session. I don't think I'll ever have to come again. You've told me that the door is open if I should ever need it but that's not for me. My therapy now belongs to the past and when I close the door behind me today, I'm going to close it on that past. I've found someone — a widower with three small kids. We want to get married — perhaps we'll even have a child together. I feel alive again and ready to face the future. You've helped me a lot, and time has done its share, too, and now I'm ready to say "goodbye."

After a few minutes of small talk, Rose left. True to her word, I have not heard from her since.

Separation Through the Death of a Child

> CL. The most awful thing that can possibly happen to parents is when they must bury their own child.

> TH. And you have had to perform this terrible duty.

> CL. Yes . . . but so have lots of others in this country. We just have to live with that dreadful threat hanging over us, and when it strikes we must bear it — we have no other choice.

Deborah spoke in this vein when she came to me a few months after her firstborn, Yitzik, had been killed. His plane had been shot down over Egypt; the remains of his body had only recently been returned. Deborah made it quite clear from the outset that she did not really believe in therapy. It was best to stand on one's

188 · THE HELPING INTERVIEW

own two feet. She came not to mourn her son — that was her own private affair — but because she was finding it very difficult to concentrate and, as a result, was no longer satisfied with her performance as a teacher in the high school where she has been teaching history and Bible studies for many years.

Clearly, the issue here would not revolve about the relative efficacy of my responses and leads. Nor could I wait for rapport to develop between us, as chances were that it would not. Deborah was a zealous patriot, strong as steel, who had taught herself over many years to play down, disregard, and repress feelings. Our contact would either turn into a real encounter or would quickly fizzle out. I admitted that I was skeptical as well; not only because of her doubts about therapy but primarily because the process of therapy sooner or later demands the exploration and expression of feelings and I was far from certain that she would be willing or capable of undertaking this.

At first she talked politics. She expressed herself as an extreme nationalist rejecting any compromise with the "enemy." Deborah scoffed at my own rather moderate position:

> *CL.* It's because of you and people like you that we stumble from war to war. You just won't grasp that the other side doesn't want and never has wanted compromise. They want us out and, if possible, in the sea. That's all there is to it. Yitzik was the only one in our family who thought like you — and just see where it got him.
>
> *TH.* Yitzik held strong convictions of his own.
>
> *CL.* He sure did and there were plenty of arguments. Today I think that perhaps we overdid it. We really fought.
>
> *TH.* Today you regret the intensity of the disputes.
>
> *CL.* It's too late now. Even the last time he was home on leave, we argued. I don't like to think of that.

Deborah then wept in my presence for the first time.

Yitzik was not mentioned again for quite awhile. Once Deborah spoke of his girlfriend and of how sad she still looked. She was bound to get over it and would eventually find someone else. Mostly, she spoke of school and of her difficulty in concentrating.

She demanded much of her pupils and of herself, as well, and now she just could not remember things the way she "ought to." At home this didn't matter so much, but at school . . . During this stage of her therapy Deborah ignored most of what I said, almost as if she were demonstrating her difficulties in concentration. And then, rather unexpectedly for both of us, the crucial session arrived:

CL. Stop hitting me over the head with the connection between Yitzik's death and my lack of concentration; everyone knows that! So what do you expect me to do — stay home and cry and try to change what can't be changed any more?

TH. Perhaps that wouldn't be such a bad idea. Maybe you never allowed yourself to mourn and get out some of those emotions you are clamping down so firmly.

CL. It's too late now and we can never set it right — not that it was so important but I simply can't get it out of my mind.

TH. Do you want to talk about it?

CL. (Deborah is silent for a long time but then bursts into sobs.) Our last parting was bad. We hadn't argued only about politics. Things just went wrong, the way they do sometimes. Friday night he had dinner at his girl's parents' house and that hurt us. It was all so stupid and pointless. We talked to him on the phone once more and things seemed O.K. again but I cannot for the life of me get that last parting out of my head.

Deborah went over the incident obsessively. She probed into every detail, recalled every word — or at least thought she did. Therapy, of course, did not bring her solace, but at least her powers of concentration returned "as if by a miracle," as she put it.

For Art, who had been pressured into seeking therapy, no response of mine proved helpful. He came and sat and wept silently. He placed fresh flowers on his daughter's grave every day and continued to assemble material for his case against the hospital — their negligence had killed her and they would pay for it. All that remained to him was the hope of vengeance and the memory of his child. He dwelt on every slight incident in the child's life, session after session. He continually berated himself for what he had done or left undone. His wife and, later on, his sons joined us but nothing helped; nothing changed. Art displayed no interest whatsoever in their store. He sat and mourned and wept. No living person could get through to him. He left me just as he had come — a broken man with a ruined life.

Separation from a Part of Self

I have known it to happen that clients will in essence guide us onto a path where our response is crucial to their real needs at the moment. The path at times forks into a direction quite distant from the traditional helping interview. When Susan felt her sanity ebbing away, she needed to call me several times a day. It was important to her to tell me what music she was either listening to or playing herself. Just prior to her hospitalization, she needed me to sit with her silently, listening to the moving strains of Mozart's great G Minor Symphony. By then, her behavior was already very erratic, but she let me know how I must respond if I wished to help.

Parting with one's sanity is undoubtedly not as conscious and self-conscious an act as is parting from one's basic beliefs. Marie had grown up in an agnostic home. She sought me out, in part, knowing my free-thinking views. Marie was no longer an agnostic and was increasingly turning toward orthodox Judaism. She was actually completely uninterested in hearing my viewpoint. Hers was becoming ever more uncompromising, and arguments and disputation, pro and con, occupied most of her days and nights. Her parents were strongly opposed to the steps she was contemplating, as were most of her former friends. But the "truth" had been revealed to her and she now had many new friends among extreme orthodox circles. From me she sought not words but rather an attitude — one of neutrality, tolerance, and patience. She needed a sounding board in order to effect closure for her past beliefs and to help her take leave of a world she had known. Her new world would be very different, and I could not accompany her thence but could, at least, listen to her farewell on the brink of separation from the old one.

Nathan came from a well-to-do Persian family. He arrived nearly penniless soon after the State of Israel was established and, shortly afterward, lost his sight. At the rehabilitation center where I was then working, he rejected all attempts at counseling. What was decreed by the heavens could not be changed and simply had to be borne. Nathan invested all his energies in the vocational area and soon became a highly adept bookbinder. Away from the workshop, he kept to himself, maintaining a polite but reserved demeanor. The one desire he expressed was to excel at bookbinding and find employment. Regarding his blindness, he had nothing to say. I took his lead and left him to follow his own course. Ever since then Nathan has phoned me on the eve of every major holiday. He inquires about my family and speaks of his. He helped me learn that sometimes our most helpful response is to leave well enough alone.

We all must learn to cope with the process of separating; however, the things different people find it particularly stressful to part with is a very individual matter. Gabriel had been released from the hospital. His recovery was deemed satisfactory, although he would have to continue taking medication. But for Gabriel things would never again be the same. He had been one of the key members of his settlement ever since its inception. Whether or not he had held an official post at any given time, his advice was frequently sought. More recently, he had been instrumental in setting up the settlement's factory and in various capacities had helped run and expand it. Gabriel had been a leader, and leadership had become a vital part of him. And now he knew that he must renounce it. His hospitalization was known to all and he felt stigmatized — perhaps unfairly, he granted, but that was how he felt. Aside from that he no longer possessed the strength to lead and even the desire was leaving him. His grief at this loss was deep and, I imagine, still endures to some extent. His way of mourning and the consequent response he required of me consisted of three stages. First, he needed to poke fun in a sardonic manner at those who were presently running the plant. From me, he asked for attentive listening and nonverbal confirmation that I had heard him. During the second stage, he allowed himself to brag a little about his accomplishments. From me, he required understanding and, to that end, encouraged questions of clarification. In the last stage he ridiculed his behavior in stages one and two, seeing in it mere boasting. What he asked of me during this last stage was not clear to me at first. "I've talked myself out;

now it's up to you." My assigned task, it soon developed, was to help him turn over a new leaf concerning a new place of work, a more subdued lifestyle, and what to do with unaccustomed time on his hands. "I used to enjoy life," he remarked. "Now I've got to get used to just existing." It did not occur to me to demean his loss by arguing about this. Gabriel fully realized what he has had to part from.

Separation Through Divorce

When both husband and wife agree upon divorce and remain on good terms, they will generally not turn to a therapist except, at times, to consult about the children. This was certainly not the case with Dalia and Simon. One morning, Dalia related, "out of the blue" Simon had announced that he was through and that their ten-year-old marriage was at an end as far as he was concerned. "I had no idea what had hit me," she continued. After a good deal of pressure, Simon agreed to come, just once, to one of our sessions. He said very little: he was moving out of town; there was no other woman involved; for him marriage had been a mistake — he needed freedom and would never marry again. Nothing more. He left town, the divorce proceedings ensued, and Dalia, bewildered and distraught, began therapy in earnest.

Now, years later and in the interim having remarried, Dalia is still bewildered regarding Simon's behavior. During the months in therapy, she kept having dreams, fantasies, and hallucinations about "things the way they used to be, about Simon's returning and about his never having left." It took me a while to discover that the only response on my part she found helpful was the confirmation that what had happened had, indeed, happened and that Simon was out of her life for good. During this period she continued to work and to look after the children, but she seemed to be functioning for the moment only — as if tomorrow "things would return to normal." To her sessions she brought the "reality" that had been and would be — simply had to be — again. And, once more, I had to disappoint her and reorient her to the present and the future. She hated me for doing that. It seemed impossible for her to fathom the fact that Simon had sat together with us in this room, had uttered a few words, and had risen and left. Although they still met occasionally because of the children, to her he had gradually become a stranger.

Ostensibly, Emma and Ernest came to work on their marriage. However, it soon transpired that there was really nothing left to work on. He still wanted her, but she could no longer bear physical contact with him and had insisted upon separate bedrooms months before. But, she claimed, she liked having him around the house and hoped the physical aversion would eventually pass. Ernest, humiliated and very resentful by now, made it clear that he could no longer go on with such an arrangement and left. Emma was furious at the thought that there might be another woman in his life, but on the other hand, she was not prepared to work on her own repugnance concerning normal conjugal relations. Friends and parents on both sides intervened but all in vain. There were no women yet in Ernest's life although there were men in Emma's. Yet she refused to contemplate divorce.

Eventually it became clear that although she was ready and willing to separate from Ernest, she could not tolerate the prospect of separating from the economic security that living with Ernest had provided — and was still providing. Were they to divorce, her standard of living was bound to suffer, and she could not face that. As for Ernest, if he would only be patient a little longer. . . . Ernest tried again to act with forbearance but finally put his foot down. My facilitation had helped to clarify the picture and to double-check our understanding of each other. But understanding is not always what is desired. Emma was far from appreciative of my efforts; even Ernest might have preferred a continued state of ambiguity.

Dealing with Obstacles

There are ways — such as checking notes, listening to tapes, and discussing interviews with professional persons — whereby one can discover to what extent obstacles to communication are present. These self-imposed tests and tasks, so to speak, are not foolproof. In any case, it is undoubtedly valid to say that communication obstacles exist to some degree in every interview. Our goal, as I perceive it, is not to eliminate them altogether, for our inability to achieve this might lead us to despair. It is, rather, to become aware of our behavior in interviews, to see where we may be creating obstacles, and to try to reduce these as much as possible, all the while recognizing that we remain humanly fallible. The five ways of reducing obstacles I am about to discuss have helped me and a good many of my students.

Talking Too Much or Too Little

If you tend to talk as much as or even more than the client, chances are that you are blocking communication from her to you. It is quite likely that you are acting as an authority, as the superior in the interview who must be respectfully listened to, and that the client perceives you in this way. You may be lecturing the client and not becoming sufficiently aware of her internal frame of reference while causing her to become too much aware of yours.

Should you find yourself talking very little — about 10 percent or less of the total talk — you may wish to look into this. Are there many pauses, awkward silences? Do you say so little because you are reluctant to get in the client's way but find that in holding back you are getting in his way nonetheless? Do the two of you seem comfortable with the fact that you are talking so little, or does the atmosphere seem unnatural and tense to you both? If you find that the little you say enables the client to release feelings and express ideas and at the same time enables you to go along with him, you may have achieved good rapport. The amount of talk is but one indication of what goes on in the interview and must be seen within the context of the entire process.

Cutting Off

Do you tend to let the client finish what he has to say, or do you often finish it for him and reply to that? Do you tend to interrupt him because you are quick to catch his intent and become impatient? Believing that you have heard many times in the past what he is now saying, do you become bored and cut him off? After your interruptions, what happens to the flow of the interview? An interruption creates a major communication obstacle. It cuts short communication that is actually taking place. Our motives may be the best: to show that we understand so well that we can finish the client's sentence for him, to demonstrate our interest by interjecting questions. Motives notwithstanding, we are actually choking off what is coming our way, although we may sincerely believe ourselves to be encouraging further flow.

At times cutting off leads to a form of duet; both partners are talking at once — the one continuing with what she was saying when interrupted and the other continuing to interrupt her. When we realize what is happening, we can probably do nothing better than stop and, if necessary, state openly what has occurred. But this explanation should be very brief lest it become, in turn, an interference. "Sorry, go ahead" may suffice. At times the client, well trained to look up to "authority," may stop in her tracks as soon as we open our mouth. Here we may have to say more: "Sorry I cut you off. I was too quick on the trigger. Please go ahead; I'll have my say when you're through."

We must become especially aware of interruptions by the client. These may well indicate that we have not understood him aright, that he has decided to add or amend, or that, for one reason or another, he finds it difficult to continue listening to us. Remarks such as "I'm talking now, so please listen" or "I've done you the courtesy of listening to you, so now please do me the courtesy of listening to me" usually add insult to injury. The helping interview is not an exercise in manners except insofar as we wish to use it to teach manners. Whatever the case, if the client interrupts us and we wish to remove communication obstacles to the greatest extent possible, sensitivity on our part to what is going on may assist us to find the causes. If we really wish to hear the client, the best thing is to stop and listen. There will always be time for us to have our say. Our need to talk, unfortunately, is often greater than our ability to listen. This is a very human failing, but since it creates obstacles to communication, it should be overcome.

Responses

Am I responding to what the client has expressed or to what, in my opinion, she should have expressed? In other words, am I responding to her needs or to my own? Do my responses enable her to express herself further? Are my responses clear? Am I getting across to her? Do my responses constitute additional obstacles to those she is already facing? In short, are my responses a help or a hindrance to the flow of her talk? We shall consider this aspect more fully in the next chapter.

Forces and Facets

Any topic discussed in an interview usually has several facets. Do I assist the client to see, discuss, and cope with as many of these as possible? When a course of action is being considered, normally certain forces push the client in one direction, while other forces pull him in another. This pushing and pulling may be going on simultaneously. Am I helping the client to explore all the aspects of his conflict, or does my behavior impede his doing so? Do I place obstacles in the way of his exploring his own life space and perceptual field? We cannot always answer these difficult questions, but the posing of them itself may remove impediments to communication.

A Helpful Communication Test

In his well-known article "Dealing with Breakdowns in Communication — Interpersonal and Intergroup," written in 1951, Rogers (1961, Ch. 17) referred to an interesting communication test that has since been frequently employed in human relations training and in various classroom situations. The test is challenging and difficult, but I have found that people value the learning experience involved and derive genuine satisfaction from it. Two or more persons are asked to discuss a topic on which they hold differing views. Each is allowed to say whatever he likes under one condition: before voicing his views, he must restate the ideas and feelings expressed by the person who spoke immediately preceding him and do so to that person's satisfaction. The assumption is that if I can tell you what you said and felt, then I heard and understood you. If I cannot, either I placed obstacles in the way or you did not make yourself sufficiently clear. Thus the test motivates the speaker to clarify his thinking and the listener to concentrate on what is being said rather than on the reply he is about to make.

The higher feelings rise in the discussion, obviously the harder it is to obey the rule. At times tempers reach such a high pitch that a moderator is required. As each participant speaks, the moderator restates to that participant's satisfaction what she has said and felt before the next participant is allowed to speak.

In the helping interview we may not always wish to restate the thoughts and feelings expressed by the client, but if we are able to recapture his message to us in this manner, it will show that minimal communication obstacles are present. In other words, if I can provide an atmosphere in which you can release your feelings and ideas without interference from mine and if I can recognize these ideas and feelings as yours, showing you that I have heard, understood, and accepted them as yours, chances are that we are truly communicating and that obstacles are at a minimum. Furthermore, in such an atmosphere you will be receptive to the ideas and feelings I communicate to you. Thus the result will be a genuine interview.

When the Client Won't Talk

Interviewing does not consist of talk alone; there is nonverbal communication as well. However, if there is no talk at all, there may be no interview at all. I am often asked, "What should I do if the client won't talk or won't continue to talk?" I am certain that in most instances the client will talk if really given the opportunity. I once met a young woman who wished to discuss her relationship with her husband. She insisted that he was the "silent type" and hardly ever spoke. We agreed that the three of us would meet. The husband talked — at least he attempted to — but each time he started, his wife would interrupt. Perceiving this, I could not help but smile. The young woman understood the smile and made a supreme effort to allow him to talk. When I last heard from her, she good-humoredly volunteered the information that her husband was no longer the silent type and that she had learned a great deal about her own behavior.

It is not always as simple as this, I admit, but if the client is interested in the interview, he will usually talk if we let him or encourage him a bit. On the other hand, he may not have wanted the interview and may feel pushed into it by others, perhaps by ourselves. In that case it may be preferable for us to indicate that we understand and accept his reluctance and then refrain from pushing him further. If and when he becomes ready, or "motivated," he will return and he will talk. Should he not return, it will not be because we consciously made the experience a threatening and unpleasant one. Not everyone wishes to be helped and not everyone can be helped in the helping interview. To have a sincere offer of help rejected is painful, but we must learn to accept this. We may even eventually learn to accept the fact that in situations in which we have "failed," another can succeed.

But what if the client won't continue to talk? Here I am assuming that communication has taken place, that contact has been established. If the client then stops, perhaps she has finished. Or maybe we have thrown obstacles into her path, the kind discussed above. Or perhaps the client has come up against obstacles in herself that hinder her from going further. The response to the ensuing silence will depend upon the therapist's perception of what is happening. I can only suggest possible ways to reopen communication.

"Is there anything else you wish to say?" (Client shakes his head.) "All right, I'd just like to make one more comment. . . ."

"I see you find it difficult to continue. I wonder if your silence is connected with anything I've said."

"I don't quite know what to make of this silence. Perhaps there is something you find difficult to put into words."

"The last time we hit a silence like this, you said it was because of something I had done. How about this time?"

Preoccupation with Self

A basic factor in communication relates more to the therapist's behavior than to the client's. As the interview proceeds, you, the therapist, may be asking yourself what to say or do next. This concern with your own role may so absorb your attention that you will not be genuinely listening to the client. You will be preoccupied with that small voice inside that insists on knowing how to act next. This inner voice constitutes a clear obstacle to communication. It is not to be confused with the other inner voice that brings you closer to the world of the client — that "third ear" with which you suddenly understand something haltingly expressed. The voice that insists on knowing what to do next is a block between you and your partner in the interview. It is concerned more with you than with him, more with the impression you will make on him than with the impressions he might make on you if you were listening and trying to understand with him.

Should you, then, not be concerned with what you are to do or say? Naturally you must be, but not consciously while the client is expressing herself. When you really listen, almost inevitably a moment's silence will intervene between the client's pausing and your carrying on. Whatever you say or do next will be unpremeditated. It may not be polished or carefully thought through, but it will be genuine. It will come forth spontaneously as the result of your having truly listened. At any rate, you will not have planned your action at the expense of having lost track of the client. You will not sound like the "ideal" therapist, but you may well sound like yourself. The ideal therapist does not exist, but you do; and if the client can sense the genuine, unplanned, spontaneous you, she will have an experience rare in our society. She might even dare to learn from this experience.

On the other hand, should the client sense that we are occupied not with what he is saying but with our eventual response to it, this could be very harmful to the relationship between us. He might imbibe from this a lesson I doubt we wish him to learn: in the interview the important thing is not to be listened to but to be responded to. Were he to act on this conclusion, he would not listen to us either but instead would plan his responses. Perhaps this sounds absurd, but I have known it to happen.

When not stemming merely from lack of experience, this preoccupation with self, I fear, has deep roots somewhere else. We are concerned with how we shall appear instead of being satisfied with what we are. We are concerned with demonstrating our role rather than revealing ourself; with being perceived as superior rather than behaving as an equal; with presenting a show of authority rather than letting our authority — if it exists at all — come through naturally in the ongoing exchange of ideas and feelings.

I reiterate my conviction that the therapist's preoccupation with self at the expense of the client creates a serious obstacle to interpersonal communication. If we can accept ourselves as fallible, we shall err less. If we can learn to rely on our spontaneity, sensitivity, and basic common sense, we shall listen better and understand more. Our behavior influences that of the client more than we know. Behaving openly ourselves, we shall encourage him to do likewise.

Providing Information the Client Needs

At this point I want to discuss an obstacle to communication that often is not perceived as such or is entirely overlooked. I am referring to certain aspects of the process involved in providing information to the client.

First of all, however, let us note the following special circumstances. Sometimes when the client asks the therapist for information, the therapist may not wish to furnish it because he thinks that the client already possesses it or can easily obtain it by himself. For example:

> *CL.* Am I blushing?
>
> *TH.* Do you feel embarrassed?

> *CL.* Can you tell me whether this course is being offered next fall?
>
> *IER.* The new listings have just been published; you may wish to look them over.

In the first instance the therapist may not have wished to reply either yes or no because he assumed that how the client felt was more relevant than any information he could supply about the color of her cheeks. In the second example the interviewer may not have wanted to give a definite answer because he wished to encourage the client to do for himself what he could easily do while gaining additional information in the process. However, the failure to provide certain types of information may create obstacles to communication.

Concerning this major category of information that if provided may impel the interview forward and if withheld may block smooth progress, I shall first discuss information requested by the client. This is knowledge that the therapist or interviewer possesses and the client does not have but feels she needs and cannot obtain by her own resources. In such situations a straightforward reply is helpful. In the following examples the mere reflection of feeling or the verbalized recognition of the fact that the client is seeking information would not have sufficed:

CL. Did you speak to Mr. Adams the way we agreed?

TH. Yes, I did. He and I had quite a talk. There are some things on which you see eye to eye, but there are others that make it hard to believe both of you are speaking of the same incidents.

CL. Do you know whether I got the scholarship?

IER. No, not yet; but as soon as I know, I'll tell you.

CL. Will I feel the operation?

IER. You shouldn't feel anything during the operation, but there will be some pain afterward for a few days. We'll try to make you as comfortable as possible, but you won't feel very comfortable at first.

CL. Do they know at the factory that I was at X hospital?

TH. To the best of my knowledge they don't. I wonder how you feel about that.

CL. If I should need you while you're on vacation, will I be able to get in touch with you?

TH. No, you won't, but Miss C. will be available during my absence. I see you have mixed feelings about my going on vacation. You want me to go away and rest, but you want me nearby as well.

In some of the above examples the therapist or interviewer goes beyond providing the requested information. She relates it to the client's internal frame of reference and thereby shows her interest in what the information may mean to the client or how it may affect him. When appropriate, this seems to me as helpful a response as can be made.

The therapist or interviewer may also profitably provide information that the client has not requested. He may do this to reduce tension. On occasion the client may wish to ask but may neither dare to nor know how to go about it. Perhaps the client may not even be cognizant of the fact that if he were provided with some necessary information, he would feel more relaxed. All the following statements by therapists exemplify this approach:

"The money hasn't come through yet; I know you must be anxious."

"I'm the person who meets with the parents of the children staying with us. You can reach me here by phone, and we can make an appointment whenever you feel you wish to discuss matters relating to Peggy's stay. Once a month there is a meeting of all the parents at which . . ."

"Mr. S. is sick today. I'm pinch-hitting for him. I'll be happy to talk with you unless you prefer waiting for his return."

"I have the impression you are wondering whether I know more about you than you have told me. As a matter of fact, I do. Mr. D. told me of your illness, and he wanted me to inform you that he had done so. I'm glad I know because this enables me to understand the situation better. I wonder how you feel about it . . . my knowing, I mean."

"I am free till noon so we have plenty of time, and you can tell me everything you wish without hurrying."

One last point. I may remove a communication obstacle by telling the client frankly what I am doing or propose to do and for what reasons. This will eliminate any aura of mystery surrounding my status and indicate that here in the helping interview he can be equally frank. Some examples:

"I should like to write and ask them about your records; then we'll be able to compare. O.K.?"

"I won't be in next Tuesday because I have an earlier commitment. How about Thursday instead?"

"I'll give you the injection now. It will hurt very little. Then you'll have to lie down for ten minutes or so till we can go on with the examination. No cards up my sleeve, so you can relax now."

Occasionally I may be unable to furnish certain information because I do not have it, and may wish to inform the client of this fact. For example: "I can't tell you about summer camp for Janet yet because the committee hasn't reached its decision. We'll just have to wait."

7 • RESPONSES AND LEADS

In this chapter the focus is on responses and leads. I shall deal with those already mentioned but not placed into the present context, as well as with others not yet touched upon. Inasmuch as the number of possible responses and leads is all but limitless, I shall not even attempt to be comprehensive but shall merely consider those most frequently used. Although I shall not pretend to be impartial, I shall try to be fair.

The difference between response and lead cannot be unmistakably defined, for a response may change into a lead, and a lead may be meant as a response and be interpreted as such. However, there is a basic difference in the way individual therapists and interviewers lead and respond, and this will become evident when one examines the particular style each develops and finds most congenial. Extracts from random interviews may present an erroneous picture. The extracts I shall cite, therefore, are for the purpose of identifying and analyzing the particular response or lead and will not deal with the interviewer's style. Developing a style is a task each interviewer, if interested, must undertake for himself.

The essential difference between response and lead is denoted in the definitions of the two words themselves. When I respond, I speak in terms of what the client has expressed. I react to the ideas and feelings he has communicated to me with something of my own. When I lead, I take over. I express ideas and feelings to which I expect the client to react. Leading, of course, may also be in response to what has already occurred in the interview or to the last statement made by the client; however, it generally involves a quite different attitude. When leading, I make use of my own life space; when responding, I tend more to utilize the life space of the client. Responses keep the client at the center of things; leads make the interviewer central. Philosophically speaking, those interviewers who usually employ more responses than leads seem to believe that the client has it within himself to find the way. Those who tend to lead seem to act on the conviction that the client needs the way pointed out to her. It is evident that much blurring and overlapping exist here. The interviewer's intentions are important, but the way the client perceives them is decisive. For each interviewer there is the forest and there are the trees. The forest is his overall style; the trees, his leads and responses. In this chapter we shall examine only the trees in the hope that this may help us eventually to look at the forest more closely and see it more clearly.

Some years ago Robinson (1950) presented a gradated list of responses and leads ranging from what he termed most nondirective to most directive, that is, from those most centered in the client's internal frame of reference to those least centered in it. I shall base my model on his approach while keeping clear of the nondirective-directive controversy (Rogers, 1942), which, I submit, belongs to the past. (For elaboration on this point see Rogers, 1961; Bugental, 1965; Beck [ed.], 1966.) We realize today that a very directive lead may be helpful in a situation in which neither recognition nor reflection of feeling is helpful, and we know the reverse is true as well. In addition, enough research evidence is available (Fiedler, 1950a,b, 1951) to show that it is the therapist as a human being whom the client perceives — above and beyond any theory of interviewing the therapist advocates or any leads and responses he employs.

One additional point must be stressed. I am convinced that it is a mistake to assume that the therapist who talks little and uses more responses than leads is passive or that one who talks much and leads often is active. Listening with understanding is not, as I see it, in the least passive. Familiarizing oneself with the client's life space is activity indeed. A therapist who talks and leads extensively may not be active in this sense at all. What makes the difference is the therapist's degree of involvement with the client — with his thoughts and feelings, his hopes and fears, his perceptions of the world. Thus the therapist can be very actively involved and say almost nothing or he can be passive though speaking and leading most of the time. The question remains, With whom is the therapist most involved? To repeat, the therapist who is involved largely with himself is active or passive in a way clearly unlike that of the therapist who is involved primarily with the client.

Blurs, overlappings, and ambiguities notwithstanding, responses and leads will be described in a certain order. Not from "good" to "bad" or from "right" to "wrong" but not haphazardly or nonevaluatively either. I do find that the more we tend to use the responses and leads listed last in this chapter, the less we are truly taking into account the client and her world. The more we employ the responses and leads listed at the beginning, the less likely we are to impose ourselves and our world on her. This is not a clear-cut issue. It may not even be a matter of consistency. However, all of us follow a distinct trend that is expressed in our style whether we are aware of it or not. It is our way of being human. There are many such ways, and I have not concealed the one I feel to be most facilitative to growth.

Client-Centered Responses and Leads

Silence

I have discussed silence previously in another context. It is listed here first because it can be a response, although this fact is frequently overlooked. The response is nonverbal, of course, but can express a great deal. A gesture on the therapist's part may communicate: "Yes, I'm with you, go on" or "I'm waiting, sensing that you have not finished" or "You've said that before; I'm beginning to get bored." Our gestures mean much; so do our glances and the way we move about in our chair. Just as words have meaning, silence has meaning. Through it both partners in the interview may be drawing closer, sharing something; or silence may show them just how wide the gulf between them really is. Silence may point up misunderstanding. It may be neutral or very empathic. It may be the result of confusion. It can say, "We have really finished but haven't yet admitted it." As a deliberate response, silence implies that the therapist has decided to say nothing, regarding this as the most helpful thing she can offer at this point. She decides not to interfere verbally, but she is there in the interview, and her presence is felt by the client. It is as if the therapist were saying: "You know I am listening. The best way in which I can be of help right now, I believe, is to keep quiet. I am not afraid of the silence because I feel that this is what you want." Often her gestures will communicate this to the client quite clearly.

Unless the therapist is very sure of her ground, she should avoid extensive silences; a minute of meaningful silence is quite lengthy. If it is true, as the proverb would have it, that words are silver but silence is gold, then we ought to value silence as a response more than we do. Perhaps we can become more aware of our own feelings about silences in the interview and determine how we use them. As an intentional response properly utilized, silence can be an important facet of the experience the client takes away with him, saying to himself, "Here I was really listened to."

"Mm-hm"

"Mm-hm" is a verbal response. Though not a word, it is clearly an uttered sound. It is generally considered to indicate permissiveness on the part of the therapist, expressing, "Go on, I'm with you; I'm listening and following you." However, its usage is not quite so restricted. By an "mm-hm" the therapist may instead indicate approval of what the client is saying or of how he is going about handling his situation. It may tell the client that the therapist likes what he is doing and, therefore, encourage him to continue in that direction. "Mm-hm" may also at times suggest criticism, as though to say: "So that's how you feel!" or "So that's what you're thinking!" In other situations it may imply suspended judgment, as if the therapist were saying, "Well, let's see what you are going to add; I want to wait a bit."

The possibilities are manifold. "*C'est le ton qui fait la musique.*" This is true for all responses and leads, including "mm-hm." We may wish to become aware of how we use "mm-hm," that is, if we use it, and study how the client interprets it. In the following excerpts it has various meanings:

> *CL.* I don't know what would be best for me; I keep going back and forth and don't seem to be able to make up my own mind.
>
> *TH.* Mm-hm.

> *CL.* I don't like the way this agency functions. You people promise a lot, but it's just words with nothing behind them.
>
> *TH.* Mm-hm.

> *CL.* If my mother would only stop picking on me everything would be all right. She doesn't pick on my brother, just on me.
>
> *TH.* Mm-hm.

In the first instance the therapist meant to be permissive, to let the client explore her own indecisiveness. In the second, he felt disapproving of the criticism expressed. In the last, he wished to wait and see what would develop. Now let's look at the following examples. When the therapist examined her feelings, she concluded that in the first instance she felt approving and in the second disapproving. How the client perceived her is not clear.

> *CL.* Last month I followed your suggestion, and it worked. I managed much better with the budget, and there was less drinking.
>
> *TH.* Mm-hm.

> *CL.* I've tried the hearing aid — I really have — but I can't get used to it. So I brought it back; let someone else have it.
>
> *TH.* Mm-hm.

Other responses might have been used, but this is begging the question — other responses can always be employed. The "mm-hm" seems noncommittal on the therapist's part but does not necessarily imply that he refuses to commit himself. That may come later. Meanwhile, he wishes to let the client know by uttering this sound that he is prepared to listen further. Although apparently a nonjudgmental sound, "mm-hm" has many nuances, which the therapist may be aware of and which the client will perceive correctly or incorrectly. It may be hard to believe that a little "mm-hm" is open to such a wide range of meaning and interpretation; but a careful perusal of interviews will show, I believe, that this is the case.

Restatement

Now, at last, the therapist speaks. He uses actual words, but they are those of the client. Restatement can be accomplished in various ways, but the rationale is the same: to serve as an echo, to let the client hear what she has said on the assumption that this may encourage her to go on speaking, examining, looking deeper. When the therapist utilizes restatement, his own perceptual field either does not enter the picture at all or enters it to a very small extent. Restatement communicates to the client: "I am listening to you very carefully, so carefully, in fact, that I can restate what you have said. I am doing so now because it may help you to hear yourself through me. I am restating what you have said so that you may absorb it and consider its impact, if any, on you. For the time being, I am keeping myself out of it."

Restatement can be effected in four basic ways:

1. Restating exactly what has been said without even changing the pronoun the client has used.

   CL. I felt cold and deserted.

   TH. I felt cold and deserted.

2. Restating exactly, changing only the pronoun.

   CL. I felt cold and deserted.

   TH. You felt cold and deserted.

I find the latter form more genuine than the first. The exact repetition, pronoun and all, seems to me artificial and affected. If the therapist is to keep himself out of it to that extent, the use of a tape recorder would be preferable, in my opinion.

3. Restating part of what has been said, the part the therapist feels to be most significant and worth having the client hear again.

> CL. So Joe and Mike and Chick ganged up on me, and before I knew what was going on, they knocked me down and ran.

> TH. They ganged up on you, knocked you down, and ran.

4. Restating in summary fashion what the client has said. This is a selective process. As she selects, the therapist does use her own perceptual field, of course. However, she keeps herself emotionally and intellectually uninvolved and simply summarizes what she has heard. At times this results in her stressing one aspect of what the client has just stated more than another and thereby goes beyond pattern three above and also, technically, beyond restating. We have come a long way from the tape recorder now. Contrast the following two examples:

> CL. I just couldn't tell him because we were never alone — the guys may have known what was up or . . . I don't know. All I know is that whenever I tried to tell him, there were people around; and I just couldn't tell him then . . . what with all of these people. . . .

> TH. You couldn't get him alone long enough to tell him.

> CL. When I got home that night . . . it was just awful. . . . At first I saw things blurred. Then things began to dance before my eyes, and then I could just feel that I was seeing less and less. I closed my eyes and reopened them. It was as if a gray curtain had descended all over the world; the world I knew collapsed that night.

> TH. A curtain descended on the world you had known, and it collapsed all about you. You had gone blind.

It is possible, of course, to employ restatement in other ways —
sarcasm or disbelief, for example.

> CL. I didn't do it.
>
> TH. You didn't do it!

Even with the pronoun changed and some summarizing, I find
restatement to be a powerful and forward-thrusting response. It is
a clear and genuine echo, allowing the client to hear aloud what
he has uttered. Its impact is probably more cognitive than emotional, inviting further thought and further relating. It stimulates
verbalization and rarely leads to silence. It has been my experience that restatement is particularly helpful when the client is
examining a conflict. It is then that he tends to think aloud.

When Carol examined her conflict with John she found herself
saying:

> CL. It's pointless to continue. I have to bring this marriage
> to an end.
>
> TH. It is pointless to go on. You have to finish.
>
> CL. I've tried and tried but nothing works.
>
> TH. You have tried hard but nothing works.
>
> CL. John and I should never have gotten married.
>
> TH. You and John should never have gotten married.
>
> CL. He's too weak to admit it but I'm not. It's all over.
>
> TH. It's all over.

Toward the end of therapy Fran said:

> CL. That struggle is over for me for good. I'm going to live.
>
> TH. Your struggle regarding life or death is at an end and life
> has won out.
>
> CL. It felt so good just to fade out, but now I see life can be
> fun.
>
> TH. Life can be fun, you find.

CL. Yes, I'll have to work at it, I know, but I think I'll make it.

TH. You think you can make it.

Clarification

Clarification is commonly understood to mean the therapist's clarification for the client of what the latter has said or tried to say. There is another side to the coin, but let us look first at this one, which has two possible designs:

1. The therapist remains very close to what the client has expressed but simplifies it to make it clearer. It is then, of course, up to the client to decide whether this response has been facilitating, whether it really clarified what she had in mind. For example:

   CL. The only thing that's clear to me is that I'm all mixed up. I want to try, but I can't. I want to be strong, but I'm acting weak. I want to make up my own mind, but I'm letting everybody sway me in every direction. It's one big mess. . . .

   TH. You see quite clearly that you are mixed up and not doing what you wish to be doing.

2. The therapist in his own words tries to clarify for the client what the latter has had difficulty in expressing clearly. The therapist submits a tentative synthesis of the client's verbalized ideas and feelings for his approval, amendment, or rejection. It is as though the therapist were translating the client's words into a language more familiar to them both.

   CL. I'm not sure whether it was really nice that he came. It was friendly and kind and generous on his part, but I don't deserve it if he did it for me — and if he didn't do it for me, I'm still glad he came because really I don't deserve it. But that's how he is, and I couldn't get anything out of him. I couldn't even tell him how I feel. I got all confused. . . .

   TH. You couldn't express to him how undeserving of his attention you feel.

CL. It's easy to get used to being crippled, but you never get used to it. It's not clear, I know, but I can't make it any clearer. Do you get what I mean?

TH. I understood you to say that it is possible to manage as a crippled person, but it never quite feels the way it used to feel before. . . .

CL. That's right. You can manage all right; that's simple enough. It's the other thing you never get used to — remembering and comparing and . . .

The other side of the coin of clarification concerns the need of the therapist to have things clarified for him. This aspect of clarification as a response is often overlooked entirely or else glossed over. Hence it needs pointing up. The therapist cannot be expected to understand everything. He is humanly fallible, and it will help the client to know that the therapist realizes and accepts this. Such an attitude will facilitate communication.

CL. He just threw me for a loop when . . .

TH. I'm sorry — my English is still not very good — what did you say he threw?

The client explains, and the interview continues. In this case the question was a genuine search for clarification, not mere flippancy, and rapport was thereby improved. Here are some more examples:

CL. . . . and she said she meant it, but it didn't sound too kosher to me.

TH. I thought that *kosher* referred to dietary laws. What did you mean by using it the way you just did?

CL. You'd go crazy, too, if you lived in a house like mine. You couldn't stand it either. You wouldn't think any more of it than I do.

TH. (in a light, almost jesting manner) You are imputing to me all sorts of thoughts and feelings about your home. Honestly, I don't know what it is like. I think I know how *you* feel about it, but perhaps you could describe it a little so that I can try to understand what upsets you so about goings-on there.

Reflection

This is a very difficult response to achieve. To reflect the feelings and attitudes of the client demands deeply empathic listening and understanding. To serve as a mirror in which the client can see her feelings and attitudes reflected requires a facility in recognizing and verbalizing those feelings and attitudes. When restating, the therapist tells the client what she has said. When reflecting, he verbalizes what the client feels. Reflection should not be confused with interpretation, which will be discussed shortly. Reflection consists of bringing to the surface and expressing in words those feelings and attitudes that lie behind the client's words. The therapist echoes feelings not expressed as such by the client but clearly sensed by the therapist from what the other has said. The therapist perceives these feelings and verbalizes them. Functioning like a mirror or an echo, the therapist adds nothing of his own except — and this is all-important — his sensitivity and empathic interest, which enable him to put into words what the client has meant affectively but stated intellectually or descriptively. In a manner of speaking, the therapist acts like a very attentive hostess who senses, understands, and expresses the wishes of her guest when he hesitates to state them openly because he does not know whether this would be appropriate to the situation.

Reflection is very similar to restatement except that the former is more loaded emotionally. Revealing, as it does, the emotional nuances behind the cognitive content, it invites the client to express feelings. Reproducing both thought and feeling, it is like a stereophonic echo to which the client almost always relates and through which he is propelled forward. Carol said:

CL. Divorce is not pleasant to contemplate.

TH. It upsets and scares you.

CL. Very much so. And since John is so weak, it'll all be on my shoulders.

TH. And you'll have to be the strong one.

CL. John will use the child's "best interests" as a spoke in the wheel.

TH. You feel that you won't be able to count on him to help.

CL. Not John — he'll play it safe and clean.

TH. The rough and the dirty he'll leave to you.

CL. In divorce as in marriage, I'll have to bear the brunt of it.

TH. You feel that it will be up to you to make all major moves.

CL. Oh yes, I know John's delaying tactics so well.

TH. You know him so well that you can predict how he'll behave.

CL. I wish I were a year older.

TH. You wish the divorce were behind you.

Even after her decision, Fran was fearful of the future:

CL. I talk as if everything were clear and settled.

TH. You talk big but feel small.

CL. Very small — like a baby sometimes.

TH. You feel as if you were starting from the beginning.

CL. But with a big strike against me.

TH. A feeling of having failed somehow.

CL. Having failed myself, and people won't forget and will hold it against me — the suicide attempt, I mean.

TH. You feel you won't get the support and understanding you'll need.

CL. I often think I should dare to move away and start afresh somewhere else where nobody knows me.

TH. But you're not sure you feel strong enough to do that.

CL. I'm not ready for such a move yet. It's too scary.

TH. You can't see yourself moving away from home and friends and beginning anew somewhere else — at least, not yet.

When reflecting, the therapist neither guesses nor assumes. She voices what is there behind the word content and brings it to the fore as the emotional content, which has been present all the time but unexpressed by the client. This in itself is hard to accomplish. The possibility of an additional complication should be recognized: The reflection presented may be distorted and consequently rejected by the client. In this case it was not reflection but another response, probably interpretation. However, even true reflection may be rejected by the client when he perceives it as threatening. Therefore, it is not always easy to be certain that your response was indeed reflection. Consideration of the interview as a whole will usually help you ascertain this. I shall hazard this general rule: True reflection will be accepted by the client because it simply consists of putting into words the feeling tone of what he has just said. Or, to put it another way, what the client verbally expressed was accompanied by an affective message that the therapist received and then translated into words, thus in a way completing the client's communication. The following examples will illustrate:

CL. I was fired yesterday . . . general layoff . . . after all those years at the plant. . . . No idea what to do next.

TH. After many years of steady employment you are jobless now, and you feel totally bewildered.

CL. I just can't take it any longer and must do something.

TH. You're completely fed up and feel you've got to find a way out.

CL. It's so hard knowing she's in the hospital and that there's nothing, absolutely nothing, I can do.

TH. You feel anxious and entirely helpless right now.

CL. You're listening to me all right, but that doesn't do me any good.

TH. You feel that I'm paying attention to what you're saying but that this doesn't get you any closer to solving your problems.

CL. If it had been my sister who had done that, my mother wouldn't have said a thing. It's never been any different.

TH. You feel your mother has always discriminated against you, and you resent it.

CL. Well, I don't know . . . treated us differently. . . . I suppose you're right. I must have felt the discrimination right along; but when you said it, my first impulse was to come to Mother's defense.

Here the client at first found it hard to accept the feeling tone of her own words. In the following excerpt the client rejected the affective content of his words:

CL. You have the right to do what you like. I don't care. Just don't give me all that bull about wanting to help. You don't have to . . . but you don't want to, and that's different.

TH. You feel quite angry with me right now.

CL. No, I don't. You have every right . . .

When the therapist uses reflection, he responds not to his own inner frame of reference but solely to the feeling tone of the client. Thus in the last example the therapist reflected the client's anger instead of reacting to his assertion that he, the therapist, did not want to help. Nor, of course, did the therapist dispute the assertion. He believed that sufficient evidence to the contrary existed but that to bring it out would be harmful at this point because the client's deep anger, not cold facts, was at issue. This the therapist was prepared to face, though the client was not as yet. Later on when the client could accept and explore his anger, he himself recalled the instances of help and began to understand what his anger had really been about.

Interpretation and Explanation

Now, at long last for those who have missed it, the therapist's frame of reference comes into focus. In all the responses so far, he has not expressed himself. If he has spoken at all, he has restricted himself to verbalizing what the client has said or felt. This limitation of self is constricting for many therapists. They wish to get across to the client on their own terms, in their own personal way. To keep silent, say "mm-hm," restate what has been said, or reflect the feeling tone of the client is not enough for them; and to some it is downright uncongenial. Personally I like these classical, nondirective responses and am convinced that clients find them helpful when the therapist feels at ease with them and does not merely employ them as a technique. To my mind, the greatest merit of these responses is that they are, they are bound to be, client-centered. Using them, we respond to him. It is his internal frame of reference that is all-important.

At this point in our discussion the emphasis shifts. The therapist's frame of reference makes its appearance and, as the discussion proceeds, gradually takes over. We move slowly but surely from responses to leads. We are bringing ourselves onstage. The danger is obvious — that we take over at the expense of the client; that we perform instead of her. We may end up enjoying this role so much we do not realize that we have turned her off; that we have put her into the audience, so to speak; that we have made of the client-subject a spectator-object.

There are two kinds of interpretation. The first is based on the internal frame of reference of the client; the second, on the internal frame of reference of the therapist. When I interpret what I have understood from the client's communication to me in terms of his life space, I am responding to him. On the other hand, when I interpret it in terms of my own life space, I have crossed the Rubicon and am expecting to have him respond to me. I am beginning to lead. This distinction is often overlooked but ought not to be. It makes quite a difference whether I translate in terms of how things seem to him or how they seem to me. The Rubicon is a narrow river, but for Caesar it was immense. In the examples of interpretation that follow, therapist responses gradually move in the direction of leads; the frame of reference shifts from client to therapist.

CL. It doesn't matter too much either way. I can get a babysitter for Tuesday if that's more convenient.

TH. I hear you saying that you can come on either day but that Tuesday involves getting a sitter. Thursday is quite convenient for me, so let's make it Thursday. Is that all right?

CL. I haven't had to look for a job in such a long time that I'm sort of overwhelmed by the prospect. I can't quite see myself looking for employment.

TH. I understand you to say that, being used to steady employment right along, you find it difficult to shift over, to see yourself as unemployed and having to act accordingly. It is hard to shift roles in this way and to realize that it is *you* all the while.

CL. . . . I can't cut down on sports. . . . Everyone's been piling on the homework lately, and it's just too much.

TH. You seem to be saying that the teachers are to blame when you don't do all your homework because they give too much and you cannot be flexible about your sports activities.

CL. The truck's been coming late every week this past month, and they haven't been giving me as much work as they used to. I've got the same expenses, though, and you people ought to make good the difference. After all, it's your trucks and all that. . . .

IER. No one else has complained. I'll look into the truck service and the work deliveries, but I'm wondering whether the work satisfies you the way I thought it did.

CL. My older brothers are all working, and my big sister is married and out of the house. So Mother and Dad pick on me because there's no one else around to pick on. I bet they didn't treat the others that way when they were my age. It's not right.

TH. You find it hard to be the baby of the family.

CL. You never know exactly what people are telling you when you can't hear well. When you've got your back turned, well ... then you don't know at all, and they're bound to be talking about you because they know you can't make it out. That's why I don't want the hearing aid. It would only make things worse. Then they wouldn't just guess, they would know, and I'd be sunk. Everyone would take advantage. ...

TH. You're quite suspicious of people, I notice. I wonder whether you realize that you may be causing the very results you fear. Your behavior would antagonize me, too, if I didn't know you better.

Explanation An explanation is a descriptive statement. It may include evaluative overtones — whether intended as such or not — that may be sensed by the client. The therapist may utilize explanation as a lead — in structuring the interview, for example — or as a response to the client's statements and questions. As it is descriptive in character, explanation should be neutral in tone. It says that this is how things are. It implies that we must accept the way things are and behave accordingly. It tends to be impersonal, logical, matter-of-fact.

Not all therapists employ explanation to the same degree. Some hesitate to use it until the client is ready to assimilate it, when it is often superfluous. Other therapists feel that neutral explanation can help the client approach reality or remain within its bounds. Having provided an explanation, some make it a practice to ascertain whether what they have explained has been understood in the way they intended; others take this for granted. Explanation in the interview may be divided into four categories: orientation to situation, behavior, causes, and the therapist's or interviewer's position.

Orientation to Situation

TH. Whatever goes on in this room stays right here, as far as I'm concerned. Here you can feel free to say whatever you like in any way you want to say it. I'll try to help you understand and decide in which direction you want to go.

IER. We have two programs at our rehabilitation center. One is for those who sleep in; the other, for those who prefer to go home every afternoon. The first program is more comprehensive because we have more time available. The other is less comprehensive but enables the person to be with his family in the evenings. . . .

IER. I'm not the principal. I'm the school counselor, but Mr. G. asked me to meet with you. Requests like yours are turned over to me as I have more time at my disposal than the principal. I hope you won't mind discussing it with me. I shall, of course, pass on any decision we reach to Mr. G.

TH. I'm afraid I haven't made myself very clear. The doctor will see you, but only after we have the results of these tests. He is busy, but he is not indifferent. He couldn't even begin to help you without knowing what the tests indicate. As soon as we have the results, I shall arrange an appointment for you.

IER. I suppose that's true. In class I do lose my temper at times. We have forty students, so there you are one out of forty. But now I have time just for you, and I don't think I'll lose my temper. I really want to find out what happened at home last night — not because I'm nosy, but because I'd like to help if I can. I understand it all started when . . .

Explanation of Behavior

TH. Why don't you call me Fred, and I'll call you John. I like first names much better, and I do have trouble remembering family names.

IER. I want to hear what you have to say about it, but the fact is that Miss J. asked me to see you because she feels that your behavior in class disrupts her lessons. She says you either interrupt whoever is speaking or talk to one of your neighbors. She says you just can't keep still.

IER. I'm going to take a blood sample now so that we can test to what extent you are anemic. It won't hurt me a bit and you very little, and it'll help us both to know what we're doing.

TH. You're behaving in here just like that, too. You punch holes in my arguments but won't reveal your own. I don't share your husband's anger, but I'm beginning to see how he' must feel.

TH. Your behavior does seem childish — wanting to be taken care of, finding it hard to stand on your own two feet; finding it easier to play than to work. There's more to it than that, of course, but that's the picture I get. I'm not saying whether it's good or bad but only describing how it strikes me.

TH. I don't know if my explanation is the correct one, but you did say that your father's behavior had changed lately, that he didn't spend as much time at home as he used to, and that your mother said there was another woman to whom he'd become attached. This is obviously hard for you to accept, but it may just possibly be true.

Explanation of Causes

CL. I'm usually quite punctual, but now that you've pointed it out, I see I have been coming late to almost every one of our meetings. I don't get it. Do you?

TH. When punctual people come late time after time, the explanation may be that they are not too anxious to come. They may want to and yet not want to. The wanting to and not wanting to may conflict inside, resulting in latecoming. There may be another explanation, but what do you think of this one as relating to you?

CL. . . . I want you to tell me why I'm afraid of you.

TH. Well, you've indicated several times that I remind you of your mother, and, as I recall it, you were afraid of her at times.

CL. It's because I'm blind that people treat me like that — feeling sorry for me and keeping their distance. That's what the travel instructor said they did, and you can't deny it.

TH. No, I can't deny that being blind is tough on you, but I do feel that the cause of your trouble is not so much your blindness as how you relate to it: how you think and feel about being blind. This is the real cause, as I see it.

CL. O.K., I'll say it: you hate me because of my black skin — because I'm colored and you're white.

TH. To the very best of my knowledge about myself, this is not true. I do dislike you at times but for an entirely different reason: because I feel you aren't treating me as an equal. You act superior and defiant and hostile. You keep well hidden what's underneath that, but when it does come through, I like it fine. So, you see, I reject your explanation. I see it as a defense. You need to be hostile to me because you must assume that I am hostile to you. As for me . . .

Explanation of the Therapist's or Interviewer's Position

IER. I'd like you to know what my stand is because it will probably influence the board. It is that we should take your son back but on a trial basis only. I'm still not sure that this is the best place for him. I know, however, that it will be hard to find something better and so think we should all give him and ourselves another chance — but a limited one, in order to be fair to all concerned.

CL. . . . but why won't you talk to Miss M. about it? You're the school counselor, and she sent me to see you. So why won't you go talk to her?

IER. My position is really very simple. If and when Miss M. wants to discuss the matter with me, I shall be ready to do so. I feel that after all that has happened, it would be better for you to talk with her. After that, the three of us can talk things over, should both of you wish that. You and I have met several times so that I could try to help you clarify things for yourself. I think we've done that. I know my position irritates you, and I'm very sorry for that; but I honestly can't act otherwise.

CL. I can't understand how you people can allow a man like Mr. T. to work around here. He's rude and coarse and should be receiving help himself instead of trying to give it to others.

IER. It's the policy of our agency — and I endorse it fully — that anyone who comes to us has the right to like or dislike whomever he comes in contact with. On the other hand, such likes and dislikes cannot be discussed with other workers of the agency as this might lower morale and lead to shopping around by clients. So I'll have to ask you to stop discussing Mr. T. and pass on to something we can fruitfully talk about.

In many situations, these two responses, interpretation and explanation, merge and elements of both are present in the response. Very often, interpretation — whether from the point of view of the client or of the therapist — assumes more of the characteristics of explanation. In the examples that follow, explanation helps the client make sense of things that often seem confusing and sometimes even mysterious to him. It introduces reason into what may seem to be a totally chaotic situation or behavior. This use of explanation simplifies, categorizes, makes order out of chaos. It shows the client that she is driven by forces she can understand and control. It brings her nearer to reality.

Itamar finally understood his behavior. He needed the seat on each side of him unoccupied so that he could concentrate on the lecture. Were a woman to sit next to him, he would become confused and embarrassed. Women attracted him with such a tremendous force that he could not resist it, and yet he was so bashful and inexperienced that all he could do for the time being was to run away or blockade himself. As for the sharp knife he carried, the explanation seemed clear now — he never used it but could not be without it. If attacked, he planned to use it. With the knife in his pocket he felt safe and powerful. It represented the aggressive feelings he had allowed himself to become aware of only when he had to hurt people in order to save them, or when he endangered his own life carrying wounded and dead from the battlefield. The knife symbolized power and strength; its presence enabled him to control his aggression and to focus it into acceptable channels.

For a long time Emma could not explain to herself why, even though she could not bear Ernest's presence, she did not wish him to leave. She thought she was jealous, that separation would have a harmful effect on the children, that she might even get over her aversion. At long last, and even then reluctantly, she accepted Ernest's explanation that she was simply afraid of having to lower her standard of living, should they separate, and that the financial security she had enjoyed for many years would be jeopardized. Only when she finally realized that she could not have her cake and eat it too did her attitude change. But even during our last session she could not face the thought of divorce; separation was all she could cope with.

Alice and Don could not agree as to the explanation of their recent marital difficulties:

> *She.* If you would tell me things of your own free will, I would not be suspicious.
>
> *He.* Whenever I do tell you things relating to the office, you misunderstand, distort them, and unfairly accuse me of all sorts of nonsense.
>
> *She.* If you had nothing to hide . . .
>
> *He.* But I do have nothing to hide. Lately you've put your nose into business matters that do not concern you and that you just don't understand. If I tell you things there's a blowup and if I don't, you suspect me of all sorts of absurd things.
>
> *She.* Sure, your precious partners come first; the family is way behind. Maybe you don't betray me physically, but mentally you do.
>
> *He.* I don't betray you at all, but you try to run my business. I don't meddle in your school, and I'll thank you not to meddle in my business.
>
> *She.* I'm suspicious for a good reason — I just can't trust you.
>
> *He.* If you can't trust me you have a problem. But the explanation is quite different. You're jealous of the time I spend with my partners and especially of the good times we occasionally have. If you could be less of a sourpuss we could have better times together, but you'd rather just carp.

Having decided to divorce, Carol and John discussed how they should behave toward their only child, a boy of ten. They wanted to assure him that they would always love him and, even when divorced, would remain the best of friends. I felt it imperative to explain to them that this might not be the case. They might not remain good friends once both or even one of them found a new partner.

Feeling guilty concerning their son, they had a need to idealize the situation, but this was not in the best interest of any of them. They both hoped they would go on loving the boy; he should not be encouraged to expect more than that.

Joy and Andy finally agreed on at least one explanation:

TH. I understand your younger child has stopped bedwetting.

She. Yes, at long last! Andy is much better with him now and it is certainly paying off.

He. Joy is wrong about lots of things, but she was right about this. I spend more time with him at bedtime and we both enjoy it. I do miss the news on TV but that can't be helped right now, I tell myself. It's hard to break an old habit, though. Joy says I can watch the news later in the evening, but it's not the same.

She. You married me and not the screen and the boys are yours, too.

He. There you go again. I'm trying my best but I get preached at anyway. I married you and not all those books you read; but I don't tell you that even though I think it.

TH. Anyway, the bedwetting is past history.

Therapist-Centered Leads and Responses

In leading we must be conscious that we are doing so and know whom we are leading and to what end. We must be prepared to retreat once we realize that we have not been helpful. Most important, we must lead in such a way, if we must lead at all, that the client can release himself from our grasp, if he so chooses, without feeling he has hurt or offended us. We must keep in mind that in leading: we encourage the other to be led; we tell him he cannot get there on his own, not yet anyway; we foster dependency, at least for the time being; we assume the responsibility, for the moment at any rate. All this has a cumulative effect. Therefore, if we must lead, we ought to take the consequences of our actions into account. The caveat stated, I can proceed.

Encouragement

I suppose that pretty much everything we do in the helping interview we do to encourage the client in one way or another. Our attitude, our approach, our responses — all are meant to support and reinforce her in her efforts to change in a direction meaningful and worthwhile for her. We wish to assist her in coming closer to reality and to her own self in order that she may explore her present situation and determine her future goals. Our slightest "mm-hm" is meant to spur her on. It tells her: "That's it. Go on. You're on your way. I'm with you. I care." This manner of encouraging is an integral part of our philosophy. Like empathy it is not stated in words; but if it is present in us, the client will sense it. If it is not, our saying that it is will not make it so or deceive her into believing that it is.

Now, however, we shall discuss encouragement of a different sort — a type of lead (at times it is a response) in which encouragement is verbally and openly expressed. What encourages another person? We do not really know. Is he encouraged when we tell him that others suffer more than he does and that they somehow learn to make the best of things? Is he encouraged when we say that time is a great healer and that in a short while the world will seem a more cheerful place to him? Is he encouraged when we aver that we shall support him just as long as he feels he needs us — the implication being that he can lean on us because we are strong and he is weak? Whether or not he is fundamentally encouraged and strengthened, we do not know.

These questions I believe to be of basic importance. Every therapist finds operational answers to them. My stand, I trust, is made clear in Chapter 3. It necessarily colors my approach throughout this book, particularly regarding the leads to be discussed (we shall be concerned mostly with leads from now on). These leads are in general usage because the assumption is that they are helpful. Undoubtedly they sometimes are. Nevertheless, they do tend to push and pressure the client from the outside, from the frame of reference of someone else — a someone who is looked upon and sees himself as superior, as an authority figure. These leads may be internalized by the client and thus serve to strengthen him; on the other hand, they may not. He may pay lip service to our various attempts to help, feeling cornered by them instead of strengthened or really helped, and wishing nothing more than to escape the situation as unscathed as possible.

In the past, I refrained from the use of encouragement just because of the pressuring it involves. I thought then that all had to come from within the client. I know better today. True, the ultimate decision is hers and she will have to be the one to execute it. But sometimes she is a little hesitant, uncertain of her capabilities and eventual success. Since deciding in itself is not always sufficient, I am willing to verbally encourage her to act. Once having acted, it will be easier to act again, to act more readily and more successfully.

Morris had felt so frustrated about teaching music that he had stopped composing. He moped around till the early hours of the morning feeling sorry for himself. He missed composing and, especially, hearing new compositions of his on radio and TV. If he could once more compose, he was sure he would feel better and function more effectively in other areas of life. When pressed, he admitted that he could compose if he would just get down to it. Together, we worked out a schedule of hours for composition. I suggested that he bring his new songs so we might listen to and discuss them. I accepted no excuses for procrastination. Morris began working in earnest again. When the first fruits of his renewed labor were performed on a prime-time TV program, he admitted that he hardly minded teaching any more.

Dora decided to drive on her own again. She had become sick and tired of being chauffeured about but still felt very insecure about driving on her own. At my suggestion she came with a list of places in her immediate neighborhood that she would like to be able to get to by car, and we worked out a program she felt she could follow. She now drives a little every day and is gradually expanding the radius of her drives. Dora is still not prepared to drive alone to our sessions, but we have begun to plan this as well.

Harry was fed up with his job. He played around with the idea of enrolling in a course for tourist guides, but that would entail attending classes three times weekly after work and traveling a rather long distance to the town where the course was being given. He vacillated, fearing that his lack of concentration might impede progress. He also worried about the possibility of renewed headaches, as well as intensification of the spots he still saw occasionally. With a little encouragement he was able to apply, was accepted, and did very well. He could concentrate far better than he had expected and after a short time the spots "miraculously" disappeared.

Assurance-Reassurance

We use assurance or reassurance as leads to tell the client in words that we believe in his capability to act and overcome obstacles, to face up to his situation successfully. In effect, we are also showing him that we can see further ahead than he, that he can safely place his trust in us, that it is up to him to act but that he requires a little pat on the back from us to help him on his way. Thus we indicate that he needs an external influence to keep him going or get him started and that this we shall provide. The following examples range from mild to heavy reassurance, openly expressed:

> CL. I can't face him.

To this different therapists may reply:

> TH. You haven't tried; it may not be as bad as you think.

> TH. I'm not so sure you can't; I rather suspect you can.

> TH. Can't you? That's one man's opinion; this man thinks otherwise.

> TH. Of course you can. I can't come with you, but I shall be there in spirit.

> TH. It's hard, I know; but you can and you must.

> CL. . . . I really don't know if I'll come again.

> TH. Well, it's up to you, but I think you should. You've done very nicely today, and next time I'm sure you'll do even better.

CL. I'll never get a job — the way I look.

TH. Not so fast there, young man. Rome wasn't built in a day. We've just begun to explore the possibilities, and you already want to throw in the sponge. Let's see now . . .

CL. (sobbing) It's just awful!

TH. I know . . . it's been pretty rough going. . . . Try to stop crying now. You'll feel much better tomorrow, and the world will look brighter.

CL. She hates me; I have proof.

TH. Now stop this, your mother does love you. She herself has told me so. She means to be nice to you, and I know you want to try hard to be nice to her. I assure you everything will work out if we all just get in there together. She is willing, and so am I. You'll see. . . .

CL. My legs will be all right, won't they? They must be. If they're not, I'm going to kill myself!

TH. Now, just relax. Everything will be all right. The doctors are doing everything they can, and you know that medicine today can perform miracles. You'll be O.K. I'm just sure you will be. As for . . . well, I know you didn't mean that. Everything will work out fine.

Often heavy reassurance, stressing conscience, borders on moralizing. It may suggest disbelief as well — as though the therapist were saying, "You couldn't possibly" or "I can't believe you would." These leads will be discussed later.

Suggestion

Suggestion is a mild form of advice. Its overtones tend to be tentative and vague. In it the therapist proffers a possible line of action. Suggestion does not demand compliance or threaten the client with rejection should he not follow it through. I am speaking of genuine suggestion, of course, not of masked command. Suggestion provides the client with the therapist's considered opinions but leaves her leeway to accept, refuse, or propose ideas of her own. Indeed, its purpose may be to stimulate the client to think and plan for herself. When this is the therapist's sincere intention, suggestion communicates: "I think my idea is a good one and may work. It's up to you, of course, to decide." If clearly stated as suggestion and genuinely intended as such, it is open rather than closed, provisional rather than final. It is equal speaking to equal, one of whom may possess more information, knowledge, or experience but is not determined to force it on the other. Suggestion may be offered at the client's request, or it may be unsolicited.

> CL. . . . I can't come up with anything else. Do you have any ideas?

> TH. I was thinking that it might be helpful to take him out of nursery school for a while and keep him at home so he could see just what you do with the baby, instead of imagining all sorts of things the way he has been doing.

> CL. I can't make up my mind whether to get married in the spring or to finish college first. You know what I mean. . . .

> TH. I think I do and suggest you try to talk it over with Bob from your viewpoint. He might surprise you after all. Then when you come in next week, we can discuss it further. How does that sound to you?

> TH. I have a suggestion to make if you'd like to hear it. It's just an idea I have, and I'll offer it for what it may be worth. If you took that job at the X company, which involves fewer hours, you might be able to take enough credits at night to finish in two years and yet be financially independent. You might even get a loan from the university. I'm sort of thinking out loud. How do you feel about all this?

> TH. My suggestion is to go in there and do it. You've been hesitating quite awhile, and we've looked into all of the angles. If you don't make up your mind soon, you'll miss the boat. They don't care about how you feel but about what you can do; and you can do it. So I suggest you get started. That's the way I feel, in any case.

Advice

Whether or not to give advice has been and remains a controversial issue that, unfortunately, cannot be resolved here. Again it is a matter of personal philosophy. Advice, essentially, is telling someone else how to behave, what to do or not to do. It may be offered directly or indirectly; nonthreateningly or as an ultimatum. It may be tendered because we really feel that this is what the client should do in his own best interest or because we feel compelled to release ourselves from a difficult situation and the easiest way is to give "disinterested" advice. We may proffer it to fulfill our need to dominate or to satisfy his need to submit. When the client cannot make up his own mind and, even after having examined the alternatives as thoroughly as possible, still cannot move in any given direction, I may proffer advice — naturally, only when requested to do so and when able to comply. In this situation, I am making a decision with the client but, to some extent, for him. If, when having understood the advice, he accepts and tries it out, it is imperative that we follow up on it afterward, examining the results as nondefensively as possible. Only then can the client derive maximal benefit from the advice. I must, of course, be very careful to keep my mind open and my perceptions keen and enable the client to adjust the advice to his own needs and capabilities, not to mine. In other words, he must remain at the center of our deliberations; the advice must be discarded should this prove necessary.

Before looking more closely at advice giving. I want to relate a personal experience that occurred some years ago and to this day aids me in decisions concerning advice. A woman once came to see me and began the interview by declaring: "I've consulted with many people and received lots of advice. I didn't like any of it, and so now I've come to you to see what you've got to say. My problem is . . ." Because I am convinced that all of us give advice much more often than we realize and because this issue is a basic one in the helping interview, I want to outline my views regarding it. Let me begin by considering advice that has actually — or at least verbally — been requested by the client. The first step, I believe, is not to comply immediately with the request but rather to discover what the client herself thinks about the situation under discussion and what alternatives — if any — she has considered. When the woman in my story learned that I refused to play at her game, she eventually suggested herself the "advice" she had been waiting to hear from someone else. However limited may be the application of the lesson I learned that day, still I feel certain that when the therapist is asked for advice, it is essential that he first of all enable the client to identify and delimit the areas in which she seeks advice. The client should be encouraged to verbalize her hopes and fears regarding these areas — in brief, to throw as much light as possible on her own situation.

"I wonder what alternatives you have been considering."

"I realize that you are terribly concerned about this. Perhaps if you can tell me the various alternatives you have considered and how you feel about them, we may be able to arrive at something that makes sense for you."

"I wonder if you have discussed this matter with other people and how you feel about what they had to say. Perhaps if we understand what you exclude, we may be able to come up with something positive."

"I feel that all of us can profit from advice only — if at all — when it falls on fertile soil, so to speak; if you can tell me more about your own thoughts on the matter, we may be able to come up with something fruitful for you."

Obviously, innumerable ways to express this exist, but the aim is always to gather all possible thoughts and feelings from the client concerning the subject on which he wants advice. At times this alone is sufficient to enable him to reach a decision. At other times slight clarification on our part will lead to positive results. In the event that the client cannot reach his own solution, at least we shall have obtained from him as much information as we are likely to receive. No one can benefit from advice unless it is meaningful to him, unless he understands it in terms of his own frame of reference, and until he has expressed himself sufficiently so that he can really listen to the advice he claims he wants. Only then can he look upon it as meant for him in his particular life space.

Now arises the question of whether I, the therapist, feel I have the right on moral, professional, or simply human grounds to give advice. If I conclude that I do not, I should say so openly and clearly.

"It's hard for you to decide, but I feel I have no moral right to do it for you. These are your children, and the decision as to whether to leave them with your wife's parents or to stay with them is one, I'm afraid, you'll have to make on your own."

"This lies beyond my professional competence. All I can do is to recommend a qualified physician who may be able to give you sound advice. But even here, different doctors have different approaches; and my guess is that, ultimately, you will have to make up your own mind."

"What should I do in your place? Honestly I can't say. I've tried to understand how things seem to you, but I cannot say whether they would look like this to me if I were you. As you will have to live with your decision, I don't want to influence it unduly. I have a feeling, however, that we have not yet considered all the aspects of the home in X. . . ."

Sometimes, giving advice is easy. Bob telephoned from abroad. No, he didn't intend to return yet. Once again he had gambled and lost and was ashamed to return for the moment. First he would earn the money to repay his debts but . . . should he tell his parents? He could not face them even on the phone; yet they would worry terribly. I strongly advised calling. He demurred. I advised that under these circumstances I should call them. To this he gave his consent.

Anne could not decide. Bert was leaving on an extended lecture tour in the States and wanted her to join him. At first she laughed off the idea. To fly to the United States and then to fly from city to city, moving from unfamiliar hotel to unfamiliar hotel — that was much too much for her! On the other hand, Bert was so disappointed. She was afraid to go and afraid not to. In answer to her question I strongly advised that she join Bert. She was afraid, but fear is part of life; it can be dealt with and, if not overcome, tolerated — certainly with Anne this was so. We planned and role-played and considered possible emergencies. As their day of departure approached, Anne became more enthusiastic and, at the same time, more fearful. Before and during flights and, at first, in unfamiliar surroundings she was anxious but she coped, enjoyed the trip, and returned extremely proud of her achievement.

I have a hunch that when clients ask for my advice, they know beforehand quite well what it will be. They request it because it is exactly the line they wish to pursue but require external assurance and encouragement. They receive the advice they are actually seeking — another form of encouragement.

It is essential that the therapist ask herself whether she has a need to give advice, in specific instances or generally. Such a need may interfere with the client's struggle to decide what is best for him. The therapist's need to advise may prematurely cut off the joint examination of the matter under discussion. If the therapist can become aware of this need, she may think twice before giving advice and ask herself whether it has been solicited and whether it is, in fact, required.

I feel it is also important that the therapist examine to what extent the client feels he cannot decide alone. The client may have learned to regard himself as someone who requires the advice of others, who is incompetent to choose, who must always be dependent on a "specialist." Am I then really helping by tendering the advice he seeks? May I not be reinforcing his negative concept of himself? Will he be able to build upon my advice, or will advice seeking lead to more advice seeking, dependence to more dependence? Does he possess the inner resources required to carry out someone else's advice, or will he ask for more in order to reinforce it? Would I possibly be of more assistance by withholding advice, by attempting to show him what is involved in his seeking it and enabling him to change his self-concept?

When rapport is good and the therapist is genuine, he can allow himself to say to the other: "No, I will not solve your vocational dilemma for you. You seem to see yourself as a poor, unfortunate cripple, but I don't. If I were to tell you what to do, you would have a basis for thinking that I consider you one. Then there would be two of us with that opinion. I'd rather there be none, but if there must be one, it won't be me. So let's get down to business and consider what you ought to be doing with the rest of your life as far as work is concerned."

It is often easier to advise than to become more deeply involved in the struggles of another. This interviewer acted not from weakness but from strength. He did not take the easy way out, and his refusal to succumb was in the end justified.

Sometimes, especially when the contact is brief and superficial and we sincerely believe that we cannot help the client effect a change in herself, it may seem unavoidable to give advice and be done with it. Unfortunately, many of us feel we must act in this manner at times. A stone wall confronts us, and all we have in the way of tools is a chisel.

> CL. You're the counselor here . . . you've got to know what my son should study. I don't know, and I don't care as long as it's an honest living. You're getting paid for giving advice. If I knew what school to send him to, I wouldn't waste my valuable time coming to you. I've got better things to do.

> IER. Perhaps you'll let me discuss this matter of schools with your son. He may know in which direction . . .

> CL. Oh no! You're going to tell me, and I'll tell him; and he'd better listen to me if he knows what's good for him.

Having weighed all these considerations, the interviewer must still ask himself a few final questions before, at long last, he provides the best advice he can. "Do I know enough about what is involved to give advice? Do I possess enough factual information, as well as sufficient knowledge of the expressed thoughts and feelings of the client, so that my advice will be sound and meaningful for him? Have we arrived at the stage where my advice may truly aid him?" A single example will suffice.

> IER. Well, I believe we have looked into this matter of housing for you and your family quite thoroughly. Considering everything you have told me and the housing situation as I know it, I feel that it would be best not to move at this point. This isn't an ideal solution for you, I know, and it will be particularly hard on Jim; but, on the other hand, you seem to feel sure that you can handle his school difficulties for another year. By then, things may have changed. . . .

Now that advice has been provided, how does the client perceive, understand, and react to it? The best way of ascertaining this may be to ask him to restate it in his own words. In the above instance, Jim's mother felt the interviewer had put into words her own uncrystallized thoughts. The advice seemed sound to her, and they agreed to meet again the following year to consider what ought to be done then. If an interviewer gives advice within the framework delineated above, she will wish to elicit an open reaction to it. She may say: "I wonder how you react to this" or "It would be helpful to both of us if you would tell me what you really think of this advice. Since it is meant for you, it is important to know whether you feel it will be useful to you."

Occasionally therapists and interviewers fall into a trap. The client seeks advice to prove that it is worthless and, by implication, that the giver is as well. If we are caught, it will not be because we have had no warning, and we shall have to devise our own means of escape. This reflection leads me to a more general consideration: How do we feel and react when our opinion, judgment, advice are rejected? Do we take it as a personal affront, or can we cope with it? Do we perhaps even enjoy watching the client make his own decision by tearing ours down? Do we thrust these "pearls" of ours upon him, or do we display them in order that he may examine them and decide for himself which, if any, to acquire for his own use?

How do we feel when our advice is accepted — and doesn't work? At least, the client claims it doesn't work for her. Do we then have to defend our own wisdom, or do we seek to understand what is happening to the client? What if our advice works for the client and, glowing with gratitude, she returns and requests more advice, guidance, and direction? We are so wise. Why not pour out just a little more of that profound wisdom? When we feel that this is a bit too much, whom do we blame, with whom do we become angry? We can resolve our doubts quite nicely by categorizing her as an ungrateful nuisance and a dependent being. We, of course, meant only to help, but some people, we tell ourselves, just take advantage. And that solves it — for us.

Those interviewers who insist on giving advice even when it is unsolicited, I have found, tend to be the ones who resent it most when the advice is rejected or misunderstood. Underlying the advice seems to be a kind of ultimatum: Take it or leave me. However, even if the interviewer has no need to control others, he may still find it necessary on occasion to offer advice not specifically requested. He may hit upon something the client does not know, has not considered, or regards as out of the question for him. If he can offer such advice and not feel rejected should it be turned down, if he offers it deliberately, keeping the reservations referred to in mind, he will not be endangering the relationship.

> *IER.* Have you ever considered becoming a professional photographer? You obviously like photography and spend a lot of time at it. In terms of your disability, this might work — and you might do for a living what you seem to enjoy doing as a hobby. Perhaps you want to think it over. We could discuss it when you come in next week. If you think of anything else, we could also discuss that.

One last word. When advice has been given, it should be followed up. I feel we should meet with the client again or at least communicate in some way to ascertain to what extent our advice has proved helpful. If it has not aided, we may wish to explore the situation with the client to learn what went amiss. This will provide an indispensable source of feedback for the interviewer interested in professional growth and personal development. Also, it will indicate to the client that advice giving is not necessarily the final stage in our relationship — unless he decides it should be because he no longer needs us. Should he wish to return and we have not left the door wide open, he may hesitate, fearing that we shall be displeased with the way he carried out the advice. We must convince him by our behavior that we are far more interested in him than in any advice we have given. More often than not, people accept advice and leave; and we never hear from them again. The advice may or may not have been useful. In either event we should want to know. If we have left the door open, we can always continue where advice giving left off or start afresh. Closed doors constitute a barrier to further communication.

Urging

Urging, which is so closely related to persuasion and cajoling that I shall not try to differentiate between them, is a lead or response the purpose of which is to prod the client, to not let her escape what, in our opinion, she should not evade. Urging involves supporting in order to strengthen the client's determination to carry out whatever it is that both partners have discussed and the therapist, at least, feels would be beneficial to the client. It relates to the practical aspects of a theoretical discussion or agreement. For example, both may agree that the client ought to resume her studies. This remains theoretical as long as the therapist does nothing about it. The therapist urges, cajoles, and persuades the client to spur her into action, to turn theory into practice.

Frequently, urging takes place after advice has been ostensibly accepted by the client or at least has not been rejected outright. This is the very point at which urging may be dangerous. We have given advice in good faith and assume the client has accepted it, but nothing further happens. He does not move to carry it out. So we urge, cajole, persuade. We build on what we believe to be the solid foundation of our advice without checking to see whether this foundation is of sand or stone. What is needed here is less urging and more examining of the life space of the client. Perhaps this is his way of rejecting our advice. Perhaps this is his way of letting us know that theoretically the advice is sound but that practically, for him at least, it is irrelevant. This refusal to budge may well be his way of communicating that we must seek another alternative, one that will prove more meaningful for him.

Sometimes, I admit, urging has positive results. Ultimately, our support and belief in the client may strengthen him sufficiently to enable him to act. Even in this event, I am certain that we must always check whether we are supporting and showing belief in the client or in our own advice. Behind the client's rejection of or resistance to our advice, expressed in hesitation or inaction, may just possibly glimmer the sparks of self-initiated action. By recognizing this tiny flame and kindling it, we give the most significant help of all.

In summary, I propose that when you discover that you are urging, take note of the effect this produces on the client. Are you inadvertently forcing her to the wall? Are you urging *your* case, assuming it to be hers as well? What is *her* case? What can you both learn from a situation in which a line of action theoretically agreed upon breaks down when the time comes to carry it out? Are you so engrossed in urging that you cannot see anything else, even the client's attempt to come to grips with her own problem in her own way? Are you listening to her with all the understanding you can muster, or do you insist she listen to you and get moving? Following are a few illustrations:

> TH. I thought we had agreed you would write that letter. Of course, talking about it won't get it written. You thought it such a good idea just a few days ago, and here you are, and the letter isn't written yet.

> CL. It was a good idea of yours and still is. I tried several times, but I tore them all up. They just weren't right. Perhaps I just can't do it.

> TH. But of course you can. It needn't be a literary masterpiece. It just needs to be written. I have pen and paper right here. Why don't you try to write it now, while we're on the subject?

> CL. I just can't. I've been thinking things over, and ... I thought it might be better, after all, to tell it to him in person. It'll be hard to say it; but since I can't write it, perhaps I have no other choice.

Here the client proposed a course of action more meaningful to her. The therapist, in spite of her initial urging, was able to listen and to pick this up. The two of them examined it together, and eventually the therapist was able to support the client in this course. The letter remained unwritten, but the conversation took place. Although it was far from satisfactory, it was better than nothing. In time, more conversations followed between the client and her estranged son. However, not all clients are as determined, nor are all interviewers as perceptive and as prepared to retreat in order to advance afresh. For example:

> IER. Well, how did it go?

> CL. It didn't ... I mean, I never showed up. It was very nice of you to make the appointment but ... I just couldn't go.

> IER. It wasn't easy to arrange that appointment for you. I really don't understand. After all, you agreed it would be best to see the head of the department, and so I went out of my way to get him to see you and now ...

CL. I'm very sorry, but I just couldn't face up to it.

IER. Being sorry doesn't help us. He's an extremely busy man, and I don't know if I can arrange another appointment. However, I'll try. I'll let you know if and when he will see you. I won't give up and won't let you throw up your hands either. He's a nice man in his own way, and, in any case, he won't bite.

CL. That's really very good of you; but on thinking it over, I've kind of given up the . . .

IER. Well, one can't give up that easily. I won't, and you won't. It may be slightly embarrassing for me to explain — but I don't care. I'll get another appointment for you, and this time you'll go. Once you're in that office talking to him, you'll see that it isn't half as bad as you anticipate it to be right now. We've come so far, and we can't give up now.

CL. I don't even know whether I want to work there . . .

IER. Come on now — of course you want to work there; that's all we've talked about for weeks now. You're hesitating, but I'm not. Right now it seems difficult, but some day you'll appreciate all this. It took us such a long time to make up your mind in any direction that we must keep at this till we succeed. You'll see; it won't be bad at all, and once it's over you'll be all set.

The appointment was duly made; the client did not appear. The interviewer thought he recognized irresponsibility, ingratitude, and lack of cooperation. The contact was broken off.

Below are two final examples of urging in which previous advice giving was not involved:

CL. I could do homework at my friend's house.

TH. You could study there, but you don't.

CL. I think my mother would be insulted — you know, like my house wasn't good enough for me, or something.

TH. We could check on that, but I'm sure your mother would be pleased with the arrangement. In our last talk she told me how hard it was for you to do homework with all the little ones around. As for studying at Bob's house, that might help Bob, too. You know it's hard for him to settle down before late in the evening, and this way both of you might profit.

CL. Well, I never really tried it.

TH. Why don't you, and see how it goes? You could ask your mother, too, and let me know if I understood her correctly or not. If you try it this week, we could talk about it next week. Do you think you are going to try?

CL. If Mother agrees, I'll try it.

TH. I really think you ought to. I'll see you next week.

Contrast the above example with the following:

TH. This is the setup at our center. It may seem rigid, but you must go through all the prescribed activities so that the instructors can evaluate your performance and determine what you are best suited for.

CL. Yes, but so much of this stuff is childish and . . .

TH. I can only urge you again to make the best of things. If instead of complaining you had gone ahead, by now you might already be done with the simpler tasks. No one wants to hold you back, but there are certain procedures . . .

CL. I think I could do better at . . .

TH. If you would only conform, it would be to your best advantage.

Moralizing

Moralizing is a mixture of advice giving and urging with one significant addition. When the therapist simply advises and persuades, she relies on her own judgment. For her, at least, this suffices. When she moralizes, however, she resorts to new weapons; she brings more powerful ammunition into action. She arrays these forces against the client to make him "see the light."

The main weapons the therapist chooses are those two the client will find most difficult to combat: conscience — his own, the therapist's, or Everyman's; and morals — those sacred, social norms no one in his right senses could possibly oppose or even question.

The client is trapped. To surrender is to admit defeat. To resist is to declare himself an outlaw. Shall he bend the knee or raise his head in challenge? Thus beleaguered, he may act in a number of ways, but the chances are it will be acting, pretense. What is really happening within himself he is sure to keep well hidden. The foe is too formidable, the pressure too great, for anything but playacting or evasion.

True, it may not always be playacting; the "culprit" may genuinely feel guilty and be shocked by his own behavior. Moralizing has been known to work. His head falls upon his breast; he is deeply sorry and admits defeat. The therapist has triumphed. But has the client really been helped? What has he learned from this experience that will enrich his life and stimulate change in a direction meaningful for him? I venture the guess that he has probably learned to be more careful in the future so that he will not get caught again; or to accept the fact that resistance against an enemy so powerful is hopeless and that hence the wisest course is to submit, or comply; to give up trying to find himself and, instead, study the foe and emulate him.

On the other hand, if the client is genuinely indignant and refuses to submit, if, openly defiant, he challenges the foe to do his worst, what has he learned that will enable him to change in a worthwhile direction? Here experience tells me he has usually learned that the enemy is powerful indeed and that in order to survive he must become more powerful still. He must become shrewd to outwit him. He must become a master of strategy. He may seem to submit, temporarily disarming his opponent, at present personified by the therapist, in order to strike out hard at the first opportunity. He may, on the contrary, not give an inch but hold his ground as well as he can, never getting close to his own self because he is too busy withdrawing, defending, attacking.

You may consider my outlook one-sided and insist that moralizing is a useful agent in the helping interview at times. I shall not argue the point any further, but I must add one comment. Check and double-check, for appearances may be mislead-lug. Do not be content with present words, but observe future behavior. If you have been victorious, examine at what price your victory has been won; if defeated, think again before you reject the client as "hopeless." Moralizing can be overwhelming. At best, it helps the client see how society judges her, how others look upon her behavior. At worst, it blocks examination of self and self-motivated action and stifles further expression of feelings and attitudes. It can result in insightless submission or stubborn defiance. In the following illustrations moralizing is utilized both as lead and as response:

TH. Helping your dad for a couple of hours in the afternoon really isn't such a terrible thing. Your sister takes care of the entire household, and you want to do your share, I'm sure. I know it's hard not to play with the other boys, but you'll feel much better if you carry your share of the burden. Life isn't always a bed of roses; and, believe me, lots of boys have it much harder than you. For your departed mother's sake I know you'll want to make the effort.

CL. (silence . . . tears . . . silence)

IER. You should have let me know when you thought of giving up the job. Jobs aren't easy to come by, and other people gave their time and energy to find you this one. Anyone else in your position would be glad to have. . . .

CL. No, they wouldn't. Just because I've got a disability doesn't mean I've got to put up with all that crap. I should have let you know. Maybe some sucker could take it, but I can't and I won't.

IER. You must learn to live with your handicap. Jobs you can do are hard to find. Anyway, it couldn't have been as bad as you say.

CL. It was, but I should have let you know. I'm sorry about that.

IER. Being sorry doesn't help now.

CL. What do you want me to do, get down on my knees? If you don't have another job, just say so.

IER. No, I don't have one right now; and, anyway, first I have to consider those who are willing to make a real effort. Call me next month, O.K.?

In closing, let me cite some even more extreme examples of moralizing:

TH. You'll just have to make do with the allowance. Others manage quite well. You yourself admit that you drink a "little" and smoke too much. Saying that you're nervous won't feed your family or clothe them either. You'll just have to get control of yourself. Of course, you love your family. So you'll just have to make an effort to prove it — not to me, but to them. They'll respect you the more for it, and you'll feel less nervous.

CL. (silence)

CL: I don't like Mr. J. one bit. He yells all the time, and he's unfair. He even calls kids names.

TH. I don't understand how you can say something like that even if you feel it. Mr. J. has told me how much he likes you and how hard he tries to get you to behave. I think you really ought to be ashamed of yourself. With your attitude you won't get very far in this world. People try to help you, and you go around saying unkind things about them. I suppose you were just a little angry then and don't really mean it, do you?

CL. (silence)

CL. You don't know my mother. If she could, she'd get rid of me. She's ashamed of me and hides me whenever she can. I wish I were dead.

TH. Now stop that nonsense. You're making it all up. It isn't right to talk this way about your mother after all she has done and is doing for you. I'm really surprised, a smart boy like you. Doesn't your conscience tell you that you're wrong?

CL. (silence)

Authority Leads and Responses

Now we are about to discuss the last group of leads and responses in this survey. Here, too, I make no attempt to be exhaustive and merely point up some of the major leads and responses falling into this category. In this group the therapist perceives his role in a specific light and acts accordingly. Before we consider these leads and responses, therefore, let me say a few words about the philosophy underlying the therapist's perception.

As we have proceeded in this chapter, we have witnessed a gradual change of attitude on the part of the therapist. Except for minor deviations, we have moved along a continuum until we have arrived at the present point in our discussion. Let us look back now and examine this continuum. Although relatively fluid, it starts from a position in which the client is central throughout the interviewing process and gradually shifts to the opposite position, in which the therapist emerges as the central figure.

At one end of the continuum, the therapist sees the client as responsible for herself, as her own authority over herself. The therapist treats the client as an equal; he listens to her, tries to understand her empathically, and accepts her as she is. The therapist attempts to clarify, to describe rather than evaluate, the thoughts and feelings expressed by the client. He does his best to eliminate communication obstacles and is ready to assist the client to move in the direction of meaningful change. When the therapist considers it potentially helpful, he, as an equal in the interviewing process and as a congruent human being (Rogers, 1951), expresses his own ideas and feelings. He does not impose these on the client but presents them as coming from an interested participant. His concern is not whether his ideas and feelings are adopted but whether they can help the client come to grips with those ideas and feelings within herself that will mobilize her in the direction she chooses.

As the picture gradually changes until finally the therapist occupies the center of the interviewing stage, we reach the point where the therapist, willingly and consciously, sees himself as the authority. He accepts responsibility for what occurs in the interview and behaves and acts accordingly. He defines his role as a helping one, but for him, to help means to guide, to instruct, and, if necessary, to coerce. Inasmuch as he is the superior in the inter-

view, for what other purpose could he be there? His authority de-
rives from his knowledge, his skills, and his position and must be
openly employed for the benefit of the client. He is clear about
values. He, at least, knows right from wrong, good from bad,
proper from improper, and says so in no uncertain terms. He may
listen to the client and does his best to understand him; but he
knows that, sooner or later, he will have to act — and he is prepared to do so. Once he has decided on the course to follow, he
does not hesitate to instruct the client in which direction to
move. As he perceives it, this is the help the client came to get,
and in all fairness it is up to him to provide it. There are shadings
at this end of the continuum also, but, essentially, the attitudes
and behavior of the therapist reflect the philosophy here out-
lined. I have tried to describe the authority position without
bias; but because it is alien to my personal philosophy, I may
have overstated or understated it. (For more detailed treatment
of this subject, consult the Supplementary Reading List at the
end of this book.)

Having considered the philosophy underlying the authority position, we are ready to discuss those leads and responses that are
based on the clear assumption that under normal circumstances
the therapist will be able to solve the client's problem once he
diagnoses it — provided, of course, that the client is prepared to
cooperate, listen when necessary, and obey when ordered to do so.

Agreement-Disagreement

Here the therapist or interviewer tells the client whether in her
opinion the latter is right or wrong. Having gathered enough information from the client, as well as from other sources when necessary, and relying heavily on her own experience and background,
she states her position. Taking for granted that her judgment is
sound, she naturally wants the client to treat it seriously. Here
are some representative examples:

> CL. I still can't make up my mind. I wonder whether the
> test results can help me to decide. I still want engineering,
> but . . .

> IER. All the data lead me to think that engineering is the
> right course for you. The test results, as well as everything

else you have told me, indicate that you are on the right track. I am clear on that; but if you hesitate much longer, you may miss the boat for next year's registration.

CL. Don't you think that being blind is just the worst thing that can happen to a person?

TH. Well, frankly, I don't. It's hard being blind, I agree. But being totally deaf or bedridden, for example, is much worse. You may find this hard to believe at this point, but with time you'll see that I'm right.

CL. . . . and I'm sure it wasn't only Hitler and his guys who were responsible for starting the war, and I can't see blaming the Germans for everything that went on.

TH. You are quite wrong there. As you get older and read more on the subject, you will understand this better.

CL. Doctor, can I get up tomorrow? I so much want to.

IER. I agree. As a matter of fact, if you hadn't asked me, I would have told you to anyway. One hour out of bed tomorrow, O.K.?

CL. You said you'd let me know today whether you agree or not.

TH. I've thought it over carefully, and I personally can't agree. I'm convinced you and John can work things out, and I'm prepared to help you as much as I can. That's only my opinion of course, but there are years of experience behind it. You just think it over and let me know.

Approval-Disapproval

Approval-disapproval is similar to agreement-disagreement. However, the question not of right or wrong but of good or bad is involved. The therapist expresses a value judgment when, from his frame of reference, this seems appropriate. He evinces approval or disapproval of the client's behavior, contemplated plans, or outlook on life.

TH. Have you finally made up your mind to enter the competition?

CL. Uh, yes.

TH. That's fine. I wish you success.

CL. Jack and I are going to open our own photography shop.

TH. Good; I'm glad. Jack is such a nice fellow. I'm sure you two will make a go of it. Now I'm ready to discuss the other matters.

CL. The way I see it, if I work all summer and stop fooling around, I can earn enough to get the car and still get ready for the exams in the fall.

IER. That's wonderful. I was hoping that this is what you would decide. I'm sure you've chosen correctly; and as I told you, our agency is always glad to help fine boys like you.

Disapproval is a response I dislike but which I have learned over the years to use in good conscience. Disapproval may not promote helpful interaction but when properly employed should help prevent potential situations that might prove undesirable, harmful, or even dangerous. It tells the client: I don't go along with this line of action and I shall prevent it if I can.

Disapproving, I throw my professional weight around but I do so consciously most often in order to protect the client and his privacy. I refuse to discuss Sol with Erna, behind his back, even though she is his wife and even at the risk of her disrupting his therapy. I resist the attempts of Emma's parents to pump me concerning their daughter although, my explanations notwithstanding, that makes them angry and resentful.

Charles's hold on sanity has been precarious for years and he is well aware of the fact. But he is envious of Elsa and when she attends a week-long group dynamics workshop, he insists on doing the same. Luckily, he has enough discrimination to solicit my opinion. I ask him to come in to discuss the matter, although he had hoped the phone would suffice. I explain my opposition to his plan as clearly as possible. I disapprove in order to prevent his possible breakdown. Charles is furious but, deep down, shares my concern. Had he been confident of his intended step, he would never have contacted me.

When Sid and Diane came to me, he had just finished an affair . . . or had he? After phoning for an appointment, a young woman came in. For once, I was sorry that I do not request more information before making appointments over the phone. She introduced herself as Sid's mistress. The affair was far from over and she wished to know details about Sid and Diane and their marriage. Under the circumstances I could hardly be helpful and, when she became petulant, simply showed her the door.

Luckily for me, the need to disapprove arises only rarely. As for its opposite, approval, it takes the form of advice or encouragement and needs no further mention.

Opposition and Criticism

Both opposition and criticism were either openly expressed or implied in some of the preceding leads and responses. When the therapist opposes, she is saying no to a contemplated course of action. When she criticizes, she unambiguously expresses her displeasure with the client's "bad" conduct or "mistaken" action. The therapist, from her vantage point, is certain that this opposition or criticism is well-founded.

CL. I wish all of you would stop picking on me!

TH. I don't like your tone of voice. I for one am not picking on you, as you put it. You've been rude ever since you came in here, but I've tried to overlook it. I've tried to stretch out my hand to you in friendship, but you keep slapping it down. I won't have any more of this. Now it's up to you.

CL. I'd like to go down to the post office alone. I'm working well with my dog, and I want to get my own stamps.

IER. Sorry, but you can't. I appreciate your desire for independence, but in my opinion you just aren't ready yet. Two more days of hard practice, and I may be able to allow it. What stamps do you need?

CL. . . . I want to come in late on Monday. I've something important to take care of in the morning. Anyway, till they get things set up in the workshop on Mondays, I wouldn't miss more than a couple of hours, and I could make it up.

IER. Sorry, Bob, that won't do at all. If everybody did that, there'd be no one here. When you get out into industry, you won't be able to come and go whenever you like. Whatever you have to take care of can't be so important that it must be done first thing Monday morning. What is it, by the way?

Disbelief

Disbelief does not necessarily imply that the therapist suspects the client is lying. It does assume that the client's perception of a given situation is incorrect or distorted and that the therapist, from his position, can detect this and present an undistorted, more objective view. When employing disbelief leads and responses, the therapist may well intend to encourage the client by showing her — even through the use of sarcasm, if necessary — that things cannot possibly be as bad as she describes them. The therapist is convinced that he can interpret the point at issue more correctly than the client and thereby help her move along in a direction that her distorted perception now makes difficult, if not impossible, to pursue. In brief, the therapist informs his partner that he can evaluate the situation more soundly and authoritatively and that the client would do well to be guided by him. Thus, for example:

TH. Never on you?

CL. She calls on everyone else but never on me, I tell you.

TH. I just can't believe it. After all, you're in the class like everyone else. It just doesn't make sense, the way you see it.

CL. For the others, yes, but for me never a good word.

TH. Now, Tom, I just can't believe that. You just remember the scoldings and forget the praise. Your mother did say how sensitive you are to criticism and that you seem to take praise for granted. Perhaps if you would make a list for just a week, you would get a different picture of what really goes on in your home.

Ridicule

In intent, ridicule is related to disbelief; but the lead or response is sharper, more sarcastic. Here the therapist condescendingly instructs the client for the purpose of demonstrating how absurd he and his perceptions are. Ridicule is a form of teasing that aims at shaming the client into behaving "sensibly" like "other people" — such as the therapist. The therapist assures his partner that he, too, will evaluate the situation in the same light once he rids himself of these absurd notions and ridiculous perceptions. It is as if the therapist were saying: "Yes, I am deliberately making fun of you so that you may be able to shake yourself free of your silly conceptions and act in a manner beneficial to yourself. This you can do only if you see reality the way I see it." Contrast the following in terms of intent and therapist personalities:

CL. ... I thought about going back to work all day. ...

TH. Tried your skill at ESP. ... Thought the shop might move right into your home, I see!

CL. I couldn't practice walking yesterday because it rained most of the time.

TH. I understand. You might have melted; and if you ever get a job, you expect them to pick you up by cab when it rains.

CL. I just couldn't let you know I wouldn't make it last week.

TH. Naturally. The phones were out of order, and the mail service doesn't function in this town.

Contradiction

"It isn't so. It is otherwise. This is how it is." That is what the therapist is stating or implying when she uses contradiction as a

lead or response. She is saying "no," "wrong," "bad," to what
the client has expressed. She is certain of her ground and lets the
client know and feel this. There are no possible doubts, no two
ways of looking at things. She intends to guide the client onto
the "right" path. She even contradicts the client's expressed feelings when these are "bad" or "misguided." For example:

CL. I feel awfully warm in here.

TH. You couldn't; all the windows are wide open.

CL. I really love him and want to marry him.

TH. You want to marry him because of his wealth and his
social position. You may fool yourself, but you can't fool
me.

CL. I'm quite happy "wasting away" as you call it.

TH. I know you're not. You're just taking the easy way out.
You're miserable and lonely. No one could be happy living
the way you do.

Denial and Rejection

Of the leads and responses listed in this series, denial and rejection are the most extreme. The therapist employing them rebuffs
the ideas, thoughts, and feelings of the client, and in so doing,
he may well be rebuffing the client herself. He is telling the
client that unless her thinking, her attitudes, and her behavior
change, nothing can be achieved in the interview. Unless the
client can adapt herself to the therapist's perceptions, she is un-
worthy of any more of the latter's time, undeserving of any more
of his attention. The client is made to understand that under
prevailing conditions, she can be neither guided nor assisted. She
must either change or go. The therapist or interviewer, confident
of his rectitude, can proceed no further. Some examples:

TH. We've gone over and over this same point. You insist
that you can't and that you have tried. I insist you can and

that you haven't really tried. It's senseless to continue this
way. You can come back to see me if and when you have
something new to report

CL. ... and I hardly got started, just got my tools ready,
when the foreman told me to pack up and get out. I didn't
even open my mouth.

IER. I happen to know that foreman, and your story just isn't
true. The other times I couldn't check, but here I could and
did. You were arrogant, defiant, and uncooperative, and from
what he told me, you said plenty that was completely un-
called for. I hope you can get a job, but it won't be through
us. We're through.

CL. You just don't know what it's like, walking with a cane
or a guide dog. People stare and point at you like you were a
freak or something. I'm going to use a guide — Mother is
ready to do it — or else I'll stay home.

IER. Well, it that's your attitude, we can't help you. But just
remember that Mother won't be around forever and then —
well, it's your problem.

Open Use of Authority

We are now reaching the phase in which the therapist makes open
use of his authority. He assumes complete responsibility for what
occurs in the interview and dominates the situation accordingly.
He acts out his authority position, as it were, and by his overt
behavior goads the client in a direction that seems to him correct
beyond question. He is the determining figure in the interviewing
process. His attitudes are central, but he moves one step further:
in addition to expressing these attitudes, he acts upon them
openly and unambiguously, assuming that if the client can be
thus coerced, he may eventually be helped. He sees no other path
available and adopts this one as a last resort. I shall not consider
here those therapists who base their interviewing mainly on the
open use of authority. Rather, I shall confine myself to the discussion of these leads and responses as occasionally used — leaving

to the reader the decision as to their appropriateness and beneficial value.

Scolding

When scolding, the therapist or interviewer interprets and
evaluates the ideas, feelings, and actions of the client. Having understood these to her own satisfaction, she reacts to them negatively. "This is no way to think or feel or act," she admonishes.
The client needs correcting; and in the hope that a verbal thrash-
ing will do the trick she administers it without delay:

CL. I thought the paper wasn't due till next week.

IER. I don't know whatever gave you that idea. Everyone else
seems to have understood. You'd better think less and listen
more. There's still time to write it, so get to work.

CL. I'd rather you told him I want to change.

IER. Look here, Bill, you'd better stop that. You always want
others to do your work for you when it's unpleasant. The
pleasant things you're quite ready to do alone. We've talked
about this a lot, and I think you understand why you do it,
but understanding isn't enough. You have to act on what you
know. You'd better tell him yourself that you want to change
because I'm not going to do it for you. The time has come for
you to grow up. If you can't tell him that you want to change
from woodwork to metal, how will you ever get the gumption
to ask a girl to marry you? Go on; get moving!

CL. I meant well.

IER. So what? Meaning well isn't doing well. You hurt her
very much, and I'm quite upset about the whole thing. Next
time you'd better think of others more and yourself less.

Threat

Through the use of threat, the interviewer notifies the client of
the steps he will take should the client continue along his present

path. He says, in effect, that he will mobilize the power at his command, which is, of course, much greater than any the client can muster. What this amounts to in a broader, social context is that the interviewer warns the client of the consequences awaiting him should he persist in his erring ways. It is a distinct warning.

> *CL.* I'm telling you the truth. I didn't take those pencils!
>
> *IER.* If you persist in lying, I'll have to turn you over to the principal, and he . . . well, he'll know what to do.
>
> *CL.* I couldn't help it; my bus came late again this morning.
>
> *IER.* If you come late once again, we shall have to ask you to leave our workshop. Maybe one bus came late, but I know there was one before that which you could easily have caught.
>
> *CL.* I think my brother is just bad through and through.
>
> *IER.* You just go on thinking like that and getting him to believe it, too, and your brother may wind up in jail yet; he may want to prove you right.
>
> *CL.* . . . even though I've got the grades and the scholarship, I just don't want to go to college now.
>
> *IER.* If you keep this nonsense up, I am going to tell your parents to give you up as a lost cause. You're not going to college for me; and if you don't go, you'll see how far you can get!

Command

Here the therapist unequivocally orders the client to follow her instructions. She acts on the assumptions previously mentioned and, perhaps, this additional one: the client needs to be marshaled by a firm hand, and she, the therapist or interviewer, is best qualified to accomplish this task.

> *CL.* . . . they just come. . . . I can't control my tears.

TH. Of course you can. Pull yourself together; wipe your eyes, and blow your nose. We have lots to talk about.

TH. Stop playing with your hair; it is too distracting.

CL. I can't play ball today. My hand . . .

IER. Get out on that field. I'll be out there, and I want to see you pitching as you've never pitched before.

CL. I've got to see you today.

TH. You came an hour late for the last appointment, too. Get out now, please. I'm very busy, as you can see. You wait outside, and I'll tell you later when I can see you.

Punishment

The interviewer, feeling he must chastise the client for some impropriety of deed or attitude, brandishes the power and influence implicit in his role. He may even claim to be helping the client thereby, although the latter may not appreciate this at the moment. Here the interviewer plays his last trump on the premise that if it doesn't work, nothing will. Even when this most authoritarian of approaches is resorted to, interviewers' intent and attitude vary greatly. Contrast the following:

CL. I broke his glasses. The others just watched.

IER. I'm glad you told me, Dick, although I already knew it. You'll have to pay for them, you know. I can arrange work for you in the cafeteria if you don't have enough money to pay.

CL. All they do around here is give you the runaround.

IER. Then you'd better look for another agency. Good-bye.

CL. You all just talk, but you're really afraid to do anything.

IER. Well, I for one am not. You're suspended from all activities for a week, and you are not to leave the grounds, of course.

CL. He's my child, and I'll do whatever I like with him.

IER. You are quite mistaken. The law, in such cases, protects the child against his parents, and we'll go to court to enforce it. I'll have to show you who is stronger, and I won't hesitate to do it!

Humor

I find myself incapable of concluding on such a somber note. Luckily for me, one more reaction deserves mention. I have often found that humor when appropriately used can be as helpful as many other leads or responses, if not more so. Although I cannot define exactly what I have in mind, I definitely do not mean sarcasm, ridicule, or cynicism. Rather, I am thinking of that light touch of humor that stems from empathic listening and which reflects a positive outlook on life. It is a very individual and personal response, for which there is no detailed recipe. Sometimes it results in our spontaneously laughing with the client; at other times, in our provoking laughter in him. Now and then it is an anecdote that fits the situation — one which, the therapist or interviewer believes, will produce no obstacle to communication but may serve to ease tension and lighten the atmosphere.

I am referring, of course, to spontaneous, not artificial, humor — something very natural, not contrived. It may well consist of no more than a raised eyebrow, a smile, a gesture. When it breaks through, it brings the two partners in the interviewing process closer together by establishing an additional bond. For lack of a better term, I can only call this bond genuine caring for each other and confidence in the helping nature of human rapport.

8 • LEAVE-TAKING

When, at long last, I began putting this book down on paper after years of thinking about doing so, writing the introduction proved rather easy. Taking leave is more difficult. It is like something that occurs at times in the helping interview. When the time comes for the two partners finally to take leave of each other, they both know it is an ending, and so they linger awhile, no longer needing each other but enjoying their mutual reflections. So I find it hard to separate now, to go on my way. Not that I can't; indeed I must. But there is a desire to linger just another moment, to meditate on what has been accomplished and to consider how it has been done.

I have written this so that we might think deeply and dispassionately about the helping interview and do so with as many communication barriers as possible removed, including that of esoteric language. I wished us to consider the many ways in which therapists behave and the influence their particular mode of behavior may have on the client. Since there are practically as many modes of behavior as there are therapists, I have tried merely to depict certain patterns that seem to me predominant. The client himself remains the eternal question mark. We never know in advance who he will be; but whoever he is, we must always be prepared to try to help him.

The therapist's behavior, I am convinced, strongly affects both the client's perception of her as a person and the client's reaction to the interviewing process. If our behavior did not matter, there would be little point in writing about it. It does matter, however, and will as long as human beings try to help other human beings through personal contacts such as the interview. Should nonhuman interviewers — computers — take over this function my premise will no longer hold. I hate to contemplate the implications of such a change and return posthaste to the human therapist, for whom I have written.

I believe that what is true for the client is true for ourselves, the therapists, as well. People can change; people do change. Without this conviction on our part, the interview, our tool, would disintegrate. The debate rages as to what brings change about — what promotes it and what hinders it. We can change our behavior if we can allow ourselves, first of all, to find out how we do actually behave. By analyzing our own behavior non-defensively, we can learn a great deal. No longer feeling threatened, we can permit ourselves to examine our work closely. Through the use of tapes, notes, observers, supervision, discussion, client feedback, and self-examination, we can arrive at the point at which we are able to describe our behavior in the helping interview. Having described it, we can then consider whether this is, in fact, how we believed we were behaving and whether we wish to continue to behave thus. My hunch is that we shall always find a gulf — or at least a fissure — between what we are actually doing, what we thought we were doing, and what we ideally wish to do.

It is my conviction that we can change our behavior in the direction of our philosophy. In other words, we can change toward the self we wish to become. However, change involves arduous work, of the kind no one can perform for us. A pertinent book may aid us; so may a perceptive supervisor, notes, tapes, role-playing, and frank discussions with colleagues. Ultimately, change involves never-ending work that each one of us must perform within himself.

Alternatives to Therapy

Therapy, of course, is only one method of effecting change within ourselves. Even within our own culture, some people are not aware of its existence, while others prefer not to expose themselves to its hardships. Some make an honest attempt at it but leave disappointed. Over the years I have become familiar with some of the alternatives to unsuccessful therapy that clients I have worked with have tried. To round off the picture, I shall describe some of them here.

A few months after we had parted, Sol called to inform me that he and Erna were now very happy. They had just adopted two adorable babies. This wasn't orthodox therapy, he added, but perhaps for him it would work better. I know of at least two other couples who found in adoption a better solution to their problems than therapy.

Recently, I met Itamar on the street walking his big dog. With a happy grin, he confided that at last he had a girlfriend and was sure that for him this was infinitely preferable to therapy. He is by no means the only one. A potential client turned to me to consider therapy. Before we started, however, he called to say that he had decided to get married and that, therefore, therapy would be superfluous.

Joy and Andy did not look for a substitute for therapy. They had gotten out of it what they could and hoped that just ordinary living with more awareness would do the rest. Olga and Glenn left therapy knowing it was not the method to help them. What alternative, if any, they have found, I do not know. Many couples cannot give therapy a proper chance because one of the partners refuses to cooperate. Some just stumble on while others separate.

Therapy, as we have seen, is often a matter of proper timing. Clients return to it — with the same or another therapist — when they feel more prepared, more motivated, more mature. Some clients try newer, less conventional therapies, while yet others leave therapy in order to throw themselves into action. For them, therapy had proved to be a defense against living rather than a method for coping. Still others turn to tranquilizers, medical treatment, and even hospitalization.

Once upon a time the Grand Tour was recommended for mending broken hearts and minds. Today, an extended stay in Israel is frequently suggested in that vein. A different locale may, at times, afford an opportunity to start all over again, and we have known this phenomenon to occur here in Israel, too. If the person involved can find his niche here and develop roots, Israel can become an absorption center for him in the same way that it has for other, more conventionally motivated immigrants. But if, on the other hand, Israel is looked upon as one big rehabilitation center, the prognosis is bleak. I have encountered clients who were sent to Israel as if to a dumping ground for the disturbed and marginal. Acquainted with neither the mores nor the language of the country, they are lonely and miserable and get worse from day to day. I try to help such clients return home as speedily as possible. If they require therapy, they should be receiving it there. There are new immigrants upon whom Israel works therapeutically, but they are not the ones who turn to therapy.

Gifts

Our tale is now rapidly approaching its end. But before parting, something should be said about a frequent accompaniment to parting. Gifts come in various forms, and I can honestly say that I have been happy with all of them and have never had to turn one down because it seemed to me inappropriate. When giving is a pleasure, it is a pleasure to receive, and when the gift is personal, I cherish it doubly and keep it near me whenever possible. The privilege of having known and worked with the client is sufficient reward in itself. But if he has the need to show gratitude in a more tangible way, I can accept this without always looking for a deeper cause or reason. Gifts during the course of therapy are rare — flowers or fruit for a holiday, no more than that. Most presents are part of the ceremony of parting.

My workroom is full of mementos. I like having them around; what they symbolize makes work even more worthwhile. There, on the floor, is Albert's massive, smooth sculpture. He recalled that I had admired it at his exhibition and presented me with it when I returned from the hospital last year. The batik on the wall is from a special education teacher, now deceased, to whom I gave supervision. Opposite, the enlarged photograph of a pastoral scene from a client whose son had died in a tragic accident. Nearer the door, a mosaic picture created by a young woman whose therapy left a strong imprint upon her life — and mine as well. Emma, who was learning to paint, brought me a canvas in appreciation of my efforts, although these were not always to her liking. And there is a plant from Rose — an unusual flowering cactus which, Rose explained, represents life.

Herman is Stiller yet. He has wonderfully capable hands and repairs my recording equipment as a token of thanks. When Judy terminated therapy she was both happy and sad, laughed and cried all at once. She had chosen a key chain for me. My office keys are still on it; I think of her and of Aaron quite frequently and still wonder whether I might have acted differently. From my very first private client, years ago, I received a vase. My wife considers it a monstrosity but I still cherish it, even though it is well hidden from sight. Aware of my love for music, some clients bring me a record when we part. Whenever I put one of these on the turntable, I think of the client who chose it and of our journey together. More often than not he has gone out of my life and I am glad of that as well.

One of the gifts I cherish most is Nathan's holiday-eve phone calls. It is such a simple gesture and yet so heartfelt that I should surely miss it were it, one day, to cease.

Years ago I had an unusual client. Actually, he wasn't unusual but the circumstances were. He was in prison and had requested rehabilitation counseling. Once a week, I was driven to the jail and met with Mark. A man in his early twenties, he had attempted to kill a neighbor in a fit of rage. Toward the end of his imprisonment, he was brought to me under escort once a week. The years have blurred the details but I remember Mark as moody and silent and very ambitious. He wished desperately to learn a trade while in prison, knowing that once out he would have to stand on his own two feet. He was without means, an orphan who suffered from diabetes and a weak heart. He had chosen printing and bookbinding as his trade and was proud of the progress he had made.

Shortly before his release Mark came to me for the last time. He was carrying a package with which he fiddled while we talked. When he got up to leave, he placed the parcel in my hands and said:

CL. I made this album for you. It's just blank pages and you can put in it whatever you like. You helped me to choose my trade and I wanted you to have something I had made. After I'm settled and working, I'll call you and let you know about it.

Mark never called. Two weeks out of prison, he had gone swimming one afternoon and drowned. His heart, it is believed, simply gave out under the unaccustomed strain. The album I have still. It is full of written mementos waiting for a rainy day, to be sorted and arranged. Every letter, every note, every scrap I wish to keep goes into the album. It contains many warm and moving words. I'm not sure I deserve them all, but Mark deserves my keeping them where I do.

Parting

In life, and thus in therapy, parting takes many forms. Of some partings we become aware only in retrospect. Lilly, who had come regularly every week, simply stopped coming. Although months have passed, I still do not know what happened. Miriam kept making appointments only to break them and then dropped out of the picture entirely. With Tom, too, no parting took place, though with him the situation was very different. He was unable to finish therapy with me; he was even unable to say "goodbye" properly. He required a woman therapist to effect that symbolic act.

For some clients, just the idea of parting is threatening. Dick and Betty make it quite clear that they do not ever intend to take that step. They may not get in touch for months at a time, but they always come back and intend to go on doing so whenever they feel the need. Betty once asserted, "I came to you even before I met Dick and I want to feel that I can continue to come, with or without him, whenever I feel like it."

When I broached the possibility, perhaps even the desirability, of considering parting, Sandy just laughed. "No, I'm not ready yet. There's still so much I want to work on and to talk about. . . . Perhaps I'll come less frequently but for now, terminating is out of the question."

Herman and I do not even touch upon the subject. As Stiller, he cannot leave and, since he cannot abandon Stiller as yet, leaving is not on our immediate agenda.

Cynthia and I had met for a while right after her marriage. After we parted I did not hear from her for years. Then, already the mother of six, she returned to therapy. This time, as we neared the end of our sessions she expressed the wish just to go without formal leave-taking. Not certain that she would not return someday, she wished to avoid what might prove to be an empty ceremony.

Sam, who as we have seen, came during two different periods in his life, put it this way when we parted recently: "I had the fantasy of bringing you a huge plant but changed my mind. I'd rather wait and see what happens. I know I can always get in touch even just to bring that plant. I'd rather be able to stay away but I don't want to slam the door."

Michelle was certain her behavior at home had changed radically and wished to bring her husband to iron out some remaining problems she felt needed their joint efforts. She was dismayed when he stated that, in fact, nothing had changed at home and that she was as hard to live with as ever. I never heard from Michelle again. Parting can certainly take manifold forms!

The "business" of therapy is seasonal to an extent. We tend to wind down toward the summer and pick up again in the fall. I tell clients well in advance of my vacation breaks and sometimes we try to bring therapy to a close just before I leave. On occasion, vacation breaks will create a break in therapy. Norman and Itamar told me they were not sure they would return in the fall. They wanted to think things over and, just in case, they thought it best to say goodbye and thank you. They did not, in fact, return.

It goes without saying that in some instances, extended vacations may bring about complications in the therapeutic process. They arouse anxiety in some clients, cause resentment in others, and lead still others to conclude that because they have succeeded in weathering the long interval between sessions, resumption of therapy is unnecessary.

It is very convenient when vacation time coincides with the end of therapy. This was the case with Alexandra. We concluded our sessions just as I was closing down the clinic for the summer.

Alexandra felt we could not have planned it better. She still wished to consider whether to go into therapy "much deeper, into the roots," but meanwhile she felt ready for our parting. Her symptoms had practically disappeared. Our journey together had been short but profitable. Alexandra did not find our parting difficult.

Just as the end is implied in the beginning, disengaging is an intrinsic part of getting involved. One of the goals of therapy, indeed, is parting so that the client can go her way alone, unhampered, lighter of heart and freer of mind. At the very outset I speak with clients of the end; not because I particularly believe in or practice what has come to be called short-term therapy, but because I want the client to realize early on that one of our aims is to help her to leave without dependence upon therapy or therapist. At times, I may even tell the client, after a few sessions, approximately how long it will take us to reach our goal. As parting nears, we both realize it and prepare to meet it.

Termination is a matter of process to the same extent as getting involved is. The disclosing, the sharing, the learning, the interacting — all this and more must now come to an end. This is not entirely so, of course — I hope the client will continue to examine, to choose, and to grow — but it seems like that for awhile. True enough, there will be no more scheduled meetings, no more set times and, we must face it, the therapist will no longer be there to support, listen, understand, and help. Generally speaking, the deeper the process of therapy has been, the more difficult it is to emerge from it and speak of, plan, and carry out separation.

Ruth was a typical "calendar client" — she began therapy in the fall and terminated at the beginning of July. Her manner of working was rather special. Whether she talked or sat silent, reflecting, she always seemed self-possessed and self-sufficient. I never knew exactly why she needed me, but she claimed that my presence enabled her to push forward. My presence perhaps, but my interventions certainly not. She worked doggedly on her own, unraveling the threads that had tied her to her mother and spinning those that tied her to her own small daughter. Once she could relinquish her search for independence in favor of that of autonomy, she felt she had reached the turning point in her therapy. Soon afterward she began to speak of leaving. As the end

approached, she invited more participation on my part, and when
she departed we both felt that she was leaving not only my workroom, but me as well.

Judy found parting very difficult. First we cut down on our sessions and then stopped, leaving the door open for her to return, if
necessary. She did come back several times. There seemed always
to remain some unfinished business to discuss and new material
to work on. She put it like this:

> CL. It isn't the parting that's so difficult; it's the staying
> away afterward. I feel strong enough and independent enough
> to get up and leave but then, some time later, I get so lonely
> and depressed and lost that I just have to come back.

Judy maintained that her parting was actually a triple one: from
therapy, from Aaron, and from her marriage. That is why she kept
coming back; she just could not separate herself from all three at
once.

She realized by now that she should never have married Aaron.
She had done so only because her self-image at the time had been
very low and since, as she saw it, no one else would ever want
her, she did not dare refuse Aaron. And now, ten years later, even
though she felt much more self-confident, she was still uncertain
whether she would ever find anyone else. She just could not see
herself continuing to live alone with the children — merely the
thought of it caused her sleepless nights. Judy pictured herself
staring reality in the face:

> CL. In my mid-thirties, a widow with small kids, not par-
> ticularly attractive or charming or even rich . . . my chances
> aren't all that good. I'm still shy and inhibited and simply
> can't see myself pursuing men — so I worry and don't sleep.

And there were the children to deal with, as well. Rumors were
spreading concerning Aaron's death and there were, inevitably,
questions. She herself had questions. There were guilt, aggression,
and regret:

> CL. I never took his "jesting" hints very seriously. Perhaps I
> should have. Perhaps I pressed him too hard but he had be-

come impossible to live with — always quietly drunk or moodily nursing a hangover. He wasn't just a nuisance but a terrible, constant burden.

TH. He lived with you but for himself only.

CL. And then he stopped living altogether but he is still living within me and I have to get rid of him because he is still making me feel guilty and angry.

Slowly Judy put order into her new life. Now parting from therapy became a challenge for her. It meant being able to put the past where it belonged. It symbolized starting afresh on her own with a more positive and more mature self-image and with new strengths with which to combat the tomorrows to come. Judy brought me a key chain and said something about keys to unlock doors and doors that always remain open. She knows mine is so for her but she hasn't needed to come back and I hope, for her sake, that she never will.

If ideal clients exist, Laura came as close to being one as I have known. She had turned to therapy after her husband left her when she had felt that her entire world was collapsing:

CL. I have nothing to look forward to. The children are miserable, I'm not functioning at my work and I just can't face anyone right now. I don't know what therapy can do for me and I certainly don't know what I can do for myself.

It took Laura time to disentangle herself from her various relationships and to really face herself. But once she did, a change took place which accompanied and guided her to the very end. She put it thus:

CL. Something very basic has changed in me. I can't define it but I feel it very clearly. It has to do with how I look at life and at myself. I used to think that I wasn't worth much and that there was no room for me at the top or even at the center, for that matter. Joe only strengthened those feelings in me, but since he has left I have been able to allow myself to look inward and explore. I've begun slowly to see that my preconceptions were wrong. I noticed it first at work. As an architect, I never felt sure of my plans and always sought the approval of others or else would try to play second fiddle to an expert. Some time ago things started to change for me. I dared more, drafted more freely, became more spontaneous. The response I got was immediate and terrific. It's as if people had been waiting for me to produce. I suppose they were ready for me right along but I wasn't ready for myself.

Laura's entire expression changed. She became vivacious and, like a young girl, delighted in every new perception. She found herself more permissive and less defensive with the children who, naturally, responded and began to demonstrate love and affection. Laura and Joe divorced but now Laura rejoiced in her newly gained freedom. Feeling more secure and competent, she could allow men to approach her again. Her passivity disappeared. She enjoyed getting up in the morning and seemed to possess boundless energy. In therapy she wept at times for the years she felt she had wasted.

No regression occurred. Movement slowed down at times but Laura always knew she was on her way. Problems at work, with the children, in her private life, did not depress her any longer, although, of course, she could not always solve them. She was coping and, one day, raised the question of ending therapy. Parting followed soon after. I remember our final exchange well:

> CL. I know that I always can come back if I need to but I also know that I won't need to.
>
> TH. You'll be able to manage without that.
>
> CL. Yes; I know there'll be ups and downs but they don't frighten me. This may sound immodest but nothing really frightens me any more. I don't feel a bit like a heroine but like a real human being. It took me a long time to get there but because of me and of you, I've finally made it!

Summing Up

Our thinking about the helping interview does not remain static. It, too, changes as we experiment and discover more about how our behavior affects that of others. As I ponder what I have written, I realize that I have not been as descriptive as I meant to be. Perhaps my own values have too often intruded. I can only repeat once more that my intention has been to stimulate thought and, possibly, change but that the direction this thought, this change, takes must be of your choosing.

When interviewing, we are left with what we are. We have no books then, no classroom lessons, no supporting person at our elbow. We are alone with the individual who has come to seek our help. How can we best assist him? The same basic issues will confront us afresh whenever we face a client for the first time:

1. Shall we allow ourselves to emerge as genuine human beings, or shall we hide behind our role, position, authority?
2. Shall we really try to listen with all our senses to the client?
3. Shall we try to understand with him — empathically and acceptingly?
4. Shall we interpret her behavior to her in terms of her frame of reference, our own, or society's?
5. Shall we evaluate his thoughts, feelings, and actions, and if so, in terms of whose values: his, ours, or society's?
6. Shall we support, encourage, urge her on, so that by leaning on us, we hope she may be able to rely on her own strength one day?
7. Shall we question and probe, push and prod, causing him to feel that we are in command and that once all our queries have been answered, we shall provide the solutions he is seeking?
8. Shall we guide him in the direction we feel certain is the best for him?
9. Shall we reject her, her thoughts and feelings, and insist that she become like ourselves or at least conform to our perception of what she could and should become?

These are, as I see them, the central issues. How we meet them today need not be the way we shall meet them tomorrow. The choice is ours.

Departing

And now it is my turn to leave. Not unlike many clients, I feel ambivalence. I am eager to get away and yet I should like to linger a while longer, as well. I am glad my task is now behind me, and yet I wish I had to begin all over again. I am too close to what I have just written to know, even vaguely, whether I have achieved my intended purpose. I feel drained and yet keen to continue.

My work is done. Deep down I know this and accept it. How the reader will react remains to be seen. As for myself, I have enjoyed writing the expanded version of *The Helping Interview* and I hope that over the years the reaffirmation of my credo will withstand the test of time. I have no desire to close the door. On the contrary, I want to leave the door wide open for comment and criticism and new ideas and continued effort and replenished faith. I need the door open wide so I can depart easily, knowing that I shall be able to return. Departing thus is almost joyful.

SUPPLEMENTARY READING LIST

References mentioned in text are preceded by an asterisk. The comments that follow some of the listings are by Alfred Benjamin.

A. General surveys of interviewing

Epstein, L. *Talking and Listening.* St. Louis: Times/Mirror Mosby, 1985.
Kahn, R. and Cannell, C. *The Dynamics of Interviewing.* New York: John Wiley, 1957.
* Richardson, S. *et al. Interviewing: Its Forms and Functions.* New York: Basic Books, 1965. A comprehensive text covering primarily the research interview.

B. Books, including casebooks, dealing specifically with the helping interview

* Barbara, D. *The Art of Listening.* Springfield, Ill.: Charles C Thomas, 1974.

* Berenson, B. and Carkhuff, R. *Beyond Counseling and Psychotherapy.* New York: Holt, Rinehart and Winston, 1967a.

* Berenson, B. and Carkhuff, R. *Sources of Gain in Counseling and Psychotherapy.* New York: Holt, Rinehart and Winston, 1967b. The authors challenge the frequently held contention that should the interview not be helpful, it will at least do no harm. They see the interviewing process as moving "in and down," then gradually "up and out," and suggest that the interviewer's behavior should change accordingly while the basic attitude of empathy, warmth, and genuineness remains constant.

Brammer, L. *The Helping Relationship: Process and Skills.* Englewood Cliffs, N.J.: Prentice-Hall, 1973.

Brammer, L. and Shostrom, E. *Therapeutic Psychology*, 3rd ed. Englewood Cliffs, N.J.: Prentice-Hall, 1977. See especially Chapter 7.

* Burton, A. *Interpersonal Psychotherapy.* Englewood Cliffs, N.J.: Prentice-Hall, 1975.

Carkhuff, R. *The Art of Helping.* Amherst, Mass.: Human Resource Development Press, 1972.

Cormier, W. and Cormier, L. *Interviewing Strategies for Helpers: A Guide to Assessment, Treatment, and Evaluation.* Monterey, Calif.: Brooks/Cole, 1979.

Danish, J., D'Augelli, A. and Hauer, A. *Helping Skills: A Basic Training Program.* New York: Human Sciences Press, 1980.

Egan, G. *The Skilled Helper.* Monterey, Calif.: Brooks-Cole, 1975. Both Carkhuff and Egan discuss thoroughly and convincingly the art and the skills that promote a helping relationship.

Evraiff, W. *Helping Counselors Grow Professionally.* Englewood Cliffs, N.J.: Prentice-Hall, 1965. I recommend this highly because the interviews included are analyzed from diverse viewpoints by several specialists.

* Fenlason, A., Ferguson, G. and Abrahamson, A. *Essentials in Interviewing*, rev. ed. New York: Harper and Row, 1962. Parts II and III are extremely relevant.

Garrett, A. *Interviewing: Its Principles and Methods*, 2nd ed. New York: Basic Books, 1972. An introductory "must."

Hackney, H. and Nye, S. *Counseling Strategies and Objectives,* 2nd ed. Englewood Cliffs, N.J.: Prentice-Hall, 1979. Highly recommended for the beginning counselor.

Ivcy, A. *Microcounseling: Innovations in Interviewing Training,* 2nd ed. Springfield, Ill.: Charles C Thomas, 1978.

Ivey, A. *Microcounseling: Interviewing Skills Manual.* Springfield, Ill.: Charles C Thomas, 1972. The above two books are essential reading for the practitioner of the helping interview.

Kadushin, A. *The Social Work Interview,* 2nd ed. New York: Columbia University Press, 1983.

Langs, R. *Resistances and Interventions.* New York: Jason Aronsom, 1981.

Patterson, C. H. *Counseling and Psychotherapy: Theory and Practice.* New York: Harper and Row, 1959. Much in line with my own approach.

Patterson, C. H. *Theories of Counseling and Psychotherapy,* 2nd ed. New York: Harper and Row, 1973.

Porter, E. H., Jr. *Therapeutic Counseling.* Boston: Houghton Mifflin, 1950. Indispensable for the purpose of interviewer self-examination, whether or not one accepts his nondirective approach. See especially "Pre and Post Tests."

Rogers, C. R. *Counseling and Psychotherapy.* Boston: Houghton Mifflin, 1942. Classic statement of the nondirective point of view.

Sifneos, P. E. *Short Term Dynamic Psychotherapy,* New York: Plenum, 1979.

Snyder, W. *Casebook of Non-Directive Counseling.* Boston: Houghton Mifflin, 1947.

Stefflre, B. and Grant, W. (eds.) *Theories of Counseling,* 2nd ed. New York: McGraw-Hill, 1972.

* Sullivan, H. S. *The Psychiatric Interview.* New York: Norton, 1970. A series of lectures delivered by Sullivan, published posthumously. Although not directly applicable, this book is most thought-provoking for the student of the helping interview.

Thorne, F. C. *Psychological Case Handling.* Brandon, Vt.: Clinical Psychology, 1968. The authoritarian position par excellence.

* Truax, C. and Carkhuff, R. *Toward Effective Counseling and Psychotherapy.* Chicago: Aldine, 1969. This book is essential reading for those who wish to become as empathic, warm, and genuine as possible and to learn to gauge their progress in these dimensions.

Tyler, L. E. *The Work of the Counselor,* 3rd ed. New York: Appleton-Century-Crofts, 1969. Chapters 2 and 3 are well worth reading and rereading.

Wicks, Robert. *Counseling Strategies and Intervention Techniques for Human Services.* White Plains, N.Y.: Longman, 1984.

C. Books dealing with the philosophy of the helping interview, plus miscellaneous books and articles

Aguilera, D. and Messick, J. *Crisis Intervention: Theory and Methodology,* 4th ed. St. Louis: C. Mosby, 1982.

Alexander, J. and Parsons, B. *Functional Family Therapy.* Monterey, Calif.: Brooks/Cole, 1982.

* Allport, G. W. *Pattern and Growth in Personality.* New York: Holt, Rinehart and Winston, 1961. Proactive approach. This theory of personality stresses coping.

Allport, G. W. *Letters from Jenny.* New York: Harcourt Brace Jovanovich, 1965. An ingenious attempt to diagnose Jenny's personality (as expressed through her letters) according to the models of the main trends in modern personality theory.

Arbuckle, D. *Counseling: Philosophy, Theory and Practice,* 2nd ed. Boston: Allyn & Bacon, 1970. An outstanding exposition of the client-centered philosophy.

Bailey, K. and Sowder W., Jr. "Audiotape and videotape self-confrontation in psychotherapy." *Psychological Bulletin* 74 (1970): 127–137.

* Beck, C. E. *Guidelines for Guidance.* Dubuque, Iowa: William C. Brown, 1966. Treats all the major contemporary philosophical approaches. See especially Chapter 48 by E. Dreyfus.

* Berger, M. M. (ed.) *Videotape Techniques in Psychiatric Training and Treatment,* 2nd ed. New York: Brunner/Mazel, 1978.

Borck, L. E. and Fawcett, S. B. *Learning Counseling and Problem-Solving Skills.* New York: Haworth Press, 1982.

* Buber, M. *I and Thou.* New York: Scribner's, 1970.

* Buber, M. *The Knowledge of Man.* New York: Harper and Row, 1965. See especially "Appendix: Dialogue between Martin Buber and Carl R. Rogers."

* Bugental, J. F. *The Search for Authenticity.* New York: Holt, Rinehart and Winston, 1965. A well-defined existentialist approach.

Butler, L. E. *Eclectic Psychotherapy· A Systematic Approach.* New York: Pergamon Press, 1983.

Cingolani, J. "Social Conflict Perspective on Work with Involuntary Clients," *Social Work* 29 (1984): 442–446.

* Coleman, J. C. *Abnormal Psychology and Modern Life,* 5th ed. Glenview, Ill.: Scott Foresman, 1976.

Combs, A. W., Avila, D. L. and Purkey, W. W. *The Helping Relationship,* 2nd ed. Boston: Allyn & Bacon, 1978.

* *Comparative Group Studies,* Vol. 3, No. 4 (1972). Entire issue devoted to nonverbal communication.

Corey, G. *Theory and Practice of Counseling and Psychotherapy.* Monterey, Calif.: Brooks/Cole, 1977.

* Ekman, P. "Body position, facial expression, and verbal behavior during interviews." *Journal of Abnormal and Social Psychology* 68 (1964): 295–301.

* Ekman, P. *et al. The Face and Emotion.* Elmsford, N.Y.: Pergamon Press, 1971.

* Fiedler, F. E. "The concept of an ideal therapeutic relationship." *Journal of Consulting Psychology* 14 (1950): 239–245.

* Fiedler, F. E. "A comparison of therapeutic relationships in psychoanalytic, non-directive and Adlerian therapy." *Journal of Consulting Psychology* 14 (1950): 436–445.

* Fiedler, F. E. "Factor analyses of psychoanalytic, nondirective and Adlerian therapeutic relationships." *Journal of Consulting Psychology* 15 (1951): 32–38.

Fine, R. *The Healing of the Mind,* 2nd ed. New York: Free Press, 1982.

Frank, J. *Persuasion and Healing,* rev. ed. Baltimore: Johns Hopkins University Press, 1973.

* Freud, A. *The Ego and the Mechanisms of Defense,* rev. ed. New York: International Universities Press, 1970.

* Freud, S. *Little Hans.* London: Hogarth Press, 1955.
* Freud, S. *The Problem of Anxiety.* New York: Norton, 1936. Freud begins and his daughter elaborates the study of defense mechanisms.
* Geertsma, R. and Mackie, J. (eds.) *Studies in Self-cognition: Techniques of Videotape Self-observation in the Behavioral Sciences.* Baltimore: Williams and Wilkins, 1969.
Goldstein, E. *Ego Psychology and Social Work Practice.* New York: Free Press, 1984.
Goldstein, H. "Starting Where the Client Is." *Social Casework* 64 (1983): 267–275.
Green, H. *I Never Promised You a Rose Garden.* New York: Holt, Rinehart and Winston, 1964. A moving account of an empathic therapeutic relationship.
Gurman, A. S. and Kniskeen, D. P. (eds.) *Handbook of Family Therapy.* New York: Brunner/Mazel, 1980.
Hanrahan, P. and Reid, W. "Choosing Effective Interventions." *Social Service Review* 58 (1984): 244–258.
Heller, K. *et al.* "The effects of interviewer style in a standardized interview." *Journal of Consulting Psychology* 30 (1966): 501–508.
Hepworth, D. and Larsen, J. *Direct Social Work Practice.* Chicago: Dorsey Press, 1986.
Hollis, F. and Woods, M. *Casework: A Psychotherapy Therapy.* New York: Random House, 1981.
Jourard, S. M. *Disclosing Man to Himself.* New York: Van Nostrand Reinhold, 1968.
* Jourard, S. M. *The Transparent Self,* 2nd ed. New York: Van Nostrand Reinhold, 1971.
Jung, C. G. *Modern Man in Search of a Soul.* New York: Harcourt Brace Jovanovich, 1955. See especially Chapter 11.
Knapp, Mark L. *Essentials of Nonverbal Communication.* New York: Holt, Rinehart and Winston, 1980.
Lebow, J. L. "On the Value of Integrating Approaches to Family Therapy." *Journal of Marital and Family Therapy* 10 (1984): 127–138.
* Lewin, K. *A Dynamic Theory of Personality.* New York: McGraw-Hill, 1935. Theoretical discussion of "life space."
* Maslow, A. *Motivation and Personality,* 2nd ed. New York: Harper and Row, 1970. Discusses coping as opposed to defense.

Maslow, A. *Toward a Psychology of Being*, 2nd ed. New York: Van Nostrand Reinhold, 1968.

Masson, H. and O'Byrne, P. *Applying Family Therapy*. New York: Pergamon Press, 1984.

Matarazzo, J. D. and Wiens, A. N. "Interviewer influence on durations of interviewee silence." *Journal of Experimental Research in Personality* 2 (1967): 56–69.

May, R. *Existential Psychology*, 2nd ed. New York: Random House, 1968.

* May, R. *Love and Will*. New York: Norton, 1969. The foregoing books expound May's powerful existentialist position.

May, R. *et al.* (eds.) *Existence: A New Dimension in Psychiatry and Psychology*. New York: Basic Books, 1967.

McGowan, J. F. and Schmidt, L. D. *Counseling: Readings in Theory and Practice*. New York: Holt, Rinehart and Winston, 1964. This collection of readings contains a rich and varied sampling of philosophical approaches.

Olan, N. *Passing Through Transitions: A Guide for the Practitioner*. New York: Free Press, 1981.

* *Personnel and Guidance Journal*, Vol. 50, No. 4 (December 1971). Special issue: "Ethical Practice: Preserving Human Dignity."

Pinsof, W. "Integrative Problem-Centered Therapy." *Journal of Marital and Family Therapy* 9 (1983): 19–35.

* Reik, T. *Listening with the Third Ear*. New York: Farrar, Straus & Giroux, 1977.

* Robinson, F. *Principles and Procedures in Student Counseling*. New York: Harper and Row, 1950.

* Rogers, C. R. *Client-Centered Therapy*. Boston: Houghton Mifflin, 1951.

* Rogers, C. R. *On Becoming A Person*. Boston: Houghton Mifflin, 1961. See particularly Chapters 3 and 17.

Rogers, C. R. and Stevens, B. *Person to Person: The Problem of Being Human*. Moab, Utah: Real People Press, 1967.

Schwartz, A. *The Behavior Therapies: Theories and Applications*. New York: Free Press, 1982.

Shertzer, B. and Stone, S. C. *Fundamentals of Counseling*, 3rd ed. Boston: Houghton Mifflin, 1980.

Steere, D. *Bodily Expressions in Psychotherapy*. New York: Brunner/Mazel, 1982.

Strean, H. *Resolving Resistances in Psychotherapy.* New York: John Wiley, 1983.

Truax, C. B. "Reinforcement and nonreinforcement in Rogerian psychotherapy." *Journal of Abnormal Psychology* 71 (1966): 1–9.

Werner, H. *Cognitive Therapy: A Humanistic Approach.* New York: Free Press, 1982.

* White, R. W. (ed.) *The Study of Lives: Essays on Personality in Honor of Henry A. Murray.* New York: Atherton Press, 1966.

* Wright, B. *Physical Disability: A Psychological Approach.* New York: Harper and Row, 1960. Analyzes coping versus succumbing.